Deep Listeners

JUDITH BECKER

Deep Listeners

Music, Emotion, and Trancing

INDIANA UNIVERSITY PRESS
Bloomington and Indianapolis

This book is a publication of

Indiana University Press
601 North Morton Street
Bloomington, IN 47404-3797 USA

http://iupress.indiana.edu

Telephone orders   800-842-6796
Fax orders   812-855-7931
Orders by e-mail   iuporder@indiana.edu

The paper used in this publication meets the minimum requirements of American National Standard for Information Sciences—Permanence of Paper for Printed Library Materials, ANSI Z39.48-1984.

Manufactured in the United States of America

Library of Congress Cataloging-in-Publication Data

Becker, Judith O.
Deep listeners : music, emotion, and trancing / Judith Becker.
p. cm.
Includes bibliographical references (p.) and index.
ISBN 0-253-34393-3 (cloth : alk. paper) — ISBN 0-253-21672-9 (pbk. : alk. paper)
1. Music—Psychological aspects. 2. Music, Influence of. 3. Trance. 4. Emotions. I. Title.
ML3838.B433 2004
781'.11—dc22
2003021168

ISBN 978-0-253-34393-2 (cloth : alk. paper)
ISBN 978-0-253-21672-4 (pbk. : alk. paper)

2   3   4   5   6   13   12   11   10   09   08

Our normal waking consciousness, rational consciousness as we call it, is but one special type of consciousness, whilst all about it, parted from it by the filmiest of screens, there lie potential forms of consciousness entirely different. We may go through life without suspecting their existence; but apply the requisite stimulus, and at a touch they are there in all their completeness, definite types of mentality which probably somewhere have their field of application and adaptation. No account of the universe in its totality can be final which leaves these other forms of consciousness quite disregarded. How to regard them is the question,—for they are so discontinuous with ordinary consciousness. Yet they may determine attitudes though they cannot furnish formulas, and open a region though they fail to give a map. At any rate, they forbid a premature closing of our accounts with reality.

—William James [1902] *The Varieties of Religious Experience*

Contents

Illustrations

Plates

Figures

Acknowledgments

By the time one reaches my age, there is no pretending that one has original ideas, that my words have sprung virgin from my mind, or that I can lay proprietary claim to whatever thoughts and ideas appear in this book. As the Australian historian, Greg Dening has said, we cannot plumb the depths of our own plagiarism. We live in a milieu of ideas that surround us, that permeate us, and that lay claim to us in ways that we can never fully comprehend. My words are only partially mine; my thoughts are probably even less my own. The bibliography of this book is one indication of the debts owed, and this short acknowledgment is another. Neither even begins to recognize the many, many thinkers who have influenced me so much that I have internalized their teachings and believe them to be my own.

That said, there are people who may not appear in the bibliography who have helped me in various ways. In New Delhi, I was given support and encouragement from the Khwaja of the Nizamuddin shrine, Hasan Sani Nizami and Dr. Ausaf Ali, then chancellor of Hamdard University. I also was given a place to work at the Archives and Research Centre for Ethnomusicology of the American Institute of Indian Studies, and was warmly received by its director, Shubha Chaudhuri and her staff. Meraj Ahmed, *qawwal*, and his extended family were also gracious and generous at all times.

In Sri Lanka, I was taken under the wing of Edin, *adura*, who patiently but firmly insisted that I learn to dance in order to understand the drumming of Yak Tovil ceremonies. He gave me lessons and arranged for me to see many Yak Tovil ceremonies that I would not have heard of had it not been for him.

In Bali, I was the beneficiary of the generosity and helpfulness of Wayan Aryati and her extended family, especially her husband, Thomas Hunter. They made my stay in Bali not only productive, but intensely pleasurable as well.

Visiting Pentecostals churches in Ann Arbor and Ypsilanti, I have always been overwhelmed by the enthusiasm of the welcome I have received. While knowing full well that conversion is on their mind, there is no doubt that Pentecostal communities exude a hospitality that is, in my mind, almost unparalleled.

Any number of my colleagues, academics from around the country, have helped in various ways. To David Huron, Ali J. Racy and Jaak Panksepp, the readers provided by Indiana University Press, I am extremely grateful for the careful and rigorous readings they provided of my manuscript. Each challenged me in fruitful ways and pushed me to work harder to make the manuscript both more coherent and more readable. I am also grateful to another set of readers, Nicola Dibben, Elizabeth Tolbert, and Steven Friedson who were solicited from the University of Michigan Press before I had settled on Indiana University

Press. Their comments also helped me to produce a more coherent book. I have been blessed with two sets of conscientious outside readers who were more than usually well-versed in my topic and willing to share their knowledge with me.

My friends, Lorna McDaniel and Rhys Isaac also read the manuscript and, as humanists, helped me to see the ways in which I had not succeeded in conveying the scientific aspects of the manuscript. If I have still not succeeded, it is not because they didn't try. Ani Patel has consistently encouraged me by his abiding personal and professional interest in music and neuroscience. Gayle Sherwood, my editor at Indiana University Press, was quick to respond to my manuscript submission and since then has put up with and assisted with my interminable queries about the labyrinthine process of getting permissions.

I am grateful to the School of Music at the University of Michigan for granting me a semester's leave in order to complete a manuscript that was seemingly never to be finished. Also, at the School of Music, I am grateful to Greg Laman who was always ready to help with any technical problem in preparing audio materials, and to Mary Huey, who always responded instantly to my many, largely self-induced, computer problems. The School of Music is lucky to have on its staff such talented and generous people.

To the Fulbright Foundation, I am grateful for the grant that allowed me to take time off from teaching to be able to go to New Delhi, to Sri Lanka and to Bali, Indonesia during my sabbatical leave. To the University of Michigan Office of the Vice-President for Research, I am grateful for a publications subvention that made possible the inclusion of a CD with the book.

Everyone thanks their spouse; it has become a trope of acknowledgments. But everyone does not have a spouse who is an authority on Southeast Asian languages and cultures, who is a mine of information about things not only Southeast Asian but also about writing, about intellectual history in general, and is the best reader imaginable (not just my opinion) who never pulls his punches. It has been our great good fortune to have been a couple, happily vexing each other for half a century. Thank you Pete.

Deep Listeners

Introduction

The interpenetration of music with trancing is ancient and universal. I suspect that most, if not all, societies have some form of institutionalized, religious trance ceremonies that also include music.[1] Trancing is often, in northwestern Europe and the United States, associated with developing world countries. The explosive worldwide growth of Christian Pentecostalism, in which trancing accompanied by music is a core feature of religious practice, belies the popular association of trancing with peoples from underdeveloped or developing nation-states only.

Trancing can be empowering for all concerned, attesting to the divine presence in one's midst, legitimizing the religious beliefs and practices of the community, and often bestowing deep satisfaction on the individual trancer. Trancers are always active and often dance—a response in part because of their deep emotionality. They welcome emotion, they offer themselves to emotion as they enact emotion. Musical immersion stimulates emotion and facilitates their special attentiveness, their special consciousness.

The connection of this kind of trancing to other phenomena such as hypnosis, multiple personality disorders, dissociative disorders, somnambulism, fugue states, catatonic states, and perhaps many more are not examined here. There may or may not be relationships and resonances with these other phenomena, but the most striking differences are the sensual richness of trancing within the context of religious ceremonies, the strong emotions of the trancer, the physical animation of the trancer, the high value placed on these events by their participants, and the enveloping musical saturation. Of all the phenomena that one might include within the category of trance, religious institutionalized trancing ranks as the most aesthetic, most widely practiced, and the most highly valued of all trances.

Meditation presents a very different complex of characteristics than do the trances presented here. Meditation is generally practiced in solitude, stillness, and silence. Trance is practiced within a communal framework, is usually accompanied by music and often involves strenuous activity on the part of the trancer. Institutionalized, religious trancing takes place within a context of sensual overstimulation; the trancer is bombarded with arresting sights and sounds. The meditator seeks to still the barrage of incoming perceptions. Trancing is emotional, while meditation aims at transcending emotion (see Rouget 1985: 6–12).

Whereas the sciences of biology and neuroscience are central to explaining the phenomenon of trancing, trance as inner experience cannot be understood entirely within a scientific framework. My object is to make trancing comprehensible within a secular humanistic framework, within a biological orientation while simultaneously acknowledging the special gnosis of trancing that cannot and need not be explained. In this way, I hope to "save the phenomenon."

"Deep Listeners" is a term I have adapted from the composer Pauline Oliveros, who uses "deep listening" as a term for her own practice of listening. On her Web site, she offers this definition of deep listening.

> Deep Listening involves going below the surface of what is heard and also expanding to the whole field of sound whatever one's usual focus might be. Such forms of listening are essential to the process of unlocking layer after layer of imagination, meaning, and memory down to the cellular level of human experience. (<http://www.deeplistening.org>)

In my own definition, deep listeners is a descriptive term for persons who are profoundly moved, perhaps even to tears, by simply listening to a piece of music. Everyone knows such a person: the roommate for whom the "Moonlight Sonata" provokes quiet sobbing, or the aunt who cries at John Lennon's "Imagine." These folks, I believe, experience a nearness to trance. Deep listeners are very emotional and often have near-religious transcendental experiences. I suspect that in cultures in which trance is not marginalized, as it is in the United States and Europe, deep listeners also might be trancers. Deep listening is a kind of secular trancing, divorced from religious practice but often carrying religious sentiments such as feelings of transcendence or a sense of communion with a power beyond oneself. Deep listening may be attributed to personal psychology as in the United States, or may be culturally situated. So closely are music and deep listening associated in Arabic cultures that the term *tarab*—which means to be moved, agitated, while listening to music (to the extent that one may cry, faint or tear one's clothes)—can also simply refer to a musical style (Racy 2003: 75). Secular musical ecstasy is the goal of performers and listeners alike for a certain segment of the urban, educated Arabic community (Racy 1991). Like *tarab*, "deep listening" conjoins musical expression and the emotional impact of musical expression. Music, trance, and emotion are, I believe, imbricated in both trancers and in deep listeners. In certain situations, the only salient distinction between the two that is obvious to an observer is the generally richer sensual and imaginary context of religious trancing.

Trancing is challenging to an objectivist epistemology, it resists representation. Within a strict objectivist view of the world, there is no way to describe trance as experience, as a first-person event. Like pain, for one who experiences it, nothing is more certain, whereas for one who does not experience it "even with effort, one may remain in doubt about its existence or may retain the astonishing freedom of denying its existence; and, finally, if with the best effort of sustained attention, one successfully apprehends it, the aversiveness of the 'it' one apprehends will only be a shadowy fraction of the actual 'it'" (Scarry 1985: 4). Nor have we had, until recently, a way to imagine the neurophysiology of trance, nor a theory of consciousness that would provide a framework to begin to study the neurophysiology of trance. Trancers are spectacularly in motion from the onset until the completion of the trance, ruling out electrodes, PET (positron emission tomography) scans, and MRIs (magnetic resonance imaging). Neurobiologists study dreams (Hobson 1994), meditation or pathological states of consciousness resulting from illnesses or injuries, situations where subjects can be examined and talked to (Squire 1987; Alkon 1992; LeDoux 1996). Trancers are on the move and not amenable to simultaneous interviews. Trance consciousness remains opaque, unstudied, and suspect as the domain of religious fanatics and the mentally unstable.

Many firsthand accounts of experienced and skillful trancers testify to the catalytic role of music in the transition into trancing, in the sustaining of trancing, and in the transition back to normal consciousness (Rouget 1985: 72; Kapferer 1991: 264; Friedson 1996: 6). But the "why" of all this remains, from a physiological perspective, largely speculation. How can one integrate richly humanistic, first-person descriptions of musical trancing with biological and neurological theories concerning consciousness?

As of today, there is no simple way of bridging the gap between the firing of neurons within the central nervous system, or the transmission of endorphins to an adjacent cell, and the complex motivations, memories, and self-understandings that we all richly inhabit. One cannot pinpoint directly any neuronal firing or chemical transmission to the experience of a Balinese trancer who, while hearing the gamelan play faster and louder, looks at a mask of the witch, Rangda, and sees fire coming from her eyes. Neurophysiological explanations are as yet primitive when dealing with human action, human perception, and human motivations. The bridge between the physical embodiment of the brain and the phenomenological experience of being-in-the-world has not yet been built.

An exploratory article written by Elizabeth Tolbert in 1992 posits some fundamental questions concerning the feasibility of integrating neurobiology, psychology, and music cognition studies within the discipline of ethnomusicology. Tolbert recognized what may be a basic incompatibility between ethnomusicology and those other fields, based as they are on scientific methodology.

> The issue of reductionism is of central concern, i.e., can one determine anything about musical meaning by reducing musical experience to an explanation of perceptual and cognitive processes? From the point of view of most ethnomusicologists, the nature of musical meaning is considered to be inapproachable by empirical studies, especially in light of ethnomusicological work that demonstrates the close relationship of musical meaning to its cultural and historical context. (Tolbert 1992: 7)

From the hard science side of the epistemological divide come similar questions and similar aspirations to bring together scientific methodology and humanistic exploration.

> One provocative possible extension of the view of cognition as enaction is to the domain of cultural knowledge in anthropology. Where is the locus of cultural knowledge such as folktales, names for fishes, jokes—is it in the mind of the individual? . . . Great leverage for anthropological theory might be obtained by

considering the knowledge to be found in the interface between mind, society, and culture rather than in one or even in all of them. The knowledge does not preexist in any one place or form but is enacted in particular situations—when a folktale is told or a fish named. (Varela, Thompson, and Rosch 1991: 178–79)

It seems clear to me that a common ground may be explored between the more humanistic, cultural anthropological approach, and the more scientific, cognitive psychological approach. I see the bringing together of the scientific and cultural approaches to the study of music and emotion, and music and trancing as one of the great challenges of our fields. Whereas the styles of argument and the criteria for evidence may remain distinct, the conclusions need to be comparable and not incommensurable. Both disciplinary areas may have to give up some of their established scholarly practices.

I seek a theory of music cognition, of consciousness that can help in understanding the complex interrelationships between trancing and music, in correlating the eye-and-ear visions and gestures of individuals in religious trance who are simultaneously being musicked. How are the outward characteristics of religious trance (dance, prophecy, speaking in tongues, speaking in voices of spiritual beings) correlated with inner physiology and what is the role of music in facilitating these events?

The prevailing models of research in music cognition, the enveloping frames of music theory do not seem adequate as starting premises for exploration into the musical cognition of an ecstatic. I wish to outline what I perceive as the limitations of musical cognitive studies as now practiced, not with the intent of restating the traditional humanistic opposition to scientific methodology but in the hope that compromise and integration can be worked through.

Problems with Traditional Paradigms of Music Cognition

Theories of the mind as reflected in studies of music cognition have a venerable history in Western intellectual traditions. In 1637, Descartes formalized a system of thinking about our minds, the elegance, simplicity, and persuasiveness of which rarely was challenged in Western intellectual domains until well into the twentieth century (Dreyfus and Dreyfus 1988; Flanagan 1991: 1–9; Damasio 1994: 247–52).[2] *Cogito, ergo sum,* "I think, therefore I am," succinctly summarizes a complicated theory of being that took issue with the prevailing doctrine of the church that knowledge depended on a disembodied soul. Descartes postulated that the soul was embodied, a function of the brain and the nervous system. Except for the more arcane aspects of Descartes's theory, such as the belief that the soul resides in the pineal gland, the broad tenets of the theory still influence the way we think about music and cognition. Descartes was a dualist who believed that our bodies were comprised of two essences, *res cogitans* and *res extensa*. *Res extensa* is the human body, which he thought of as a physical reflex machine. *Res cogitans* is the realm of the mind, the realm of reason, of imagination, of beauty, religion, and the arts. Descartes's theory allows for the richly human activities of religion, philosophy, history, and the arts while proclaiming a strict dualism and preserving from any scientific reductionism the essential human qualities of forethought, emotion, moral judgment, freedom of action, and personal responsibility: all those qualities that give meaning to our lives. The system is elegant, and was in its day liberating.

Thinking about musical meaning, before and after Descartes, centered around issues of representation, of musical referentiality, of emotion, or of divine inspiration. Musical thinking was clearly within the realm of *res cogito*, intentional, imaginative, cognitive, in the brain. Music became something "good to think with," but the physical body was excluded. The field of music cognition emerged in the mid-twentieth century with several distinct yet sometimes overlapping areas of investigation. One was learning to map musical perception within the brain, locating where melodies, harmonies, and pitch recognition were taking place (Borchgrevink 1982; Weinberger and McKenna 1988; Petsche, Lindner, and Rappelsberger 1988; Peretz and Morais 1988; Wallin 1991; Tramo 2001). Early studies led to the popular but vastly reductive idea that music was a "right-brain" activity. Those scholars for whom music cognition is the study of perception are necessarily involved in micro-musical studies within the brain, how a phrase is imaged, how intervals are understood, how pitches are heard and classified, or how musical phrases are parsed (Deutsch 1982; van Noorden 1982; Vos and Rasch 1982; Dowling and Harwood 1986; Fales 1998, 2002).

With the development of computers in the mid-twentieth century, studies in music cognition gained a powerful tool for thinking about musical meaning (Terhardt 1982; Piszczalski and Galler 1982). Music cognition as practiced by many music theorists is derived from models in which music comes to be symbolically represented in the brain and then is subjected to formal processes, or algorithms, that tell us whether what we are hearing is a first theme, an elaboration of something heard earlier, a theme that is totally inappropriate for this particular context, and so on (Meyer 1956; Minsky 1982; Lerdahl and Jackendoff 1983; Sloboda 1985; Dowling and Harwood 1986; Serafine 1988; Narmour 1990; Raffman 1993; Imberty 2000; Scherer and Zentner 2001). The shift of emphasis in all cognitive studies, especially but not exclusively psychological cognitivism, was from the "construction of meaning" to the "processing of information" (Bruner 1990: 4). Often called an objectivist approach to musical meaning, this approach to music cognition does not seem to need a body, nor does it seem able to deal with the body. Music is disembodied, able to be reduced to a string of musical symbols on which algorithmic operations are performed. Traditional music cognition as a theoretical construct is as elegant, as simple and as powerful as Descartes's formulations. Many music cognition studies also invoke universal models, making them yet more generalized and more compelling (Lerdahl and Jackendoff 1983). Structural, generative linguistics on the model of Noam Chomsky (1972) is the language corollary for both computer studies and many studies of music cognition. Grammatical structures in the brain are subject to algorithmic operations to produce the sentences of living languages. Work based on this theory in music cognition may be significant for unraveling syntactical meanings in music but not in helping to understand why Sufis in New Delhi can be brought to tears, rise up, turn in slow circles, and feel they have reached a nearness to the Divine in response to a particular poetic phrase sung over and over again. Nor does it help in trying to understand why a worshipper at a Pentecostal service gets caught up in repetitious actions of shaking her head from side-to-side with a ferocity and persistence that is almost frightening, subsequently feeling relieved, refreshed, and inspired. How do we bring together these disparate kinds of studies of musical experience?

To those who use the traditional models of music cognition, the idea of incorporating a much messier, much more complex, and uncertain model based on biology and phenomenology can seem like a giant step backward, away from scientific elegance, away from empirical controls, away from universality. Yet we experience music with our skins, with our pulse rates, and with our body temperature. To subscribe to a theory of musical cognition which cannot deal with the embodiment of music, of the involvement of the senses, the visceral system, and the emotions is to maintain a Cartesian approach of mind/body dualism.

A number of scholars have written about the inadequacy of the cognitive model for the study of language, and have pointed out that cognitive models based on computers cannot handle some of the most basic elements of language such as metaphor and metonymy, not to mention vagueness, polysemy, or shifting meanings that are integral to all living languages (Lakoff 1987; M. Johnson 1987; A. L. Becker 1995; Searle 2002). Furthermore, there is an increasing awareness within cognitive science of the importance of culture and embodiment. A growing number of cognitive scientists have stressed the importance of studying cognition as the interaction of a person with a milieu, the relevance of sensorimotor activity for cognition, and have questioned the primacy of representations in the brain as the basis for cognition. Studies of "distributed cognition" (Hutchins 1995), "embodied cognition" (Keijzer 2002; Ziemke 2002), and neural net models (Todd and Loy 1991; Griffith and Todd 1999) may offer approaches to the study of music cognition that are far less hostile to biological understandings than earlier paradigms. But the traditional cognitive model extended to musical matters as "music cognition" remains the dominant paradigm. In a highly praised book that follows a strictly formalist theory, Steven Pinker states his understanding of what a language is. This is also the model of what, for some, a musical system is.

> The way language works, then, is that each person's brain contains a lexicon of words and the concepts they stand for (a mental dictionary) and a set of rules that combine the words to convey relationships among concepts (a mental grammar). (Pinker 1994: 90)

Language consists of a set of words and a set of concepts located in the brain and a set of rules to make sentences that express concepts. The terms that are used to describe the processes of thinking are "representations" and "processors." The senses provide the representations, the mind provides the processors.

The brain becomes an input-output machine, with which, if one knows both input and processing rules, the outcome can be predicted. The "outcome" never seems applicable to what one sees and hears at a rousing Pentecostal service, entranced dancers at a Balinese temple ritual, devotees at a rock concert, or ecstatic Sufis.

There are other theoretical alternatives for the ethnomusicologist, nearly all of which are high risk, given the intellectual climate of our discipline. If one chooses a biologically based epistemology following current developments in neuroscience, one runs the risk of being accused of "scientism" or "materialism." Ethnomusicology is a discipline heavily dependent, historically, on humanistic values. With its twin forebears of historical musicology and anthropology, ethnomusicology as a discipline is firmly committed to the importance of human meanings, human evaluations, and human motivations. Many of us have an aesthetic distaste for too much "scientific" intrusion into the field, and will react instinctively to too many charts, tables, measurements, frequencies, and so on. Unlike our European forebears, we do not see ourselves as scientists but, rather, as researchers of the human spirit in the intellectual lineage of history, philosophy, aesthetics, and cultural anthropology.

Fragmentation of intellectual effort is one of the curses of the modern academy. Ethnomusicology with its multiple parentage has never had a monolithic dogma but, rather, multiple practitioners of many different kinds of ethnomusicology. I hope that there also can be many different kinds of music cognition including one that is biologically based, psychologically sophisticated, and attuned to cultural nuances, cultural knowledge.

Languaging, Musicking, and Trancing

Throughout this book, the gerunds "languaging," "musicking," and "trancing" will often appear in place of the more usual "language," "music," and "trance." My computer spell-check, a certain indicator of orthodoxy, rejects all three gerunds. Languaging is the form favored by scholars who wish to differentiate language activity from language structure, that is, to distinguish language as talking from language as primarily grammar, syntax, and procedural rules of transformation (Maturana and Varela 1987: 234; Smith and Ferstman 1996: 52; A. L. Becker 1995: 9).

"Musicking" was, as far as I know, first introduced by Christopher Small (1987: 50) for the same reasons: to emphasis the processual, active, performing aspects of music rather than the scholarly, historical emphasis on music as text. Thus it is not surprising that musicking has been accepted readily by ethnomusicologists whose involvement with music tends to be with performances and far less with music as text.

"Trancing" is preferred to the more common terms "trance state" or "altered state of consciousness," as both latter terms imply a static situation, a fixed form.

I have explored the possibility of using other terms, such as "ecstasy," a happier term, but one which also implies a "state of being in ecstasy" and does not escape the static implications of "trance." Moreover, ecstasy, as a joyful experience, does not always apply to the kinds of religious/musicked trancing that I address. In the Sufi *sama*, the musical ceremony for the attainment of a sense of union with Allah, the Arabic term *hal* is usually translated as "ecstasy," a fitting word to denote the sublime joy of the worshipper. However, depending on the psychology of the individual, *hal* can sometimes be painful and deeply disturbing.

Trances are always processual; one is either entering, continuing, or coming out of a trance. The temporal movement of both trancing and musicking from onset to conclusion can easily be followed. Trances tend to be of rather limited time duration, typically lasting from a minute or two to an hour or two; trances may reach a climax followed by a collapse. As thinking is a process, as musicking is a process, so trancing is a process and not a "state."

Multiple Senses of Embodiment

My intent is to begin to bridge the gulf between disciplines whose approach to the embodiment of experience involves different approaches and leads to differing results. There are at least three ways to think about embodied experience, none of which can be separated cleanly from the others. Each of the three can provide special insights into music and trancing and all three, separately or concurrently, will frame the discussions in the chapters that follow.

1) The body as a physical structure in which emotion and cognition happen
2) The body as the site of first-person, unique, inner life
3) The body as involved with other bodies in the phenomenal world, that is, as being-in-the-world

The first sense of embodiment is found in studies in mainstream cognitive science, including music cognition, in formalist theories of language, in psychological studies and in neuroscience. Where is music processed in the brain? What brain structures are involved in generating emotion?

The second sense of embodiment is our inner life, the traditional domain of the arts and the humanities. Human interior thoughts and feelings engage those scholars and artists who have always taken on the hard questions of human experience, the "eternal verities." Within the last hundred years, the body as the site of inner life also has become the province of the European philosophical school known as phenomenology, which has tried to bring scientific rigor into the philosophical study of inner life. There is a diverse group of scholars from various disciplines who have been influenced by the phenomenologists Martin Heidegger (who coined the phrase "being-in-the-world") and Merleau-Ponty, including psychology (Piaget 1959/1969), linguistics (Lakoff 1987; A. L. Becker

1995; Foley 1997), biology (Maturana and Varela 1987), philosophy (M. Johnson 1987), cognitive science (Nuñez 1997; Benzon 2001), and neuroscience (Edelman 1992; Damasio 1999).

The third sense of embodiment may be the most difficult as it is the sense that is least reinforced in the arts and in our intellectual tradition. The "naturalist" assumption is that human beings, like all living organisms, are constantly changing and being changed by their ongoing interactions with other human beings and with all other living organisms in their immediate milieu. William James (1842–1910) is generally credited as the founder of the modern naturalist study of mind, as well as the father of the discipline of psychology. Strongly influenced by the writings of Charles Darwin and Charles Peirce, James was the first to place the study of mind within the context of the study of all living organisms. Evolutionary development and change is subsumed within the naturalist assumption. In the naturalist view, mental life has what Flanagan calls "no metaphysically odd properties" (Flanagan 1991: 24), meaning no homunculus, no "ghost-in-the-machine" (Ryle 1949), no disembodied soul, and no mind-body dualism.

Among neuroscientists, the prevailing view is that the electrical/chemical processes of the brain are coterminous with the mind (Edelman 1992: 6–7; Panksepp 1998b: 567; Damasio 1999: 85). The brain can be considered objectively, given names for its parts and physically dissected. The mind, mental life, as process is harder to study scientifically. Although techniques for scientific mind-study are developing, mind as full inner experience can only be fully known by the one who has one; mind is a first-person, phenomenological experience. Some neuroscientists (discussed more fully later) are coming up with theories of consciousness that do not violate holistic approaches to mind, yet still maintain the biological basis of mental life.

> It is not surprising that people have treated the mind itself as a special thing or a special form of stuff. After all, it seems so different from ordinary matter that its possessor may find it difficult to conclude by introspection alone that it could arise from the *interactions* of nonintentional matter. But, as William James pointed out, mind is a process, not a stuff. Modern scientific study indicates that extraordinary processes can arise from matter; indeed, matter itself may be regarded as arising from processes of energy exchange. In modern science, matter has been reconceived in terms of processes; mind has not been reconceived as a special form of matter. That mind is a special kind of process depending on special arrangements of matter is the fundamental position I will take in this book. (Edelman 1992: 6–7)

Some humanists, musicologists, and some of those who believe in institutionalized religions find this interpretation disturbing. How could the activity of neurons, of neurotransmitters, and of neuropeptides possibly explain our rich and varied life experiences? I believe that it is not necessary to make a scientific description stand in opposition to humanistic or religious explanations of what it means to be human. All perspectives are partial perspectives and the neuroscience of the brain leaves aside ultimate questions. We will always need poets, saints, philosophers, musicians, and madmen to help us see the full range of what it means to be human. What neuroscience can do is help us understand some of the underlying mechanisms of the central nervous system that contribute to, or that make possible, the joy of the Pentecostal "slain in the spirit" while dancing to a rousing gospel hymn, or the ecstasy of the Sufi who experiences communion with Allah while listening to sung poetry, or the transcendental pleasure we may experience when entranced by music.

In the chapters that follow, I attempt to bring together fields of inquiry that normally do not interact with any intensity or frequency, such as ethnomusicology and biology, or psychology and ethnomusicology, or neuroscience and ethnomusicology. By juxtaposing these disciplines in the quest for a theory of the relationship of music and trancing, I hope that new approaches may emerge that would not be apparent were such a juxtaposing not made explicit. My aim is to begin to integrate the recent findings of the biological sciences with our knowledge of music and trance derived from first-person reports, from phenomenology, and from the psychological and anthropological literature on trance. The scientific literature on emotion and consciousness can add some striking new insights into the crucial role of emotion in musical listening and in trancing, and provides us with some ways to visualize the workings of our minds and bodies. On the other hand, recent psychological, biological, and neuroscientific studies also underscore how much we already know about music and trance. Although the language of verification is not the same, although the metaphors may be very different, scientific studies may provide parallel descriptions to the analyses of humanistic scholars of previous times and places such as al-Ghazzali (twelfth-century Sufi) and Jean-Jacques Rousseau (1712–78), both of whom thought deeply about trance and music.

Chapter-by-Chapter Summary

In Chapter 1, "Rethinking 'Trance,'" contemporary semiotic, cultural approaches to trancing are traced from Jean-Jacques Rousseau in the eighteenth century to the present. Issues of the problems of using the term "trance" cross-culturally are addressed as well as the silence of the "inner language" during trancing. Examples are given of how religious communities deal with the problem of believability (Sufis, Sri Lankan faith healers, Pentecostals). The search for an organic bodily cause for the affect of music on trancing is traced from the *tarantismo* of fifteenth-century Italy to contemporary studies of rhythmic entrainment. This chapter concludes with a definition of trance compatible with studies from humanistic and scientific disciplines.

Chapter 2, "Deep Listeners," examines the issue of ANS (autonomic nervous system) arousal in relation to musical listening and the implications for both deep listeners and trancers. Recent work on music and emotion by psychologists (Gabrielsson, Lindstrom Wik, Krumhansl) and neuroscientists (Blood and Zatorre, Damasio, Nyklicek et al., Panksepp) demonstrate that deep listeners experience the physical symptoms of ANS arousal such as changes in heart rate, skin conductance, respiration, and the phenomenon known as "chills." Feelings of transcendence, akin to those of trancers, are also frequently reported by deep listeners. An ancient Indian theory of "aesthetic" emotions (*rasa* theory) parallels recent scientific studies in linking emotion and transcendence, and the erotic dimension of musical emotion and trancing. I propose that deep listeners and trancers have "learned" to regulate or modify physiological systems of arousal that are generally believed to be *not* under voluntary control.

Chapter 3, *"Habitus of Listening,"* explores the idea that different musics are linked with different styles of listening, whether quiet and introspective as at a Western concert of classical music or a North Indian classical concert, or expectant of illumination as with Sufis at a *sama',* or anticipating rage at a Balinese Rangda/Barong ceremony. Borrowing from Bourdieu, the term *habitus of listening* is proposed to describe these differing stances of listening in relation to the musical event.

Chapter 4, "Trancing Selves," explores the idea that the normative model for a post-Enlightenment Western "self" can be antithetical to trancing. The trancer necessarily must surrender personal will and accept the penetration of her bodily boundaries. A Cartesian rational, disengaged self will resist trancing. Counterexamples to the normative Western model are presented—colonial Virginians and contemporary Pentecostals—and both are compared with the possession trance of *bissu* transvestite priests from Sulawesi, Indonesia.

Chapter 5, "Being-in-the-World: Culture and Biology," explores a biological approach to music/participant interaction influenced by European phenomenology and put forward by biologists and by neuroscientists. Based on work by Humberto Maturana, Francisco Varela, and Gerald Edelman, this approach claims that we are constantly changed by our interactions with the world while simultaneously changing that world. The term "structural coupling," borrowed from Maturana and Varela, is used to describe this enactive, biological perspective on music, trance, and emotion. Rhythmic entrainment is re-presented as an enactment of social structural coupling. Finally, structural coupling is compared to Bourdieu's *habitus,* as terms of description of the transgenerational practices that can be called "culture."

Chapter 6, "Magic through Emotion: Toward a Theory of Trance Consciousness," discusses Damasio's two-layered theory of consciousness—"core" consciousness and "extended" consciousness—and its implications for a theory of trance consciousness. I suggest that while trancing, core consciousness is unaffected, but that the autobiographical self, extended consciousness, is temporarily replaced by a trance persona, a trance consciousness. I propose that the analgesic properties of trancing may be a result of the substitution of the trance persona for the autobiographical self, the self who normally ascribes discomfort to itself. Damasio's theory links both forms of consciousness to emotion, placing emotion at the center of our sense of self. If this is so, then the emotions of trancing, emotions in part aroused by music, may play a central role in the production of trance consciousness.

These chapters are united only by my insistence that a dual perspective is the best way to approach a theory of the relationship of trancing and music. In a provocative essay on the promise and difficulty of a biological or neurological explanation of human behavior, Charles Taylor has insisted that any such explanation must "save the phenomenon" (Taylor 1985), by which he means that any scientific explanation must not violate the importance we all place on issues of human volition, human motivation, human emotions, and human interpretations.[3] Taylor does not mean that "commonsense" notions may not be overturned but that in the process no useful scientific explanation should override our sense of purposefulness, of meaningfulness, and of autonomy in our lives.

Any study of mind and behavior opens only a small window on the understanding of the complexities of being human. This work is intended to be only an initial exploration of trancing and deep listening. If it is successful, it will soon be supplanted by the work of others who will have explored these issues more deeply. As scholars, we have no "God's-eye view" and hardly any "bird's-eye view" either. I strongly believe that psychological, biological, or neurological explanations are not the enemies of more traditional religious, literary, and philosophical explanations. They are, rather, at opposite points of what the physicist Richard Feynman calls a hierarchy. Feynman's hierarchy extends from the fundamental laws of physics, to water in waves, to a muscle twitch, to a frog, to a human, to history, and [finally] to evil, beauty, and hope. He concludes:

Which end is nearer to God; if I may use a religious metaphor. Beauty and hope, or the fundamental laws? I think that the right way, of course, is to say that what we have to look at is the whole structural interconnection of the thing; and that all the sciences, and not just the sciences but all the efforts of intellectual kinds, are an endeavor to see the connections of the hierarchies, to connect beauty to history, to connect history to man's psychology, man's psychology to the working of the brain, the brain to the neural impulse, the neural impulse to the chemistry, and so forth, up and down, both ways. And today we cannot, and it is no use making believe that we can, draw carefully a line all the way from one end of this thing to the other, because we have only just begun to see that there is this relative hierarchy.

And I do not think either end is nearer to God. (Richard Feynman 1965: 124–25)

A Historical Interlude: Trance in Europe and the United States

Trance in our society suffers from our unfamiliarity with it, our historical aversion to it, and from our deep antipathy to the idea of not being fully in conscious control of our behavior. From the possessed of the early Middle Ages, to the witches of the late Middle Ages, to the women who fell under the spell of Mesmer in the late eighteenth century, to the hypnotic trances induced by the nineteenth-century Parisian doctors Charcot and Janet, to the modern-day reincarnations of these phenomena as "multiple personalities," or to the current rage for altered consciousness among Rave enthusiasts, the history of trance in our civilization is the history of a perversion. Serious trancers such as the Pentecostals are considered to be indecorous and mildly embarrassing; nonserious trancers such as many New Age followers are written off as dilettantes or, worse, crackpots. We have no reputable trance states, no awards for revelations from mediums, no summer camps for learning to trance, and no serious attention from the scientific community. In the words of Ian Hacking, trance has become a curiosity, an aberration, a "marvel" (Hacking 1995: 143). We have written off trance.

How did trance in Europe and the United States come to be classified as a pathology?

Historicizing Western trances, deconstructing the inherent bias against trance, can help us to reimagine trances everywhere. In order to move beyond the unexamined assumptions concerning trances in Western industrialized societies, it is necessary to shed light on the history of the development of those attitudes.

One of the most striking aspect of the history of trance in Western societies is that trance is gendered; trance is overwhelmingly feminized. From the Middle Ages until the present, the compelling case histories of trance phenomenon are nearly all about women. To be susceptible to trance states indicated that one did not have strong boundaries between self and nonself; one lacked clear identity; one's body was permeable, susceptible to invasion from external spirits whose provenance may be suspect.

St. Augustine (354–430 C.E.) believed that the gods of the pagans were really demons who were capable of penetrating bodies and of making accurate prophesies.

> They [demons] also influence [people] in extraordinary ways, using the subtlety of their bodies to penetrate the bodies of men without their feeling it, and intermingling themselves into their thoughts, whether they are awake or asleep, through certain imaginative visions. (St Augustine, *De Divinatione Demonum*, quoted in Caciola 1994: 220)

One thousand years later, the issue began to heat up as the Roman church began a crusade against trance possession by demonic spirits. The church needed to be able to distinguish possession by "the holy spirit" and possession by some other spirit being. In discerning spirits, or in evaluating trancing the problem is always dual: that of being able to distinguish the fraudulent actions of others, and of the "reality" of one's own experiences. We not only are constantly contesting others' embodiments but our own as well. Henry of Hassia (late-fourteenth-century Germany) addresses this problem in his treatise *De Discretio Spirituum*, on how to discern spirits.

> Since, then, there exists such a multiplicity of spirits impelling men to their action, it is rather difficult to discern which motion is our own or else from this or that spirit. . . . Therefore it is difficult for a mortal man to understand and distinguish among these things what is a supernatural inspiration and what, on the other hand, is from the causes mentioned above [positions of the stars, humoral imbalances, or even indigestion] or similar ones, or occurs naturally. Clearly, then, one should not swiftly or lightly give credence to spiritual people who continually labor at fantasizing and contemplating that in all the impulses they feel, or in every somewhat unusual thing that occurs to them, they are supernaturally moved by a good or an evil spirit. (Caciola 1994: 346)

Henry of Hassia foreshadowed the Enlightenment that would follow four centuries later with his proposal that theological study and discussion, not sensual embodiment, reveal the true will of God. Rationality, restraint, and intellectualization lead one to spiritual development, not the messy, unruly, always contestable ecstatic trances of the mystics.

Many trances involve the penetration or invasion of the body by another self, an alien spirit, the "Holy Spirit," a deity or a devil. Possession trance may take the form of a complete displacement of one soul with another, or the side-by-side cohabitation of two souls within one body. According to St. Augustine, St. Thomas Aquinas, and many canonic philosophers following them, one body and one soul will be granted eternal bliss or condemned to eternal damnation at the Last Judgment. Multiple souls in one body are theologically unthinkable. Personal responsibility cannot be sustained if there is no one center of control.

Multiple selves became a serious theological debate in relation to the somnambulists in France in the late Middle Ages. Nowadays, somnambulism refers to actions performed while one is asleep; but formerly it was more broadly used to refer to what we would now call trancing. A text dated 1313 C.E. declared that a man who committed a criminal act while in the somnambulist state could not be barred from priestly functions (communion, last rites) on the grounds that he could not be held responsible for acts performed in trance. The Thomist church majority rejected this view and insisted on one soul per person, one "substantial form" per body (Hacking 1995: 147). Well into the nineteenth century, the term somnambulist was still in use for the trance state. The most famous French multiple personality, Felida, would undergo a trance-like switch and then carry on her life "walking, chatting, sewing, loving, quarreling" as another person. In 1875, her physician used the term somnambulism to describe her second personality, her second identity (Hacking 1995: 148). Somnambulism has dropped from our vocabulary, remaining only in the cartoon characterization of the little boy with outstretched arms walking into doors in his sleep.

The problem of more than one self and how to assign personal responsibility is no less of a problem now than it was then, both in the courts and on the street. When a defendant is found not guilty by reason of insanity, the courts echo the old debate about somnabulists, possession by evil spirits, multiple personality, and trances. The discomfort of many with such verdicts also resonates with a long history of belief in the integrity of the unified self, "one self substance," one immortal soul. Trances, especially possession trances, can seem heretical, faintly diabolical and also anti-Christian.

The discrediting of trance continued throughout the eighteenth-century Enlightenment, when spirit possession and witchcraft came to be viewed as superstition and were relegated to the category of the occult. Views of trance and the uses of trance in industrial societies took a decidedly new turn with the life and work of Franz Anton Mesmer (1734–1815), a Viennese physician who became both famous and infamous throughout Europe and America. Mesmer was a child of the Enlightenment, a follower of Newton, and a believer in natural/scientific explanations for illnesses. He thought he had discovered the key to the cure of all illness in the existence of a magnetic fluid that permeates the whole universe including all human bodies. This invisible fluid is the secret force that explains magnetism, the holding together of the universe. The same fluid holds bodies on the earth, unites us with all creatures and keeps us healthy. When this magnetic fluid becomes obstructed, we become ill.

In 1775, Mesmer participated in a historic encounter with the established church in the person of an exorcist and priest, Father Gassner. Mesmer, the man of science, was invited by Prince Max Joseph of Bavaria to challenge Father Gassner, the man of religion, to a healing competition. Mesmer proved able to cure as well with his mesmeric trances and his magnetic fluids as Father Gassner with his exorcism of devils (Decker 1986: 36). Father Gassner's reputation declined and Mesmer's soared. Some viewed this event as the triumph of science over superstition, the Age of Reason over the Age of Religion. Both men healed with trances, and as in earlier times, both healers for the most part cured women.

Mesmer moved from Vienna to Paris where he hoped to have his technique confirmed and to attain recognition in the cosmopolitan center of the scientific revolution. Through the use of large oak tubs of "magnetized" water, magnetized rods, and his own magnetized wand, patients were treated for all kinds of ailments. They often fell into trances, often experienced convulsions, and, from all accounts—even those of Mesmer's enemies—often were cured as well. Mesmer's techniques subsequently would be refined by his disciples and renamed "hypnotism" rather than "animal magnetism," the term used by Mesmer. The tubs, waters, rods, wand, and the theory of magnetic fluids were all eventually

Figure HI-1. Mesmer's salon. Courtesy of the Bibliothèque Nationale, Paris.

abandoned. But the technique he developed of putting patients into a kind of trance, later called hypnotism, remained.

Although intellectually committed to scientific materialism, and believing himself to be following scientific method, Mesmer created a thoroughly ritual atmosphere in his salon in Paris. He paid the most careful attention to the stage setting and the musical accompaniment to his curing rituals (as we would now call them). He himself was dressed in a lilac taffeta robe and carried a wand. His salon at the Hotel Bullion in Paris was a large, opulent room with high ceilings, inlaid floors, paneled walls, elegant furnishings, full length mirrors and heavy draperies to keep out the sounds of the surrounding city (Buranelli 1975: 125). (See Figure HI-1.)

Silence reigned except for the whispers of Mesmer and his assistants and the music played on a piano in the corner of the room. Mesmer had learned from his Viennese teachers of the curative power of music and used music consistently in his Paris salon. While he always had a pianist playing in the corner of the room, he himself sometimes played on the glass harmonica. Figure HI-1 reveals two small (or distant?) violinists as well.

He was not interested in melody as such when he placed musical instruments in the clinic. They were indispensable to his medical practice, swaying, disturbing, calming the ill. Stormy music helped bring on the Mesmerian crisis, and soft music helped allay it. The musician shifted from one to the other at a signal from Mesmer or an assistant. One of Mesmer's followers, Caullet de Vaumorel, testifies to the exquisite sensitivity with which the mood of the patients changed as the mood of the music changed. (Buranelli 1975: 125)

Did Mesmer realize how his musical atmosphere contributed to his cures, or did he think of the pianist and his "mood music" as part of the stage setting along with his cape and wand? He wrote voluminously of his "magnetic fluid," but he never addressed the issue of music therapy.

Although Mesmer tried valiantly to establish his credentials with the scientific community in Paris, he was ultimately rejected. Two commissions were set up to investigate his claims, one by the Academy of Sciences (including Benjamin Franklin) and one by the Royal Society of Medicine (Darnton 1968: 62). Mesmer was ruled a fraud by both, even though his cures were not denied. The scientific community could find no evidence for his health-giving magnetic fluid, but the report of the royal commission gives further evidence of his use of music in inducing trances.

These convulsions are marked by violent, involuntary movements of the limbs and the whole body, by constriction of the throat, by throbbing in the chest and nausea in the stomach, by rapid blinking and crossed eyes, by piercing cries, tears, hiccups and uncontrollable laughter. These are preceded or followed by a state of languor and daydreams, a type of abatement or even slumber. The slightest sudden sound causes a startled shuddering; and it has been observed that a change of tone or beat in music played on the piano influences the ill, so that a rapid composition agitates them and throws them back into convulsions. (Buranelli 1975: 110)

Satirical portrayals of Mesmer, of Mesmer's techniques, and of his results also included musical instruments. (See Figure HI-2.)

What was this music like? We shall never know. But Mozart, who was a friend of Mesmer's and a frequent performer at the Mesmer home in Vienna before Mesmer moved to Paris, parodies the method of his old friend in the opera *Così fan Tutte* (1790). Toward the end of act I, the heroine, Despina, in a mock attempt at a cure, draws a huge magnet from beneath her robe and waves it at two gentlemen who are supposed to have swallowed poison. As she sings "Here and there a touch of the magnet, the stone of Mesmer who was born and bred in Germany, and became so famous in France," the woodwinds and violins in the orchestra play sforzando trills meant to symbolize and satirize the flow of 'animal magnetism' throughout the patients bodies (Buranelli 1975: 56). (See Figure HI-3.)

Although rejected by the scientific community from whom he so desperately wanted acceptance, Mesmer's hypnotic trance was nonetheless taken up by some members of countermovements hostile to the Age of Reason. Paris at the end of the eighteenth century was not only the heart of the scientific revolution

LES EFFETS DU MAGNETISME........ANIMAL.

Se vend chez Paris M.ᵈ d'E. stampes Sur le Boulevard du Temple vis-a-vis le Caffé d'Alexandre.

Figure HI-2. Les Effets Du Magnetisme. Courtesy of the Bibliothèque Nationale, Paris.

but also the seat of a thriving mystical community that embraced Rosicrucians, the occult writings of the Swedish scientist and theologian Swedenborg, plus an assortment of clever rogues who cashed in on mystical believers. Unfortunately for his reputation, Mesmer's hypnotic technique became associated with a range of occult practitioners. Simultaneously, he also had a serious following from some members of the scientific medical community. Thus, "Mesmerism" took two directions; one veering off into the netherworld of occultism and spiritualism associated with communication with the dead, the other a respectable development within the scientific community leading directly to the Freudian revolution and psychoanalysis. Mesmer's theory of magnetic fluids became a historical curiosity; but his technique of throwing subjects into a state between sleep and wakefulness became, on the one hand, a respectable scientific technique for recovering memory, and, on the other, a vaudeville act "sandwiched between the clowns, dancers, pantomimists, prestidigitators, and performing dogs" (Buranelli 1975: 121). The original important role of music was abandoned in both cases. The Mesmeric trance became a sideshow, and the term "mesmerized" entered the vocabulary as a synonym for the glazed eyes and dreamy look of a dissociative state.

Figure HI-3. Excerpt from score of *Cosí Fan Tutte*. Broude Brothers 1940: 206.

Often enough, "mesmerized" also meant to be under the control of a dominating male. Many suspicions were aroused by the sexual implications of Mesmer's cures. Beautiful ladies fell under the power of a male healer and responded automatically to his commands. Furthermore, a room outfitted with mattressed floors and ceilings called the "crisis room" adjoined Mesmer's healing salon in Paris. Patients in a state of collapse were taken by Mesmer or one of his assistants to this recovery room after their convulsive states subsided. At the time of the official investigations, some members of the royal French commission had sent a secret supplementary report to the king warning of the abuses to which Mesmer's techniques were prone (Fuller 1982: 32). In America, these suspicions were publicly confirmed by the confessions of a Boston magnetizer.

> He confessed to have surrendered, quite against his original intentions, to fleeting temptations and to have telepathically impressed affections for himself upon the minds of lovely young ladies. Time after time he had been unable to resist the seductive appeal of beautiful women utterly subjecting themselves to him while grasping his hand and gazing trustingly into his eyes. By skillfully employing his mesmeric powers, he had succeeded in stirring their passions toward him to such a degree that they became willing to commit indecencies. Mesmerism, he implied, was an agent eminently capable of subverting moral sensibilities. (Fuller 1982: 32)

The medieval worry about the invasion of the body, the loss of control, and the susceptibility of women comes back full circle. Hypnotic trance had severed its ties to ritual and lost its association with music but not its gendered overtones. In Europe, hypnotism became an accepted medical practice through the work of Jean Martin Charcot (1825–93), Pierre Janet (1859–1947), and others.

Charcot was a physician of "hysteria," from the Greek *hysterikos* "suffering in the womb," the same root as "hysterectomy." He had diagnosed "hysteria" as a neurological disorder rather than the earlier nosology as a disease of the uterus, a female "complaint." Both Charcot and his student Janet worked at the Salpêtrière hospital in Paris. (By this time, trance took place in hospitals.) There they developed an etiology and a nosology for trances that still echo in popular opinion today. They believed that consciousness could be split into coexistent parts that may be mutually ignorant of each other. The term "double consciousness" became prevalent, the second of which was recoverable through hypnosis. This state could only happen if a woman suffered from an abnormal "weakness," a "defect" that prevented her from keeping her consciousnesses all of a piece. The misogyny of the treatment of French "hysterics" by the doctors at the Salpêtrière hospital in Paris did not go entirely unchallenged. Some feminist writers expressed their indignation at what they saw as the exploitation of mostly poor and ignorant women by rich and famous men.

> The nurses drag these unfortunate women, notwithstanding their cries and resistance, before men who make them fall into catalepsy. They play on these organisms . . . on which experiment strains the nervous system and aggravates the morbid conditions, as if it were an instrument. . . . One of my friends told me that she . . . had seen a doctor of great reputation make one unhappy patient pass, without

Figure HI-4. Charcot's classroom. Courtesy of the Musée des Beaux Arts, Nice, France.

transition, from a celestial beatitude to a condition of infamous sensualment. And this before a company of literary men and men of the world. (quoted in Showalter 1993: 311, from the journal *Zoophilist* 1887)

Figure HI-4, the nineteenth-century painting by Pierre-André Brouillet of Charcot's classroom, confirms the description quoted above.

Various methods of hypnosis were used both in Europe and in America, largely depending on the preferences of the doctor. The simplest method was to leave the subject alone for ten minutes after seating her comfortably, telling her to close her eyes, think of nothing, and relax her muscles. James Braid (who coined the term "hypnosis" in 1840) used a bright button held near the forehead of the patient.[1] The old-fashioned "mesmerists" made hand passes downward over the face and body but without actual physical contact. Some doctors stared into the eyes of the patient, others had her listen to a ticking watch (James 1950, vol. 2: 593). The last two methods received the most attention from filmmakers.

Janet grouped hypnotic states into three main categories. The first was "cataleptic trance" brought about by hearing a sudden noise or looking at a bright light unexpectedly. The patient retains the bodily attitude in which she was when the trance "struck," a state that resembles the child's game "Statues." While in this state, the patient's eyes are staring and she is insensitive to pain. The second type, according to Janet, is the "lethargic trance," which can come about when the patient's eyes are forcibly closed or when the patient looks at something fixedly. She seems to lose consciousness and her muscles relax. The third type, called "somnambulistic trance," in reference to the much earlier somnambulists, is characterized by a patient who is wide awake, alert, talkative, and highly suggestible.

Janet was invited to give a series of lectures in 1907 at Harvard that were published as *The Major Symptoms of Hysteria*. In the lectures, Janet called the independent subpersonalities that emerge with hysteria "dissociations." He believed that memories were brought to consciousness by their associations with places, people, smells, sounds, and so on. Memories not retrievable in this way were "disassociated," were split off from normal consciousness, existed as a subordinate personality and could be retrieved under hypnosis. Possession trances, along with obsessive impulses, uses of the divining rod, and hallucinations, were also examples of "dissociation" in which the individual is controlled by a subpersonality not known to her conscious mind (Decker 1986: 48).

As a scientific enterprise, the work of Charcot, Janet and others led to the development of theories of the unconscious and of multiple personalities; ultimately to the establishment of psychology as a legitimate scientific discipline. Freud began as a student of Charcot, but apparently was not very good at hypnosis and soon abandoned it altogether (Inglis 1989: 116).

Medical and scientific developments in Europe were widely followed in the United States. William James (1842–1910), the American philosopher and psychologist, was a keen student of all the European case studies of the mind and the subconscious. Like several members of his family, James suffered from what we now call "manic-depressive illness," the symptoms of which are sometimes similar to those of nineteenth-century "hysterics" (Jamison 1993: 207–16). James brought an analytic intelligence, a deep personal empathy, and a mode of pragmatism to his understanding of the phenomena of trances. He was suspicious of clean classifications of trances, as he also was of the sharp line drawn between mental illness and normality. James was presciently aware of the power of language to shape reality and that the cultural and personal inputs to the diagnosis of disease involve the natural hopes and expectations of both doctor and patient. About the Parisian Salpêtrière system of nosology, he wrote:

> All the symptoms above described, as well as those to be described hereafter, are results of that mental susceptibility which we all to some degree possess, of yielding assent to outward suggestion, of affirming what we strongly conceive, and of acting in accordance with what we are made to expect. The bodily symptoms of the Salpetriere patients are all of them results of expectation and training. The first patients accidentally did certain things which their doctors thought typical and caused to be repeated. The subsequent subjects 'caught on' and followed the established tradition. In proof of this the fact is urged that the classical three stages [cataleptic, lethargic, somnambulistic] and their grouped symptoms have *only* been reported as spontaneously occurring, so far, at the Salpetriere, though they may be superinduced by deliberate suggestion, in patients anywhere found. (James 1950, vol. 2: 598)

Thus James believed that the "dissociated" personalities who were the patients at the Salpêtrière hospital were produced by the mutual expectations of doctor and patient and that the symptoms of "dissociation" were learned by example, which was not to imply any deception or inauthenticity. Trancing is also learned by example and reinforced by community expectations.

James also thought that mediumistic possession, by which he meant the medium who presides over a séance whose primary aim is to contact the spirits of the dead, was not a pathology. He saw it in terms of a form of alternate personality and refers to possession not as a neurosis but as a "gift."

> Mediumistic possession in all its grades seems to form a perfectly natural special type of alternate personality, and the susceptibility to it in some form is by no means an uncommon gift, in persons who have no other obvious nervous anomaly. (James 1950, vol. 1: 393)

Medical diagnoses and literary forms grew hand-in-hand. Robert Louis Stevenson wrote *The Strange Case of Dr. Jekyll and Mr. Hyde* (1886), which has become the prototypical dual personality: one genial, one evil. While writing Jekyll and Hyde, Stevenson was, according to his wife, inspired by the French doctors Charcot and Janet (Herdman 1991: 127). Offenbach's opera *Les Contes d'Hoffmann* (1880) presents three alter egos of the diva Stella: the automaton Olympia, the courtesan Giulietta, and the singer Antonia who is willing to die for art. More horrific than Hoffman's or Stevenson's multiples is the *Lady Ligeia* of Edgar Allan Poe (1840), who returns from the grave to claim the barely dead body of her husband's second wife in order to once again rejoin her husband in life. What was a medical curiosity, tied to "mesmerism" at the Salpêtrière in Paris, became a source of gothic attraction and dread in the hands of nineteenth-century writers.

The American physician and hypnotist who was most instrumental in legitimizing "multiple personality" in the United States was a friend and contemporary of James, Morton Prince (1848–1929). Like James, he came from a distinguished New England family, attended Harvard medical school, and worked in Boston. By 1890, the year of the publication of James's *Principles of Psychology*, Prince was a physician of "nervous diseases." Later in the decade, he came across a patient, "Miss Beauchamp," whom he diagnosed as a "multiple personality," whom he treated for many years, and who brought him fame through his book *The Dissociation of a Personality* (Prince 1930: 288–94). Prince propounded a theory of "co-consciousness" as distinct from "the unconscious" to explain the several personalities of Miss Beauchamp recoverable through hypnosis. "There are *very definite states of co-consciousness* of which the personal consciousness is not aware" (Inglis 1989: 137). In spite of Prince's respectability, hypnosis was too closely associated with occultism, with séances to contact the dead for full acceptance of the theory of "co-consciousness" in the medical community. Also, the scientific tide at this time was swinging in the opposite direction—away from study of the "mind" toward scientific materialism, positivism and behaviorism, all of which were hostile to the kind of inner life, mental research in which Prince (and James) were engaged. Furthermore, those who were committed to the newly emerging field of psychology were soon to be overtaken by the aggressive and dominating paradigm of Sigmund Freud. "Repressed memories," often as the result of childhood abuse, recoverable through psychoanalysis, and curable by discussion, submerged the budding theory of "multiple personality."

Not until the 1970s did "multiple personality" come back into view, and then with a vengeance—what one author calls a "multiple personality epidemic" (Boor 1982). At the 1985 meetings of the International Society for the Study of Multiple Personality, a group of multiple personality patients announced the creation of a newsletter "S4OS—Speaking for Our Selves" (Kenny 1986: 174). As in the nineteenth century, the popular media closely paralleled the concerns of the scientific community. Two movies, *The Three Faces of Eve* (1957) and *Sybil* (1976), created the popular image of the multiple personality and also reified a highly controversial theory (Hacking 1995: 40–42). The pseudonyms given to the two movie protagonists, Eve, the original woman, and Sybil, the Greco-Roman trance oracle, invoked mythic prototypes and conflated once again womanhood, mental illness, and trance.

The revival of "multiple personality disorder" in recent times had more sinister overtones for the afflicted, accompanied as it was by a more general revival of belief in satanic cults. Some multiples were diagnosed as harboring satanic selves, even when they themselves had no prior indication of any such possibility and thought of themselves as only suffering from headaches or depression. The TV program "Frontline," aired in October 1995, presented the horrifying and heart-rending stories of two women accused of harboring demonic selves intent on harming their husbands and children. Both women were able eventually to extricate themselves from their doctors' control, and to some extent, put back together their shattered lives.

*   *   *

The medically and ethically troubled historical issues surrounding hypnosis, "demonic possession," "multiple personalities," "co-consciousness," and "dissociation" in our society have created mythic stereotypes that are barriers to a fresh approach to trance consciousness. In Chapter 6, I will propose a new version of these thorny theories, a theory of trance consciousness that may not be burdened with the shades of our past but yet is not incompatible with earlier thinking.

1   Rethinking "Trance"

> My own impression is that the trance-condition is an immensely complex and fluctuating thing, into the understanding of which we have hardly begun to penetrate, and concerning which any very sweeping generalization is sure to be premature. A comparative study of trances and sub-conscious states is meanwhile of the most urgent importance for the comprehension of our nature.
>
> —William James [1890] *The Hidden Self*

Trancing is a profound mystery. You lose your strong sense of self, of ego, as you feel one with the music, you lose the sense of time passing, and may feel transported out of quotidian space. Trancers experience a kind of syncope, an absence, a lapse, a "cerebral eclipse." Syncope is sometimes viewed as a manifestation of a divine blessing, or a demonic possession, or as a pathology and called a dissociation.

Trancing and Culture

In 1980, Gilbert Rouget wrote his seminal book *La Musique et la transe: Esquisse d'une theorie generale des relations de la musique et de la possession*, translated and published in 1985 as *Music and Trance: A Theory of the Relations Between Music and Possession*. By clearing away some long-held misconceptions, he allowed for a new look at the interrelationship between music and trance. The important contributions of Rouget's book are:

1) he focused our attention on the fact that there are many different kinds of trance, some more usually associated with music than others.
2) he put to rest the assumption, both folk and scientific, that one can make a causal relationship between certain kinds of music, such as heavy, fast drumming, or repetitious melodic phrasing and certain kinds of trance. There is nothing intrinsic to the music that can cause trancing. The relationship between music and trance is not causal or deterministic.
3) he demonstrated that given the right cultural expectations, any kind of music, vocal or instrumental, can be associated with trance.

Rouget laid the groundwork for all subsequent work on music and trance and his book remains the most exhaustive treatment of the subject to date. He takes a multifaceted approach to the relationship between music and trance, stressing the ways in which music transforms one's sense of time and space while conjuring memory and associations with previous trance events. Cultural thinking about the relationship between music and trancing as presented by Rouget can be said to have begun in the eighteenth century, specifically with the writings of the French philosopher Jean-Jacques Rousseau, who insisted on the social meanings of particular musical pieces and the effects of those socially constructed, semiotically ascribed sounds on the psyches of listeners. He was particularly interested in the musical cures of those southern Italian women presumably bitten by the tarantula spider. Rousseau wrote that it was not musical sounds creating vibrations of the air that pressed on the skin that cause the humors to return to their fluid state and thus health to be restored; it was the expectation of the afflicted women that they would be cured by the melodies of the tarantellas, played by their village band, with texts sung in the colloquial dialect of their region. In contemporary terms, Rousseau posited a social/psychological, not a physical, basis for the cure.

> As proof of the physical power of sounds, people refer to the cure of Tarantula bites. The examples prove the opposite. It is not the case that absolute sounds or the same tunes are the indicated cure for everyone who has been stung by that insect; rather, each one of them requires tunes with a melody he knows and lyrics he can understand. An Italian requires Italian tunes, a Turk would require Turkish tunes. One is affected only by accents that are familiar; the nerves respond to them only insofar as the mind inclines them to it; one has to understand the language in which one is being addressed if one is to be moved by what one is told. Bernier's Cantatas are said to have cured a French musician of the fever; they would have given one to a musician of any other nation. (Rousseau 1986 [1781])[1]

With wit and precision, Rousseau staked out a position in relation to the effect of music on the mind and body that insists on the relevance of cultural associations in the production of meaning. In so doing, he was not opposing the idea of music as transcending culture, music as an autonomous object, a reading of this passage that seems natural today. Those views belong to the nineteenth century and are more associated with German idealism than with French rationalism. Rather, he set himself against a popular seventeenth- and eighteenth-century view which held that the effect of music on the mind/body was mechanistic, materialistic, organic.

Semiotic approaches continue to delineate the power of music to present to memory strong associations not intrinsic to the musical sound (Becker and Becker 1981). Indexical meanings may include bringing to memory an emotional event in our lives, the response referred to by psychologists as the "they're playing our song" response (Davies 1978). Music may be iconic; that is, within the convention of a particular musical culture, it may portray or "express" or resemble a particular emotion and thus elicit that reaction in the listener. Semiotic approaches may delineate the power of music to bring to memory associations of other realities (Feld 1982; Rouget 1985; Seeger 1987; Roseman 1991; Laderman 1996; Wong 2001). Music may mark the liturgical sequence of the event.

Beyond identification of time, place, action, or character, much of the music in trance ceremonies is also agental in bringing into existence other times, other places, other beings. Speaking of Thai ritual performers, Deborah Wong notes:

> Musicians do not say, as we might in English, that the pieces "reflect," "indicate" or "accompany" dramatic action; instead, they say that such-and-such a piece *is* (*pen*), or *means* (*maai thung*) an action. (Wong 2001: 108)

She gives the following quotation from a Thai scholar to demonstrate the array of actions, events, movements, or imaginings that the music may not just represent, but enact:

> The pieces that perform actions were implemented by musicians to *replace* actions, events, movements, or the expression of nearly anything: the animate or inanimate, people, animals, or objects, the corporeal or incorporeal, the real or the supposed, the past or present, and things of the imagination, such as deities and ghosts and demons. (Sangat Phukhaothaung quoted in Wong 2001: 108)

Music provides a link between alternate selves and alternate places and alternate times that become real places and real times in trance experiences. By enveloping the trancer in a soundscape that suggests, invokes, or represents other times and distant spaces, the transition out of quotidian time and space comes easier. Imagination becomes experience. One is moved from the mundane to the supra-normal: another realm, another time, with other kinds of knowing.

Trancing and Language

Trance experiences are socially constructed and personally experienced within a particular religious cosmology which encourages some kinds of feelings and some kinds of bodily attitudes, and constrains others. Trance processes are embedded within worldviews, within cosmic systems that are enacted by persons in trance. All trance experiences are performed within the framework of a particular understanding of the holy, and interpreted by the trancer in a way that is congruent with the understandings of her social group; they are inseparable from languaged understandings. Interpretations of trance events are taught, often by respected elders. The tie to languaged knowledge of the holy is one aspect of trance that makes the many styles of trance non-translatable. The "exuberancies" of all translations, "those things present in the translation but not in the original," as well as the "deficiencies," "those things present in the original but not in the translation" (A. L. Becker 1995: 73) give one pause about making facile generalizations concerning trance in a cross-cultural context. For example, it is not easy to reconstruct the ethos, the depths of meaning and affect, or the historical precedents when one reads in an English translation the ecstatic words of al-Ghazzali, originally written in Persian some nine hundred years ago.

> The heart of man has been so constituted by the Almighty that, like a flint, it contains a hidden fire which is evoked by music and harmony, and renders man beside himself with ecstasy. These harmonies are echoes of that higher world of beauty which we call the world of spirits, they remind man of his relationship to that world, and produce in him an emotion so deep and strange that he himself is powerless to explain it. (al-Ghazzali 1991: 57)

What does it mean to say that the heart of man is constituted like a flint that contains a hidden fire? What does al-Ghazzali mean by "that higher world of beauty"? What in the Persian terms is lost in the English translation? What are the historical precedents, the prior texts, the literary contexts of this kind of prose?

Languages may not easily be translated, but the act of languaging is universal. However, one aspect of everyday languaging stops in trance. This is what has been called "the inner language," the ongoing inner conversation one has with oneself. The inner language is often evaluating past behavior, planning future behavior, and sometimes distressingly caught in a recursive loop that repeats over and over a scenario in which we were deeply hurt or shamed (A. L. Becker 1995: 3, 13). Some theorists believe inner languaging to be the primary function of language, as an organizer of experience and thus a producer of meaning (E. Becker 1971: 68). No one knows for sure why we all talk almost constantly, silently to ourselves.

Although inner language has been a part of the human condition for who knows how long, Western scientific research into the issue only began with Piaget who studied what he called "egocentric" language in very young children (Piaget 1959, 1969). By "egocentric" language he meant all the kinds of talk that very young children use in talking not to others but to themselves, such as repeating syllables and sounds as well as later conducting real monologues and soliloquies with themselves. Piaget believed that these "conversations" only indicated psychic immaturity and that their disappearance, more or less, when a child entered school indicated the socialization of language used in its proper mature role as a form of interpersonal communication. The Russian psychologist Lev S. Vygotsky, whose works, although he wrote them a generation earlier, were only translated into English in the 1960s, took issue with Piaget. Vygotsky believed that "inner speech" had an important developmental role (Vygotsky 1986). The two-year-old infant begins language with words that are clearly social and interactive; in fact, the first words that parents try to get the infant to say are "Mama" and "Daddy." The parents want the child to acknowledge their fundamental relationship. Later, at about ages three and four, children begin to talk to themselves, often addressing themselves by name or in the third person, a clear indication that children can now understand themselves from another's perspective. Vygotsky believed that "inner speech" developed from the language of small children spoken to themselves and that, as they mature, this language becomes internalized as they no longer need to speak the words out loud. More recent research supports Vygotsky in his belief that talking to oneself, first out loud and later silently, helps the child to learn to control and to direct her own actions (Berk 1994). Most current psychological research on inner language is still focused on its development in children. It was the humanists who first made the larger claim that the development of consciousness is co-occurent with the development of language, and now biologists and neuroscientists also link inner language to consciousness (Benveniste 1971; Maturana and Varela 1987; Dennett 1991; Damasio 1999; Benzon 2001).

In trance, the inner languaging stops (Friedson 1996: 19). Similarly, for "deep listeners," simply playing or listening to music alone will halt the inner language. As an inhibitor of the inner language, deep musical listening parallels trance.

It is my hypothesis that trancers *are* deep listeners in the sense that they, too, experience strong emotional reactions to musical listening. Religious trancers differ from secular deep listeners in the degree of arousal and in differing social milieu. Trancers have been socialized within a community for whom trancing is valued as a means of interaction with the holy. They have learned to trance within that community, based on trance models of the community. Both trancing and deep listening are physical, bodily processes, involving neural stimulation of specific brain areas that result in outward, visible physical reactions such as crying, or rhythmical swaying or horripilation. Deep listeners may stop there and remain physically still. Trancers seem to experience an even more intense neural stimulation that may be expressed in some form of gross physical behavior such as dancing. Both, I suspect, are initially aroused at a level of precognition that quickly expands in the brain to involve memory, feeling, and imagination. Deep listening and trancing, as processes, are simultaneously physical *and* psychological, somatic *and* cognitive.

Universals of Trance Experience

I believe there are what can be called "limited universals" of bodily experience in trance events such as emotional arousal, loss of sense of self, cessation of inner language, and an extraordinary ability to withstand fatigue. Trance amnesia, the inability to recall what transpired during trancing, is also very frequent.[2] But I am cautious here. There is too much we do not know about trance experiences even within one culture, not to mention cross-culturally, to assume a simple-minded correspondence; and there is much that we do know that points to the uniqueness of the mystical events found within separate cultural contexts, with different prior texts (A. L. Becker 1995: 286–88), within distinct rituals and framed by differing religious beliefs (and associated with different neural patterns and body chemistries?). Given this caveat, I am still willing to apply the English term "trance" to a select group of cross-cultural experiences with certain overlapping characteristics.

Believability

Mysticism and the trance processes with which they are often accompanied present problems of interpretation even when they are not considered pathological or as perversions of an established religion. Even within trancing communities, the very ambiguity of trance leads to conflicting interpretations. Paramount is the problem of believability. Trance can be faked; it can be simulated. The legitimacy of trance is not only challenged in Western countries (Csordas 1994: 252–59); trance is always contestable. One cannot know another's inner state. Lying, pretending, or play-acting can sometimes gain one prestige and attention.

Most religious communities that practice trancing as an institutionalized part of religious observance maintain regularized methods for the control of trancers. The Sufis have, from the time of al-Ghazzali in the twelfth century, followed a rather strict set of prescriptions for the conditions of a proper *sama'* (musical performance to attain divine ecstasy) called "the laws of good conduct." Those who are present should be devout Muslims, humble of mind, not "magnifying of themselves," nor anyone "pretending to ecstasy" (al-Ghazzali 1902: 2).[3] If, by some chance, one does pretend to ecstasy, he will be gently guided by the presiding spiritual leader to sit down and be quiet, or leave. The spiritual leader usually knows well all those present and presumably can tell the difference between real and feigned ecstasy. Trances in Sufi communities are "policed" by figures of spiritual authority. The ways of dealing with fakery are as institutionalized as are the ways of expressing trance.

In the southwestern section of Sri Lanka are found dramatic rituals called *Yak Tovil,* all-night sessions to cure demon-inspired illness. For the *Yak Tovil* rituals of Sri Lanka, the problem of verifiability becomes a problem of presentation. The ritual practitioners have no doubt about the truth of what they present, yet the very outlandishness of what they present (illnesses personified as distinct dramatic personae) leads to certain inevitable suspicions among the audience.

According to the Sinhala Buddhist chronicle *Mahavamsa,* first compiled in the sixth century c.e., the Lord Buddha visited Sri Lanka three times. During his first visit he purged the island of *rakshas,* higher-status demonic beings, and *yakkas,* lower-status demonic beings. (See Plate 1.)

The *yakkas,* banished by the Lord Buddha to a distant realm, nevertheless can still afflict people with illness by their strong malevolent gaze, *dishti.* However, a Yak Tovil ritual (*Yakka Tovil*), properly performed with offerings properly presented, can coerce the demons to cease making the patient ill and to retreat to their faraway abode.

Yak Tovil rituals are now, for the most part, limited to southern Sri Lanka and practiced among the poorer segments of the population, although this was not true in the past. Ritual healers belong to the *berava* cast (*bera* means "drum," *va* means "to sound"), a caste associated with rituals and the arts: painting,

Figure 1-1. Yak Tovil drummers Eralis, Sarath, and Jayaneti playing *yak bera*. Photo by J. Becker.

carving, music, dance, architecture, astrology, marriage matchmaking, tailoring, and the making of tourist curios. They are a low-ranking service caste, below merchants and farmers. Each ritual troupe is led by a healer, *adura*, assisted by three, four, or more drummers and dancers who together perform the curing ritual which lasts from sundown to sunrise.

A *Yak Tovil* ritual usually takes place in the courtyard just in front of the house or inside the house of the patient. While it is performed as a continuous series of events, the night-long ritual is divided into named sections and subsections that includes the chanting of mantras, the singing of the origin stories of the demons, praising and flattering the demons, welcoming them with dance and song, and the presentations of offerings (Egan 1969; Halverson 1971; Kapferer 1991; Tambiah 1985).

The instruments used in the ritual are cylindrical, double-headed drums about one yard in length, suspended from the shoulders of the musicians and played on both heads. The drums are called *yak bera*, or "demon drums."

Figure 1-1 is taken from a videotape of a *Yak Tovil* ritual recorded in Sri Lanka in 1996.

At the most tense moments in the ritual, sometime around midnight when the demons appear, or when a dancer or the patient enters trance, the drumming becomes the loudest and the drum sequences that were previously metric become nonmetric, like spoken sentences.

> When the yakka's poem is recited with the drumming, the yakka's power is being put on the patient. Then the patient will dance with that power according to the rhythm of the drum and the poem. (W. Edin, interview 1996)

At these moments, even members of the audience are likely to feel they have "been hit with sound," *andagahanava*. Figure 1-2 is a transcription of a brief section of a sung poem summoning the great demon Kalu Yakka.[4]

A partial translation of the text sung by the *adura* to summon Kalu Yakka is as follows:

> Through the power of that act, I am giving you this sacrificial offering.
> Therefore, put your *dishti* into the offering, the resin, and the coal fire.
> Come from the eight corners.
> Come from the eleven places.
> Come from the three directions.
> Come in seven ships.
> Come across the Seven Seas and the Seven Oceans.
> Come from the Flower Ocean.
> Come from the Ocean of Milk.
> Come from the Ocean of Sands.
> Come from the Seven Ponds.
> Come from the Seven Waterfalls.
> Come from the Seven Mountains.
> Come from the Seven Pandals.
> Come across the Seven Rivers.
> Come from the center of the mountain.
> Today, yield to me, for I am the son of the god, Ishvara.
> Take away and cure this patient's bodily complaints.
> Cure the pains in his bones, joints and veins.
> Cure any hidden diseases, and any diseases I have failed to mention.
> Come, flying! Come flying Yantra-Mantra *dishti*!
> Cast your *dishti* on the offered food.
> O Kalu Yakka, Come! Come! Appear! Appear![5] (Egan 1969: 2.41)

One of the times at which trancing may occur is during what is called the "double-torch" dance. One member of the healing troupe, with a torch flaming at both ends clenched between his teeth, will enter trance believed to be precipitated through the recitation of mantras by the ritual officiant, through inhaling incense, through his own rhythmic movements, and through the impact of strenuous nonmetric drumming. At the end of the "double-torch" dance, the dancer collapses. There is a great show of several men trying to get the torch out of the grip of the teeth of the entranced, now collapsed, dancer. I don't believe that there is any reason for the struggles of the men with the dancer to be held in full view of the audience except for the problem of believability. There is a small hut in the ritual area from which all the characters including

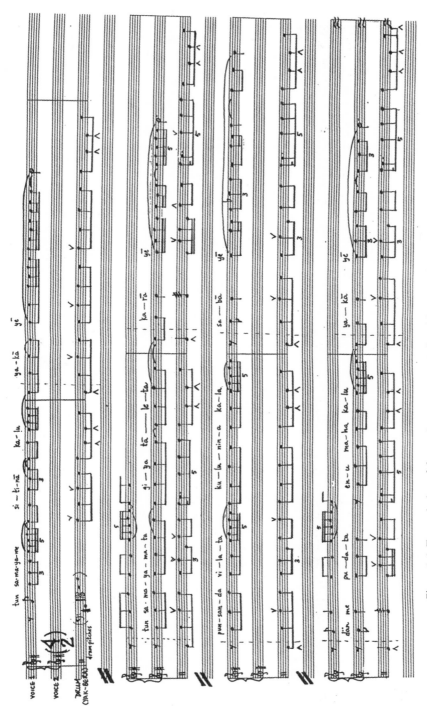

Figure 1-2. Transcription of drumming to summon Kalu Yakka. Reproduced with permission of Erik Santos.

the demons (played by members of the healing troupe) enter and depart. The struggle to release the double torch from the clenched jaws of the dancer could just as easily be done inside this building, away from view. But it never is. When it comes time for this part of the ritual, those in the audience will knowingly tell you beforehand that they will not be able to get the torch from the dancer's mouth. The clenched jaws of the still-entranced dancer confirm the trance, and thus also confirm the whole proceedings. Everyone is reassured. Believability is firmly established.

The problem of believability for Pentecostals in relation to speaking in tongues or "slain in the Spirit" is a matter of discernment. Demons can torment Holy Spirit–baptized believers by faking the deeds and actions of the Holy Spirit.

> By far the most fearsome aspect of the netherworld lay in Satan's ability to fake the Holy Spirit's deeds—and sometimes it was nearly impossible to tell which was which. Working through the influence of these imps, individuals could speak in bogus tongues, perform bogus miracles, and initiate bogus healings. (One helpful test, however, was to see if the demon-influenced person could say "Jesus is Lord.") (Wacker 2001: 92)

The Kaluli peoples of New Guinea look to the aesthetic skills of the medium to help them discern between authentic or false practitioners.

> As a basic minimum, the songs had to be well composed, poetically well constructed (with proper framing of place-names within a range of poetic devices), well sung, and capable of occasionally moving audience members to tears. Furthermore, the voices of the various spirits had to be recognizably different from the medium's natural voice and from each other. Various vocal pyrotechnics, such as bird calls (representing spirits who arrived in the form of birds) and other kinds of vocalizations thought to be only producible by spirits, lent further verisimilitude to a séance. (Schieffelin 1996: 67)

Since there is no foolproof way to discern between genuine and faked trancing, faith may be the ultimate touchstone. No amount of evidence can persuade the confirmed skeptic, nor can believers be dissuaded by any degree of contestation. One may accept the possibility of trancing and yet resist accepting a particular instance of it; or, one may accept the possibility of trancing, accept a particular instance of it, and yet not accept the trancer's interpretation of the event. All these degrees of acceptance and nonacceptance can be found within faith communities as well as the general public.

Trancing and the Body

The search for a physical cause or for the underlying physical mechanism for the impact of music on the trancing body has a long history and continues today. The strange outbreak of "tarantism" which peaked between the fifteenth and seventeenth centuries in Apulia, the heel of the Italian peninsula, provided a rich field of data for scientists and scholars to debate the physical and "moral" (read "psychological") effects of music on the mind/body. An alternate name for *tarantismo* was *carnevaletto delle donne* "the women's little carnival" (Mora 1963: 423), indicating the gendered nature of the dance of the tarantella. Although there were many variations in the symptoms, in the progress of the ailment, in the firsthand descriptions of the victims, and in the music that cured them, a typical case history can still be reconstructed.

During the hot season, July or August, a woman would lie down for a midday siesta in the field where she had been working. She would wake up, believe herself to have been bitten by the tarantula spider (often she did not actually see the spider) and fall into a depressive state, characterized by a "stuporous and absent expression, loss of appetite and sexual drive, general apathy" (Mora 1963: 418). The only cure known was for her to "dance it off." A small band of musicians, often composed of a violinist, a flutist, and a drummer who knew the *tarantella* dance tunes had to be hired, and quickly. Victims were said to have died within an hour or a few days if music was not forthcoming. Bands of musicians roamed the countryside during the tarantism season, knowing good money was to be made (Sigerist 1944: 219). On the appointed day, the room in which the victim was to be laid out was decorated with brightly colored draperies and gleaming mirrors. The patients were known to respond to beautiful glowing colors. The musicians, once they had arrived, would begin going through their repertoire, trying to identify the particular tune that would make the apathetic, depressed woman dance. When they hit the proper tune, she would rise, begin to dance more and more vigorously, sometimes tearing her clothes apart, sometimes touching her genitals or performing obscene gestures unthinkable in her normal state (Mora 1963: 418–19). She often would leave the house with the musicians following and go to the marketplace, where she would be joined in her wild dance. The music and the dancing were contagious, at least to those who had been bitten in previous hot seasons. The cultural belief was that the effect of the poison of the tarantula could be brought into remission in one season by the music and dancing, but that the sound and sight of another victim dancing in another season would trigger a relapse in a former patient. A host of dancers might thus aggregate.

> Sometimes their fancy leads them to rich clothes, curious vests and necklaces and suchlike ornaments. . . . They are most delighted with clothes of a gay color, for the most part red, green, and yellow. . . . There are some of them that, during the exercise of dancing, are mightily pleased with the green boughs of vines or reeds and wave them about in their hands in the air, or dip them in the water, or bind them about their face and neck. (Baglivi 1723 [1695]: 346–47, quoted in Sigerist 1944: 218–19)

The musical repertoire mainly was comprised of variants of the dance form tarantella and included oft-repeated lyrics. Song texts testify to the strong eroticism that underlay this curing ceremony.

> Carry me to the sea if you wish to cure me.
> To the sea, to the sea, thus my beloved loves me.

To the sea, to the sea,
As long as I live I shall love thee.

It was neither a big nor a small tarantula.
It was wine from the flask.
Where did it bite you, tell me, beloved, where it was.
Oh, if it was your leg, oh mamma!

Where did the tarantula bite you?
Under the fringe of the skirt. (Kircher 1643: 763, 760, quoted in Sigerist 1944: 220)[6]

Songs and dances were played very fast and repeated over and over again. With breaks for rests, the music and dancing could go on for the whole day, or several days. Finally, the victim would collapse from exhaustion, be given food by her relatives, and put to bed for a long sleep. When she awoke, she would remember little or nothing of what had happened to her and would take up her life again where she had left it days before, during her siesta in the fields.

The seventeenth-century physician Epiphanium Ferdinandus practiced medicine for over twenty years in Apulia. In his collection of medical observations written in 1621 he referred to the fact that some people did not consider tarantism a disease. He refutes this belief by observing that if it were not a disease, then why would so many poor women spend so much money on musicians (Ferdinandus 1621: 254)? Why indeed!

Tarantismo was a secular trance, in that sense more like contemporary rave trances than like the healing, religious trancing performed in *Yak Tovil. Tarantismo* trancing was often solitary. Aside from the fact of its being an established cultural practice, unlike ceremonial trancing there seem not to have been strong social pressures to trance. A peasant woman's life in southern Italy in the seventeenth century probably included a lot of very hard labor, too much child-bearing, too few pleasures and almost surely an overbearing husband. It is easy to imagine what a joyous relief a temporary trance state would offer. Enveloped in music, and dancing with abandon, she was given temporary license to be a more sensual, more frivolous, more extravagant human being. The stories of the victims of the bite of the tarantula remind one of the centuries-later cases of "multiple personality disorder." In both instances, there seems to be a large amount of self-interest and personal gratification involved for the patient in the diagnoses of their doctors and consociates. A minority opinion of the time claimed that tarantism was, in fact, not a disease but "some kind of melancholy" or even a fiction (Sigerist 1944: 224). Empirical skepticism lost out to the popular imagination and the search for the secret of the illness and its musical cure continued for centuries. The debate was not the question of the credibility of the illness but the question of how the musical/dancing-cure worked.

Giorgio Baglivi, a seventeenth-century scientist who wrote a long monograph on *tarantismo* (Baglivi 1723 [1695]), had an Apulian tarantula sent to Naples and allowed it to bite his rabbit. Although musicians were called and they played enthusiastically for the beast, it did not dance and died five days later. In spite of this empirical failure, Baglivi was sure that the action of music on the body/mind was of a mechanical, automatic, physical nature. He believed in the four humors (blood, phlegm, yellow bile, black bile), whose balance in the body assured good health. Blood originated in the heart, phlegm in the brain, yellow bile in the liver, and black bile in the spleen. The poison of the tarantula caused "coagulation of the humors" that music can correct.

> It is probable, that the very swift motion impressed upon the air by musical instruments, and communicated by the air to the skin, and so to the spirits and blood, does, in some measure, dissolve and dispel their growing coagulation; and that the effects of the dissolution increase as the sound itself increases, till, at last, the humors retrieve their primitive fluid state, by virtue of these repeated shakings and vibrations; upon which the patient revives gradually, moves his limbs, gets up on his legs, groans, jumps about with violence, till the sweat breaks and carries off the seeds of the poison. (Baglivi 1723: 366–73)[7]

Baglivi was restating in seventeenth-century terms the Aristotelian idea that the affects of musical listening were a purely physical phenomenon that resulted from intrinsic and acoustic properties of the melodies themselves; certain melodies played in certain modes had intrinsic properties that would produce certain dispositions in the listener. Aristotle (*The Politics*) wrote that ritual melodies in the Phrygian mode played on the *aulos,* a type of oboe, could propel the congregant into a state of trance (Strunk 1950: 18, 21).[8] The idea that melodies contain intrinsic properties, or that a particular musical timbre, such as the sound of oboes, or the playing of drums, contain intrinsic properties that can trigger trancing has remained a popular theory of trancing from Aristotle's day to our own (Neher 1961/1962; Needham 1967).

The assumption that drumming can claim a particularly potent role in triggering trancing has not abated in spite of Rouget's attempts to refute it (Rouget 1985: 172–76). The sheer frequency with which drumming is associated with trancing contributes to the persistence of the belief in a causal connection between the two. Linking drumming and trancing to acoustic and physiological phenomenon, Pfeiffer makes the following claims:

> Drums produce the sort of "steep-fronted" sounds, sounds emitted abruptly and explosively, best suited to stimulate the auditory cortex, the part of the brain's outer layer concerned with hearing. The sounds are also emitted over a wide range of frequencies, high overtone notes as well as low notes, effectively ensuring the arousal of large areas of the auditory cortex and interconnected centers. (Pfeiffer 1982: 212)

The long-standing argument between trance as basically physiological or as culturally constructed is based on the idea that it is possible to separate minds from bodies, psychology from physiology, "nature from nurture"—all dichotomies that are becoming increasingly irrelevant. It is undeniable that strong rhythms and drum timbres have a direct impact on our bodies as physical organisms. There is no necessity to insist on the primacy of any one of the senses of embodiment over the others. We can transcend outdated epistemologies and approach trance as an embodied enactment happening within and because of dense cultural networks of knowing and feeling. We need not be trapped within confining dualistic ideas, the mind-body separation that we have inherited. Sound properties of music accompanying trancing can be both biological and cultural.

Defining Trance

"Trance" is an English word with cognates in French and German, a term favored in anthropological writings of the last hundred years rather than close synonyms like "ecstasy" or "altered state of consciousness." Like most words in natural languages, trance has a range of meanings, some more central than others (Lakoff 1987: 39–54). One of the most common uses of the term "trance" is to describe the absent-minded, dreamy state one gets into when driving a car alone and listening to music on the radio. It has been suggested that the pleasure of this intensely private state is one of the reasons why people are so resistant to car-pooling in spite of all the ecological reasons for doing so (Hacking 1995: 145). We sometimes enjoy the feeling of nothing but our own bodies in a space that holds no other human being. Being with other people demands communication; talking, laughing, and listening make demands not only on our time, energy, and emotion, but also on our sense of ourselves. Our self-esteem is always being negotiated. Being alone makes fewer demands, and creates no external challenge to one's own sense of self. Listening to music while being alone further allows one to fantasize another self, to envision an even more romantic, glamorous self with which to dance. This dreamy introspective experience is perhaps the most common vernacular definition of trance.

Although we have an ideology of "the essential me," "the real me," an inviolate inner self that, if we are "true to ourselves," is constant in all different kinds of human interaction, some of us may feel as if we are many selves that do not always seem tightly bound together. No one has ever suggested that I should consult a psychiatrist and yet I feel my "self" to be very much situationally determined. I, like all adults, have played and continue to play many roles in my social life beginning with the role of child and sister, then moving on to friend and student, eventually wife, mother, teacher, colleague, and now grandmother, not to mention other more transitory roles such as musician in the gamelan ensemble, hostess, guest, and foreigner. It has never seemed to me that all these roles were perfectly integrated. They called on different abilities, different modes of presentation, different kinds of denials, different sorts of rewards, different challenges, and very different emotional stances. This kind of multiplicity, changing one's self ever so imperceptibly as one moves through life or changing roles within a given day, is our common experience.

But trance consciousness is very different from the sensation of more than one self cohabiting our everyday, wide-awake consciousness. Roseman and Friedson speak of "double-consciousness" as a description of the trance of

Temiar mediums or Tumbuka healers respectively, trance consciousness as though it were side-by-side normal quotidian consciousness.

> Mediums . . . speak of a double-consciousness, as if their own heart souls were moved slightly to the side while the spirit guide sings through them. (Roseman 1996: 253)

> In order to be possessed by the *vimbuza* spirits, there must be a space created in oneself in order to accommodate the possession. . . . there must be an opening, or clearing, of interior space in oneself to accommodate the new spirit personality. (Friedson 1996: 21–22)

The term "double consciousness" may be descriptively apt. Yet it evokes a history in Western pathological terminology that is certainly not intended by Roseman and Friedson. "Double consciousness" was an early term used in the eighteenth and nineteenth centuries for a diagnostic category that would later include "multiple personality" and "schizophrenia" (Hacking 1995: 150–55). It referred to persons who had two distinct, often contrasting personalities, such as a merry self versus a melancholy self who alternately direct the person to whom they are attributed for rather long stretches of time, from a few hours to a few days. All these women shared some symptoms with trancers such as memory loss of the "other" self and fainting as a prelude or postlude to the assumption of the double. "Multiple personality" first appeared in medical terminology in 1885 to describe not a double but a mental patient with eight distinct personality states (Hacking 1995: 172). These multiples have, like the doubles, fully developed, distinct personalities that are in place for long periods of time. Other terms for doubles and multiples in medical history are "alternating personality," "co-consciousness," and *état second*.

None of these terms as they have been medically defined comes close to describing the religious trancer or the deep listener whose consciousness is not diseased, who is in no need of medical attention, who feels in contact with a spiritual realm, who may be endowed with extraordinary physical or mental powers, and who often feels privy to a new, special knowledge more impactful and powerful than any she has ever experienced. And all this is happening within a richly sensual physical environment of sights, smells, and especially music that envelopes and permeates every pore of her body, that rhythmically entrains her with many other bodies. Religious ecstasy suffused with melodies and rhythms cannot be compared to the sad litany of unhappy persons called "doubles" or "multiples" in medical reports. A Balinese medium with a medical degree who is the director of a mental hospital in Den Pasar enthusiastically describes her own trance persona below:

> If we *kasurupan* we can have strength that is extraordinary. We become clever beyond our abilities. We more quickly understand other people. It is a kind of teaching. We can see how it works. "If you wish to behave well, do like this." We can learn to control ourselves. Evidence is that many people are chosen to *kasurupan*. It is a teaching from God that anyone can receive. According to my belief, ceremonies are not entertainment but a message. A kind of transformation

from God to mankind. Not many people here read books, thus this is a way of teaching. (Interview with Dr. Luh Ketut Suryani, Den Pasar, Bali, Indonesia, 1996)

The differing extent of trance vocabularies between different societies seems to reflect differing degrees of acceptance of trance consciousness. In Bali, where trancing within established religious practices is a generally accepted and fairly common event, there are about a dozen different words that are translated into English as "trance," each distinguishing a different configuration of possession trance. It matters whether one is entered by a deity or a demon, whether inadvertently or voluntarily, the setting of trancing, and to what purpose. A few of these terms can be defined as follows:

bebuten: possession within a ritual context by a low-ranked, demonic spirit.
dasaran: to become a medium, fully conscious but not in control of one's words or behavior.
kakalan: to be possessed outside of a ritual context by a low-ranked, demonic spirit (Suryani, interview 1996).
kalinggihan: to become the "sitting place" of a highly ranked deity such as a holy ancestor (Kamus Bali-Indonesia 1991).
kasurupan: "to be entered"; a general term for possession trance. (Suryani, interview 1996).
katakson: to be entered by a spirit that gives one special powers, particularly related to performance traditions in which a performer's special gifts are attributed to an entering spirit (Bandem 1994).
nadi: "to become"; a general term that can be used for most any type of trance (Eiseman 1989: 154).

One must resist the urge to reify the English word "trance" into an abstract Platonic category of which both English notions and Balinese notions are subcategories. English words such as "trance," "mystical state," "ecstasy," and "dissociative state" have contexts and histories. Their meanings are inseparable from the milieu in which they are used and from the "whats" to which they refer. The Balinese context for *kalinggihan,* referring to a ritual trance in which one is possessed by a deity, accompanied by gamelan music, preceded by an incensed blessing by a priest in the inner sanctum of a temple, simply has no corresponding context in the twenty-first-century United States. One should ask, "Can the Pentecostal experience of coming forward to the altar, accompanied by gospel music on piano, synthesizer and drum set, being touched by the pastor, becoming rigid, crying out, weeping, and knowing oneself to have been entered by the Holy Spirit be equated with *kalinggihan?*" Without a similar defining context, without a similar set of prior texts, *kalinggihan* can be translated as "trance" only with the broadest of license.

Yet many people, Western and Eastern, feel that "trance" is a cross-cultural constant. Through his study of the Western secondary literature on mysticism of the last hundred years, Steven Katz (1978) found "the almost universally accepted" claim that the experience of one mystic can be equated with the experience of another; and that this belief takes three forms. In an ascending order of what Katz considers increasing sophistication, he lists these claims as follows:

1) All mystical experiences are the same; even their descriptions reflect an underlying similarity which transcends cultural or religious diversity.
2) All mystical experiences are the same but the mystics' *reports about* their experiences are culturally bound. Thus they use the available symbols of the cultural-religious milieu to describe their experience.
3) All mystical experience can be divided into a small class of types which cut across cultural boundaries. Although the language used by mystics to describe their experience is culturally bound, their experience is not. (Katz 1978: 23)

According to Katz, (1) "all mystical experiences are the same," is commonly found in the early literature on mysticism, often written by missionaries, that looks for a common ecumenical grounding for various religious trances. Underlying this belief is the idea that in spite of overt differences, all religions are at base the same. This view can be used oppressively, that is, all religions, while trying to attain to the same ends are attempting to attain the sophistication and subtlety of *my* religion; or generously, that is, all religions are, in truth, equal to mine.

(2) "only reports about trance experiences are culturally bound," reflects an awareness of the different styles of languaging used to describe mystical states but declares an underlying unity regardless. It is a view that rescues viewpoint (1) for someone with an understanding of cultural differences. It is also a view with deep resonance with prior generative linguistics and "deep structure." An underlying unity can still be posited in spite of all the differing descriptions of mystical trance one encounters in the literature. This view also often assumes an ecumenical, theological wrap. Viewpoint (2) denies that all experience is mediated by language, by bodily interaction with one's milieu, by interaction with other people, and that as humans we cannot escape the conditioning of our culture on our experience. To hold the view that we do not all have the same life experiences is sometimes understood as a form of racism. Thus this ecumenical view, that we use different styles of languaging to describe the same experience, often carries with it a stance of moral superiority.

(3) "mystical experiences can be divided into a small class of types," broadens the base of the drive toward universality found in (1) and (2). There may be not just one kind of mystic trance but only a few which "cut across cultural boundaries." This view also invokes a linguistic prior text that claims there are only so many sounds that can be made by humans for use as language, and that each language selects its phonology from that set (Pinker 1994: 163). This view, it seems to me, almost works for language but does not substantiate a universalism of trance states. Viewpoint (3) still leaves us with a kind of Platonism but with several categories of trance rather than just one.

I would like to move beyond these abstractions, add (4), and insist that cultural expectations always play a part in trance behavior, that the trance experience is never unmediated and is intimately tied to its own ontogeny. Before trancing happens, one has expectations as to what is *supposed* to happen: What does one believe concerning the ontology of trance? In what kinds of events is trance a possible or appropriate behavior? How does one move one's body in trance? How does one come out of trance? An important cultural variable in the trance experience is the relationship between the entranced and the agent of entrancement. How are God, deities, demons, and spirits conceived? The transcendental theism of Judaism, Islam, and Christianity does not generally allow for the possession of a devotee by the supreme deity. A God such as Yahweh or Allah maintains distance between Himself and humankind. Aside from one notable exception, God does not incarnate in man. Nor does Allah. One may attain a spiritual union with God or Allah in a state of mystical ecstasy, but one does not ever *become* God. A Balinese, on the contrary, may become a deity for a period and speak with his/her voice and communicate his/her wishes directly, without intermediaries. Likewise, a Tibetan *rinpoche* may temporarily incarnate a form of the Buddha and bless with the power of a Buddha.

Trance behavior, within a community, is highly predictable. A Balinese trancer acts differently in trance from a Sufi trancer, who acts differently again from an American Pentecostal trancer. One's society teaches one, quite precisely, how to act in trance. Behavior in states of religious ecstasy are more predictable than everyday behavior. Whether restrained and silent like the enchanted concertgoer, or wildly whirling like the Sri Lankan healer, trancers reenact the behavior of their cultural predecessors.

It has been demonstrated that one learns not only how to imagine trance and how to behave in trance but also how to go into trance (Wacker 2001: 56). Al-Ghazzali even goes so far as to say that one must begin by pretending, what he calls the "forced affecting of ecstasy." As one "gets the hang of it," one can give up pretending and "really" attain an ecstatic state that "becomes nature through custom."

> Of this forced affecting of ecstasy there is that which is blameworthy, and it is what aims at hypocrisy and at the manifesting of the Glorious States in spite of being destitute of them. And of it there is that which is praiseworthy, and it leads to the invoking of the Glorious States and the gaining of them for oneself and bringing them to oneself by device: for the Glorious States may be brought through such gaining for oneself. . . .
>
> So there is no path to gaining for oneself anything possible for the soul and the members except by effort and practice at first; and, thereafter, it becomes nature through custom. . . . Thus it is with the Glorious States. (al-Ghazzali 1901: 730–31)

Trancing is a learned bodily behavior acted out within a culturally pregiven religious narrative. Trancing is seldom spontaneous. Religious trances with music occur in particular places at particular times with fully articulated theories of what is happening. I believe that trancers have "learned" how to control or to affect processes of body and mind that are normally not under voluntary control. I believe they are thus able to determine the time and the place of their trancing through control over autonomic physiological processes, similar to the control over heart rate or body temperature that can be learned through bio-feedback techniques. This hypothesis will be addressed more fully in Chapter 2.

Were I to add a fourth view to Katz's three, it would read something like this:

4) All trance experiences are surely not the same. The languaged reports about the experience and the bodily having of the experience must differ cross-culturally. Whatever we mean by "trance," it must be historically located and locally defined. The trance experience and its description and interpretation is a matter to be negotiated between the trancer and her society. What might be called "madness" from one viewpoint is "sanctity" from another. Every culture has a set of named trance events, each with a particular complex of recognizable symptoms, its own etiology, nosology, and interpretation.

Having said that, I still believe that it is possible to extract from all the cultural richness and variability of trances a few characteristics that occur with enough frequency to approach the notion of "defining characteristics." I attempt in this study to bridge the chasm between scientific and humanistic approaches to trance study and thus must embrace the tension between a reductive, universalist description and an open-ended, holistic cultural description. In order to establish some parameters to the subject that will allow the participation of psychologists, music cognitivists, and neuroscientists, I define trance as a bodily event characterized by strong emotion, intense focus, the loss of the strong sense of self, usually enveloped by amnesia and a cessation of the inner language. Following James, I wish to include that trance is an event that accesses types of knowledge and experience which are inaccessible in nontrance events, and which are felt to be ineffable, not easily described or spoken of.

> Although so similar to states of feeling, mystical states seem to those who experience them to be also states of knowledge. They are states of insight into depths of truth unplumbed by the discursive intellect. They are illuminations, revelations, full of significance and importance, all inarticulate though they remain; and as a rule they carry with them a curious sense of authority for after-time. (James 1982: 380–81)

Can trance events be of different kinds and degrees such as the mild trance of the performer who feels herself to be one with the music she plays, or the trance of the listener whose whole attention becomes focused on the music, or deep possession trance in which one's own self appears to be displaced and one's body is taken over by a deity or a spirit, or the ecstatic trance of the Christian or Sufi mystic who feels himself unified with God or Allah? Are there many degrees of trance or is trancing digital, either on or off? Are there many kinds of trance as Rouget has proposed or do they all presuppose an underlying psychological, neurological basis? And what difference does that make in terms of a theory of consciousness?

For the time being, I wish to say that trance can best be thought of as a category not defined by "singly necessary" and "jointly sufficient" properties but, rather, should be thought of as a Wittgensteinian category, a set of similar events that bear "family" resemblances to one another, a family of events that have some overlapping, and some nonoverlapping external symptoms (Wittgenstein 1958: 31–32). Trance, like most natural language categories (Lakoff 1987), is a cover term for a set of events that more or less resemble each other.

Over and over again in India, Sri Lanka, and Bali, I was told that all religions are the same in terms of their basic beliefs but only differ in terms of surface ritual practices. Yet, ritual practices and their languaged explanations differ wildly, not to mention the nature of the deities, physical forces of the universe, and beliefs regarding the afterworlds. Each system is logically coherent and presents a totalizing view of man's relationship to the forces and powers beyond himself. All proclaim a universe that can be orderly if one observes the appropriate disciplines of inner and outer behavior, including the appropriate rituals. None leaves the individual standing naked and alone in an incomprehensible universe where "the silence of cosmic space strikes terror" (Steiner 1984: 284).

2   Deep Listeners

Part 1. Contemporary Deep Listeners

The arousal of emotion within the trancer, in part inspired by music, links trancers and deep listeners: trance consciousness and the transcendental experiences of deep listeners both rest on powerful emotional excitement. The United States would seem at first blush to be a place generally hostile to trance, providing few positive role models for trance. And indeed it is. Yet, in spite of this, and ignoring the many communal trances of religious groups such as the Pentecostals, it would appear that many nonreligious Americans have had similar kinds of "oceanic" experiences, the near-trance experiences of deep listeners that resemble in affect the trances of many religious domains. In their exploratory article "Are We a Nation of Mystics?" Greeley and McCready (1979) expressed their surprise at the results when they inserted into a survey on "ultimate values," distributed to fifteen hundred American adults, a question concerning "religio-mystical experience." They received back the response that a full 50 percent attested to having had such an experience. For most, it was an intensely joyful experience, often accompanied by the sense of new understanding and knowledge. A good quarter of these forty- to fifty-year-olds had a sense that their own personality had been taken over by something more powerful than they.

In the Greeley and McCready study, music as an emotional trigger is not specifically mentioned. But in a number of recent Western studies of music and emotion, musical emotions alone are the focus for the studies of the psychological and physiological affects of musical listening. For the most part, the researchers quoted in this chapter focus on the senses of embodiment as (1) the body as a physical structure in which emotion happens and (2) the body as a site of first-person experience. These Western listeners may or may not be religious, but they testify to the power of music alone to stimulate what are clearly transcendental experiences. Not all music listeners are deep listeners, nor will all participants in religious ceremonies trance, but deep listeners and trancers are both predictably emotional and prone to numinous experiences.

Before proceeding to relate the neurological and psychological findings of recent music and emotion studies, "emotion" itself needs to be defined.

In his famous and controversial theory of the emotions, William James claimed that the physiological component of arousal is primary and precedes the interpretation of the subsequent emotion (James 1950, vol. 2: 442–85). The "feeling" of anger is the feeling that results from an increased heart rate, an increase of blood to the face, an angry facial expression, an aggressive bodily

COMMON SENSE:

PERCEPTION:
RABID WOODCHUCK

$\downarrow$

EMOTION:
FEAR

$\downarrow$

BODILY RESPONSE:
DRY MOUTH, POUNDING
HEART, SWEATY HANDS

JAMES-LANGE:

PERCEPTION:
RABID WOODCHUCK

$\downarrow$

BODILY RESPONSE:
DRY MOUTH, POUNDING
HEART, SWEATY HANDS

$\downarrow$

EMOTION:
FEAR

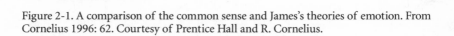

Figure 2-1. A comparison of the common sense and James's theories of emotion. From Cornelius 1996: 62. Courtesy of Prentice Hall and R. Cornelius.

stance, shallow breathing, and so on. Anger, the emotion, *is,* according to James, what one *feels* when enacting this display.[1]

> If we fancy some strong emotion and then try to abstract from our consciousness of it all the feelings of its bodily symptoms, we find we have nothing left behind, no "mind-stuff" out of which the emotion can be constituted, and that a cold and neutral state of intellectual perception is all that remains. . . .
> What kind of an emotion or fear would be felt if the feeling neither of quickened heart-beats nor of shallow breathing, neither of trembling lips nor of weakened limbs, neither of goose-flesh nor of visceral stirrings, were present, it is quite impossible for me to think. Can one fancy the state of rage and picture no ebullition in the chest, no flushing of the face, no dilation of the nostrils, no clenching of the teeth, no impulse to vigorous action, but in their stead limp muscles, calm breathing, and a placid face? (James 1950 [1890], vol. 2: 451–52)

In Figure 2-1, the psychologist Randolph Cornelius has constructed a whimsical illustration presenting the two opposing views of the genesis of a Victorian gentleman's reaction to a "rabid" woodchuck.

James never adequately allowed for the reverse process in the generation of emotion, that is, the idea that strong emotions initially can be generated by thought and then be reflected in the body. In Western theatrical traditions, the Jamesian approach to emotion was followed by the Polish director Jerzy Grotowski and his disciples, who taught actors to imitate the outward signs of emotion in order to feel them inwardly (Grotowski 1968). Asian theatrical traditions, especially Kathakali from South India, have long trained actors to "feel" emotion by first embodying its physical characteristics. Supportive of the theatrical pedagogy followed by Kathakali instructors, the work of Ekman, Levenson, and Friesen (1983) has demonstrated specific, differentiated ANS responses to facial expressions of fear, anger, happiness, and disgust.

Following James, but with much more sophisticated knowledge of the neurophysiology of emotion and a more nuanced and inclusive theory of emotion, Damasio claims that the term "emotion" should be applied to the autonomic arousal of specific cortical and subcortical structures, and that "feeling" which generally follows "emotion" should be applied to the complex cognitive, culturally inflected, and secondary interpretation of "emotion."

> The term *feeling* should be reserved for the private, mental experience of an emotion, while the term *emotion* should be used to designate the collection of responses, many of which are publicly observable. (Damasio 1999: 42)

"Arousal," here, means the activation of the autonomic nervous system, or ANS. "Autonomic" means that particular physiological processes are controlled by sections of the brain that, for the most part, operate independently of our willing them, many located deep within the interior of the brain (the encephalon) and within the brainstem (Figure 2-2, Figure 2-3), the oldest part of the brain believed to have evolved more than five hundred million years ago.

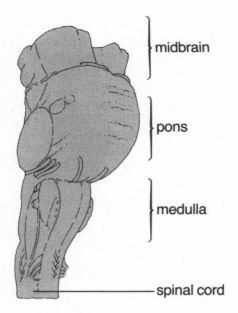

midbrain

pons

medulla

spinal cord

Figure 2-2. The brain stem. From Ornstein and Thompson 1984: 4. Illustration copyright © 1984 by David A. Macaulay. Reprinted by permission of Houghton Mifflin Company. All rights reserved.

The brainstem handles basic bodily functions such as breathing and heart rate, determines levels of wakefulness and alerts the organism to important sensory information that might indicate a threatening situation. (Ornstein and Thompson 1984: 4)

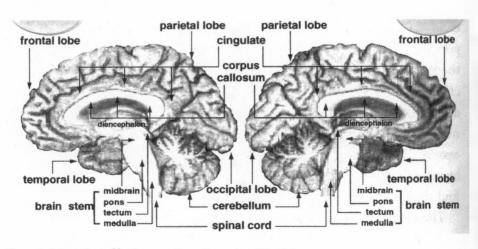

Figure 2-3. Location of brain stem. From Damasio 1999: 326. Courtesy of Harcourt/H. and A. Damasio.

Respiration, heart functions, other visceral functions such as digestion, the involuntary muscles of the body, as well as skin temperature are all regulated by the ANS. The heart beats faster, the pulse rises, breathing becomes more shallow, the skin temperature rises, the pattern of brain waves becomes less regular as we react to some perception that has emotional resonance for us. All these changes have been observed without any necessary reference to the affective, interpretive component of arousal. Someone who has just been exercising will respond more strongly to sexual stimuli or to musical listening than when just arising from a nap. Arousal, at some basic level, is culturally primitive and most clearly evident in crisis situations.

ANS arousal (emotion) while listening to music may be manifested in shivers, goosebumps, changes in breathing and heart rate, tears, weeping, changes in skin temperature, all involuntary reactions that precede language and evaluation. The term "feeling" is used to refer to the cognitive evaluation of these bodily changes resulting in the language labels "joy," "anger," "fear," "grief," "surprise," "disgust," and so on.

Primary and Secondary Emotions

Neuroscientists, following Darwin (1872), subscribe to the "common-sense" notion that emotions are biologically adaptive processes (Plutchik 1980: 139; Panksepp 1992: 555; Damasio 1994: 118; LeDoux 1996: 17). Many neuroscientists and psychologists also believe that there are core or primary emotions that are hardwired and secondary emotions that are more likely to be culturally conditioned (Lewis and Michalson 1983: 31–38; Lewis and Saarni 1985; Ortony, Clore, and Collins 1988: 27). As a neuroscientist, Damasio separates emotions into primary and secondary emotions according to the degree to which they necessarily involve the upper regions of the brain, the neocortex. Primary emotions include those most crucial to the survival of the organism such as fear, anger, surprise, or disgust, whereas secondary emotions or "social emotions" would include embarrassment, shame, guilt, pride, or jealousy. Secondary emotions are clearly culturally conditioned. Primary emotions are as well, but perhaps to a lesser degree.

> In all probability, development and culture superpose the following influences on the preset devices: first, they shape what constitutes an adequate inducer of a given emotion; second, they shape some aspects of the expression of emotion; and third, they shape the cognition and behavior which follows the deployment of an emotion. (Damasio 1999: 57)

In any case, primary emotions (Figure 2-4) extend far down the evolutionary chain, whereas secondary emotions seem to be more specifically human, or at least mammalian.

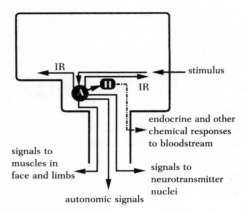

Figure 2-4. Primary emotions. From Damasio 1994: 132. Courtesy of Putnam/H. and A. Damasio.

The black perimeter stands for the brain and brain stem. After an appropriate stimulus activates the amygdala (A), a number of responses ensue: internal responses (marked IR); muscular responses; visceral responses (autonomic signals); and responses to neurotransmitter nuclei and hypothalamus (H). The hypothalamus gives rise to the endocrine and other chemical responses which use a bloodstream route. . . . [T]he muscular responses with which we express emotions, say, in body posture, probably utilize structures in the basal ganglia. (Damasio 1994: 132)

Both categories of emotion involve only selected portions of the brain and both involve many of the same portions of the brain. Secondary emotions (Figure 2-5) add the involvement of prefrontal and somatosensory cortices to the limbic and brain stem areas of the brain that are active in expressing primary emotions.

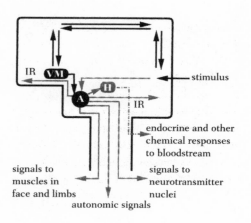

Figure 2-5. Secondary emotions. From Damasio 1994: 137. Courtesy of Putnam/H. and A. Damasio.

The stimulus may still be processed directly via the amygdala but is now also ana- lyzed in the thought process, and may activate frontal cortices (VM). VM acts via the amygdala (A). In other words, secondary emotions utilize the machinery of Primary Emotions. Again, I am deliberately oversimplifying, since numerous pre- frontal cortices other than VM are also activated, but I believe the essence of the mechanism is as shown in the diagram. Note how VM depends on A to express its activity, how it is piggy-backed on it, so to speak. This dependence-precedence relationship is a good example of nature's tinkering style of engineering. Nature makes use of old structures and mechanisms in order to create new mechanisms and obtain new results. (Damasio 1994: 137)

A shared biological core underlies both primary and secondary emotions as well as what Damasio calls "background emotions" or moods.

1) Emotions are complicated collections of chemical and neural responses, form- ing a pattern: all emotions have some kind of regulatory role to play, leading in one way or another to the creation of circumstances advantageous to the orga- nism exhibiting the phenomenon; emotions are *about* the life of an organism, its body to be precise, and their role is to assist the organism in maintaining life.
2) Notwithstanding the reality that learning and culture alter the expression of emotions and give emotions new meanings, emotions are biologically deter- mined processes, depending on innately set brain devices, laid down by a long evolutionary history.
3) The devices which produce emotions occupy a fairly restricted ensemble of sub- cortical regions, beginning at the level of the brain stem and moving up to the higher brain; the devices are part of a set of structures that both regulate and represent body states.
4) All the devices can be engaged automatically, without conscious deliberation; the considerable amount of individual variation and the fact that culture plays a role in shaping some inducers does not deny the fundamental stereotypicity, automaticity, and regulatory purpose of the emotions.
5) All emotions use the body as their theater (internal milieu, visceral, vestibular, and musculoskeletal systems), but emotions also affect the mode of operation of numerous brain circuits. (Damasio 1999: 28)

Although I accept the basic premise that certain emotions such as anger and fear are evolutionarily ancient, I also believe that from the moment of birth all human emotions are continually being shaped by culture (Geertz 1973a) and that at some point it ceases to make sense to talk about emotions that are cul- turally conditioned and those that are hardwired. The world is the context of the maturation of the infant, the world is the context of our ever-evolving lives; our continual interaction with that world begins at birth or before, and contin- ues until we die.

Musical Emotions

Musical emotions in this study narrowly refer to emotions aroused in deep listeners or performers, not necessarily those the listener believes are *ex-*

pressed by the music.[2] The studies discussed below were focused on the strong emotional reactions of the listener, the physiology of musical listening. Musical emotions are different from life-experience emotions. Basic survival doesn't seem relevant. Nor do musical emotions carry the same consequences that life situations do. Nor do they normally involve subsequent changes in behavior or actions directed toward regaining emotional equilibrium (Krumhansl 1997: 336). For all the differences from other kinds of emotion that may have evolved as a strategy for survival, musical emotion is still rooted in basic physiological arousal felt in the body and displayed by tears, chills/shivers, goosebumps, palpitation of the heart, and perspiration (Sloboda 1991; Panksepp 1995; Gabrielsson and Lindstrom Wik 2000: 103; Blood and Zatorre 2001).

Emotions in response to musical listening, often called "aesthetic emotions" (James 1950, vol. 2: 468; Arnheim 1958; Lazarus 1991: 292) are mostly selectively focused on some form of happiness or sadness, or mixed emotions such as "bitter sweetness" or "beauty and pain" (Gabrielsson and Lindstrom Wik 2000). "Happiness," meaning some kind of strong positive emotion, is the feeling most frequently cited in association with musical listening and may constitute one of the universals of cross-cultural studies of music and emotion. From the "polka happiness" of the Polish-American parties of Chicago (Keil 1987: 276), to the !Kung of the Kalahari desert, "Being at a dance makes our hearts happy" (R. Katz 1982: 348), to the Basongye of the Congo who "make music in order to be happy" (Merriam 1964: 82), to the extroverted joy of a Pentecostal musical service, music has the ability to make people feel good. The "happiness" of listening to music, however one construes "happiness," is in part the simple result of musical arousal. We tend to feel good when we are musically aroused and excited. Notably, musical emotions tend to be positive, whereas primary emotions tend to be negative.[3]

High Arousal

If, as I believe, arousal is fundamental to the triggering of trancing, then those emotions that signal high arousal should figure prominently in trancers, not the "lower-key" emotional reactions to music described as "calm," "peaceful," "soothing," or "comforting." The emotions of trancing, regardless of cultural conditioning, seem to fall overwhelmingly into the scientists' category of primary emotions. Joy, fear, and rage predominate. Feelings of solace, humility, and peace may occur after trancing, but these feelings do not seem to trigger or sustain trancing. Trancing needs high-energy, high-arousal emotions. Although I suspect that trancers experience higher degrees of ANS arousal than do deep listeners, studies of deep listeners in laboratory situations establish the presence of considerable ANS arousal. Panksepp (1995, 1998b), Krumhansl (1997), Nyklicek et al. (1997), and Blood and Zatorre (2001) have all tested for and found ANS arousal in deep listeners.

Blood and Zatorre (2001) conducted an experiment in which the subjects selected music that predictably invoked intensely pleasurable responses (chills). Changes in heart rate and breathing as well as changes in the electrical activity of skeletal muscles were significant when the subjects were listening to their self-selected, pleasure-inducing musical examples. The same subjects underwent PET scans which showed the involvement of opioid systems in musical listening.[4] The experimenters Blood and Zatorre observed regional cerebral blood flow increases in paralimbic regions, regions associated with arousal, and in regions associated with motor processes.[5] They noticed that this blood flow activity in the brain is "similar to that observed in other brain imaging studies of euphoria" (Blood and Zatorre 2001: 11821). From this they postulate that the reward processes for musical listening, as for food and sex, involve dopamine, opioid systems, and other transmitters as well. That "music recruits neural systems of reward" (Blood and Zatorre 2001) is a scientific finding that only confirms a phenomenal truism: Pleasure motivates deep musical listening.

Panksepp also predicts that the social bonding chemicals oxytocin and the opioid systems "may be major players in the production and control of chills" in deep listening. Opioids are known to participate in social bonding, in play, and in sexual pleasures. Panksepp believes that they are operative in emotional listening as well. In any event, the chill feels as if a fountain of neurochemicals has been released in brain areas that control our bodily feelings (Panksepp 1995: 200).

Most people assume that sadness is less arousing than happiness. One of the nonintuitive findings of Panksepp (1995: 172, 1998b: 317) and Krumhansl (1997: 344) is that sadness in relation to a musical example can be more arousing than happiness. PET scan studies also support the idea that sadness may produce more arousal than does happiness (Panksepp 1998b: 317).

> The fact that sadness can provoke chills seems outwardly perplexing from the perspective that most people find the experience to be positive emotionally. No doubt, this is only a superficial paradox that disappears when we consider the deeper aspects of human emotionality . . . As neurological evidence indicates, the basic output circuitries of grief and joy (as indexed by crying and laughter) are intertwined in the human brain. These powerful emotions, which emerged early in mammalian evolution, were designed to solidify and elaborate the mandates and possibilities of social bonds. (Panksepp 1995: 197)

The study of Nyklicek et al. (1997) was based on cardiorespiratory responses to musical listening and they, like those discussed earlier, discovered differential visceral and ANS responses to musical examples. But, contrary to the findings of Panksepp and Krumhansl, in this study "sadness" is a depressive, not an arousing, emotion.

> The two bipolar dimensions most frequently found in factor analytic studies of emotional reactions are valence (pleasantness vs. unpleasantness) and arousal (high arousal vs. low arousal) . . . specifically, happiness represents a high arousal and

pleasant emotion, sadness a low arousal and unpleasant emotion, serenity a low arousal and pleasant emotion, and agitation a high arousal and unpleasant emotion. (Nyklicek et al. 1997: 305)

Regardless, deep listeners experience strong ANS arousal in listening to music that may result in chills or tears, changes in their heart rates, in their skin temperatures, in their respiration, and in their brain chemistry resulting in a heightened sense of aliveness, an alertness, and, mostly, a joyfulness.

Deep Listeners and Transcendental Experience

Trancers and deep listeners share the ability to respond with strong emotional arousal to musical stimulation. Both, I suggest, are deep listeners in their attention to music and in their expectation that they will be moved by it. Deep listeners' statements about their experiences are often indistinguishable from those of ecstatic trancers. Expressions of transcendence, of gnosis, of out-of-body sensations abound.[6]

> This is the moment when I got my musical experience. The first notes made me almost pass out. . . . I felt that I disappeared for a moment and then woke up like in a dream but aware of the music all the time. Somehow I was soaring above the audience that was merely there but could not be heard and did not disturb. It was like a dream, I was soaring and they played just for me. It is very hard to explain the feeling I had. (Gabrielsson and S. Lindstrom 1993: 124)

Feelings of nearness to the sacred, loss of boundaries between self and other, experiences of wholeness and unity occur in relation to emotionally aroused musical listening.

> I find it very difficult to find words for this music that I have experienced so strongly at *one* occasion. The closest description I can come up with is that it was a cosmic wholeness-experience beyond time and space. The body and the music became a whole, where I knew that I was dead, but it was a death that also gave birth to something that was liberating and light. A light that did not belong to this life. I disappeared even from this life, so I can't remember anything of my surroundings. I feel hesitant to write what it was, because it has never been important, since everything that happened had no connection to this world. (Gabrielsson and S. Lindstrom 1993: 129)

Often, the deep listener feels great joy:

> I was filled by a feeling that the music started to take command of my body. I was charged in some way . . . I was filled by an enormous warmth and heat. I swallowed all tones . . . [T]he music became so distinct. I was captured by each of the instruments and what they had to give me. . . . Nothing else existed. I was dancing, whirling, giving myself up to the music and the rhythms, overjoyed, laughing. Tears came into my eyes—however strange it may seem—and it was as a kind of liberation. (Gabrielsson and Lindstrom Wik 2000: 437)

But pain can also predominate:

I have had similar experience of other music . . . but none so terribly deep as "Pathetique": in certain passages it evokes sobs and I feel totally crushed—my listening is fully concentrated, the rest of the world disappears in a way, and I become merged in the music or the music in me, it fills me completely. I also get physical reactions . . . wet eyes, a breathing that gets sobbing in certain passages, a feeling of crying in my throat and chest. Trying to find words for the emotions themselves, I would like to use words as: crushed, shaken, tragedy, maybe death, absorption, but also tenderness, longing, desire (vain), a will to live, prayer. The whole experience also has the character of a total standstill, a kind of meditative rest, a last definite and absolute end, after which nothing else can follow. (Gabrielsson and S. Lindstrom 1993: 123)

Pentecostal worshippers do not often mention the music that accompanied their ecstasy, but it is ubiquitous in Pentecostal worship services and acknowledged as a cornerstone of religious practice. Pentecostal descriptions of ecstasy parallel deep listeners descriptions of their euphoria.

Being sanctified was indescribable! . . . It was as if a thousand bulbs had been turned on in me. After that it was possible to see the meaning in the Bible in things where I had never seen anything before. (Wood 1965: 24)

When I received it [Baptism in the Holy Spirit] I felt light-hearted and happy—more than at any other time. . . . Have you felt so joyous that you didn't know what you were doing? Well, it's that way—except more. . . . I didn't know what was happening at first, but when I began to speak in tongues I did. (Wood 1965: 26)

My heart was filled with light, love and glory. . . . I seemingly was taken out of myself and thought I was within a few feet of the gates of Heaven. . . . It was utterly indescribably. (Wacker 2001: 55)

Sanctification is just more of the same thing as being saved; but the Holy Spirit is different—it knocks you about and you don't know what is going on. The most wonderful experiences of my life have been over in that church. When the Holy Spirit hits you it is like getting over your head in water. One doesn't know what is what when he gets the Holy Spirit. (Wood 1965: 24)

It seemed as if human joys vanished. . . . This is something I never had before. It seemed as if the whole world and the people looked a different color. Jesus had come to me. (Blumhofer 1993: 91)

The anger of the Balinese *bebuten* trancer contrasts with the joy of the Pentecostals, but both share an intensely emotional moment. Similar to deep listeners' euphoria and Pentecostal ecstasy, *bebuten* trancers see things and feel things that far exceed the sights, thoughts, and feelings of everyday life.

When I come up to that tower, when the curtain opens like that, as soon as I step up to approach Rangda [the witch], I see a strong fire coming from her eyes. . . . I want to attack her! (I Wayan Dibia, interview, 1996)

What is happening within the brains and bodies of these enraptured persons? What is the physiology that supports the phenomenal experience of extreme joy or furious rage?

Initially, strong ANS arousal that recruits neural activity in the brainstem nuclei, hypothalamus, amygdala, basal forebrain, and ventromedial prefrontal cortex—brain structures that are ancient and for the most part deep within the lower part of the brain. These changes, deep within the brain, lead to visible, perceptible changes such as increased heart rate, perspiration, and faster breathing. Almost immediately, news of these perturbations are sent via the thalamus to many parts of the cortex recruiting memories of former history with the ritual, knowledge of appropriate behavior in this situation, valorizing of the event and one's participation in it, and, I suspect, enlisting the know-how to control and modulate ANS response and thus how to propel oneself into trance consciousness. Without a rich history of immersion within the beliefs of each faith, as well as a readiness for, an acceptance of a changed consciousness, trancing won't happen. Nor will it happen without strong ANS "bottom-up" arousal, further intensified by belief—magnified by reverse neural activity from the neocortex, "top-down" arousal. It is as if the electrical storm, the concomitant chemical bath and the skill to control them all are the necessary preconditions for trance.

If, as I am proposing, trancers and deep listeners share intense reactions to musical stimulation, then one may predict that the physiological studies of deep listeners also may apply to trancers. Because most studies of deep listeners have been about positive emotional responses, the physical correlates may apply more to Pentecostals and most Sufi trancers rather than the angry *bebuten* trancers, although there is bound to be much overlapping, as the general emotional circuitry of the brain is enlisted in any case. The increases in blood flow to the paralimbic regions of the brain associated with arousal and with motor functions surely happen with trancers as well as with deep listeners. Trancers often are distinguished by their agitated and strenuous physical movements. The similarity of this blood flow pattern with brain imaging patterns for euphoria also suggests that the chemical bath of dopamine, oxytocin, and other transmitters is experienced by trancers. If chills and tears are the phenomenal experience of the deep listener to these physiological changes, then trance may be the response of the even deeper listener.

Part 2. Ancient Deep Listeners, *Rasa* Theory

The focus of the scientific studies reported earlier is on the physical impact of aesthetic emotion on the listener. The perceiver is also the focus of the oldest and best-known non-Western theory of aesthetic emotions, *rasa* theory of ancient and medieval India: a theory that makes transcendental claims about the importance of the arousal of primary emotions when listening to music, when viewing beautiful statues in a temple, or when relishing a theatrical performance.[7] *Rasa* theory is also like current scientific studies of music and emotion in ignoring cultural influences. Both ancient Indian philosophers and contemporary scientists, for different reasons, proceed with universalist assumptions of the fundamental psychological sameness of all peoples.

The earliest written document including rasa theory was composed by Bharata in his treatise on theater, the *Natyasastra*, written sometime between the first and fifth centuries C.E. Later, in the Middle Ages, Indian Tantric philosophers, Buddhist and Shaivite, further developed *rasa* theory, the aesthetic experience, and expressly linked it to the pursuit of enlightenment. The best-known Indian philosopher who wrote extensively on this theory of aesthetics was Abhinavagupta, a Tantric Shaivite who lived in Kashmir, India, in the eleventh century. Abhinavagupta incorporated works of earlier theorists into his own works, clarifying and systematizing aesthetic terminology. After his death, his influence continued in the writings not only of his students but also in the incorporation of his ideas into the writings and teachings of philosophers from other schools as well (Masson and Patwardhan 1977: 290).

The English term "aesthetics" has come to mean the study of the basis of evaluating objects designated as "artistic" that have been isolated from their cultural context (Sparshott 1983: 3). But that was not its original Greek meaning (*aesthetikos* "of sense perception"), nor is it the meaning of comparable terms used in India and Southeast Asia. The idea of aesthetic appreciation in Tantric teachings has to do with a special kind of perception, of paying full attention to whatever is before one at the moment. The Tantrics of medieval India linked the study of perception and cognition with aesthetics. One is taught constantly to strive to be in the present, not mentally reliving the past nor rehearsing the future. One strives to be mindful of every moment and to see, hear, taste, smell, and touch without preconceptions, without the intervening overlay of the memory of past experiences. To see things as they are, to hear music as it is, without precognition or judgment, is to perceive aesthetically. Refinement of perception, according to Tantric philosophy, can lead to a refinement of cognition and a dissolution of the boundaries between oneself and the thing perceived. Aesthetics as clarified perception becomes a cornerstone of spiritual practice and an important source of meaning in a performance or a ritual.

> Rasa is not a thing in itself, formed previous to the act of consciousness by which it is perceived, but the consciousness itself (and therefore the perception) which, freed from external interference and from all practical desires, becomes Rasa or aesthetic consciousness. The subject, when immersed in this state, finds, in it, the fulfillment of all his desires: in this sense, therefore, Rasa is pleasure, beatitude, rest, lysis. Aesthetic consciousness has no end outside itself. . . . Aesthetic experience postulates, of necessity, the extinction of every practical desire and, therefore, the submersion of the subject in the aesthetic object to the exclusion of all else. (Gnoli 1956: xxii)

What was to be perceived? The emotion portrayed in the music, the dance, or the theatrical persona. A dance, a musical composition or a theatrical presentation should be centered on one of the "permanent" emotions, which is to be experienced by the receiver "without obstacles," by which is meant received experience without individual memories, associations, the colorings of one's own personal history. The aim is to feel the designated emotion, along with all other listeners or viewers, united in a "field" of emotion, removed from autobiography, without consequences, and transformed into "aesthetic rapture" regardless of the positive or negative nature of the emotion portrayed. From the eight basic emotions (nine by the Middle Ages) the artist chooses to portray one *rasa*, or "taste," corresponding to one primary emotion.

The *rasas*	The "permanent" (primary) emotions
1. *srngara:* the erotic	*rati:* love (sexual)
2. *hasya:* the comic	*hasa:* laughter
3. *karuna:* the compassionate	*soka:* sorrow
4. *raudra:* the furious	*krodha:* anger
5. *vira:* the heroic	*utsaha:* energy
6. *bhayanaka:* the terrible	*bhaya:* fear
7. *bibhatsa:* the odious	*jugupsa:* disgust
8. *adbhuta:* the wondrous	*vismaya:* wonder
9. [*shanta:* the peaceful—added in the medieval period]	(Rowell 1992: 329)

With the possible exception of "wonder," I would designate all the primary emotions of Indian *rasa* theory as high arousal emotions. Among *rasa* theorists, as often as they are called "emotions" they are called "mental states" or "forms of consciousness."

Indeed every creature from its birth possesses these nine forms of consciousness. In fact, on the basis of the principle that all beings "hate to be in contact with pain and are eager to taste pleasure," everyone is pervaded by sexual desires [Delight]; believes himself to be superior to others, whom he is thus led to deride [Laughter]; grieves when he is forced to part from what he loves [Sorrow]; gets angry against the causes of such separation [Anger]—but still is desirous of overcoming the danger which threatens him [Heroism]; is attacked, when judging a thing to be displeasing, by a sense of revulsion directed just toward this ugly object [Disgust]; wonders at the sight of extraordinary deeds done by himself or others [Astonishment]; and, lastly, is desirous of abandoning certain things [Serenity]. (Abhinavagupta in Gnoli 1956: 91)

Most of the "transitory mental states" or secondary emotions of *rasa* theory appear to be in the low arousal category. Some of those states included in the secondary, transitory category such as death, sleeping, or awakening would not be likely to appear in a Western list unless "emotion" is defined generally as a "feeling state."[8]

Transitory Mental States/secondary emotions

1. discouragement	18. dreaming
2. weakness	19. sleeping
3. apprehension	20. awakening
4. weariness	21. shame
5. contentment	22. epilepsy
6. stupor	23. distraction
7. joy	24. assurance

8. depression
9. cruelty
10. anxiety
11. fright
12. envy
13. indignation
14. arrogance
15. recollection
16. death
17. intoxication

25. indolence
26. agitation
27. deliberation
28. dissimulation
29. sickness
30. insanity
31. despair
32. impatience
33. inconstancy (Gnoli 1956: 30)

An artist is ideally expected to portray one central, primary emotion, and a subset of lesser, secondary emotions. For example, the primary emotion may be *srngara* (erotic love) and the secondary emotions might be joy, arrogance, and distraction. Or the primary emotion may be *srngara* with a different set of secondary emotions such as apprehension, anxiety, and despair. *Rasa* theory also includes a discussion of what would now be called the outward, visible manifestations of ANS arousal, in this ancient theory called "consequents" of the emotion, or "involuntary states." Many of these ancient "involuntary states" closely parallel the physiological responses of deep listeners. "Paralysis" and "fainting" seem to suggest trancing as well.

Involuntary States

Paralysis
Fainting
Horripilation [goosebumps]
Sweating
Change of colour
Trembling
Weeping
Change of voice (Gnoli 1956: 29–30)

In its insistence on the primacy of strong emotional arousal in musical listening, *rasa* theory has parallels with the "strong emotions" of the deep listeners in the studies of Gabrielsson and Lindstom Wik, Krumhansl, Nyklicek et al., and Panksepp. But there may be a significant difference. *Rasa* theorists posit a distancing of the receiver from the emotion received, an impersonal and disinterested pleasure in order, in part, to transform pain into pleasure.

Aesthetic experience, being characterized by disinterested and impersonal pleasure, is a modality *sui generis* of the unbounded beatitude that appears to the yogin in his ecstasy and, in his eyes, transforms *samsara* into *nirvana*. The mysterious conversion of pain into pleasure, which accompanies the full realization of one's own Self, is to be found equally in aesthetic experience, which possesses the magical power of transfiguring the greatest sadness into the disinterested pleasure of contemplation. Pain, which is mobility, inquietude, has no place in aesthetic experience, which is rest, lysis and the fulfillment of all desires—unless it is converted magically into pleasure. (Gnoli 1956: xxiv)

In this respect, *rasa* theory may be applicable to some deep listeners but not to trancers. The trancer, for certain, is not mentally distanced from the inducer of her arousal.

For medieval Tantric Shaivite and Buddhist scholars, there is a clear distinction between the aesthetic experience and the experience of God. The aesthetic experience is merely a stepping-stone toward a more perfect enlightenment. It seems that for Abhinavagupta, the difference between aesthetic consciousness and enlightenment lies in the object into which the listener is absorbed—whether absorbed in the music or absorbed in God. Significantly, he posits a group of listeners in a ritual context, not an individual listener as the ideal forum for aesthetic consciousness. The type of consciousness experienced by the sensitive listener in a group ritual context "expands," as opposed to individual consciousness, which he describes as "a state of contraction."

> The consciousness, which consists of, and is animated by, all things on account of the difference of bodies, enters into a state of contraction. But, in public celebrations, it returns to a state of expansion—since all the components are reflected in each other. The flow of one's own consciousness in ebullition (i.e., when it is tending to come out of itself) is reflected in the consciousness of all the bystanders, as if in so many mirrors, and, inflamed by these, it abandons without effort its state of individual contraction. (Abhinavagupta in Gnoli 1956: 70)

Writing about aesthetic experience a millennium ago, Abhinavagupta seems to be invoking the phenomenon I would call structural coupling and rhythmic entrainment (see Chapter 5). Solitary listening would not have been the norm in his place and time. His deep listeners would usually be in groups, in "public celebrations," in which structural coupling and rhythmic entrainment would facilitate his expansion of consciousness.

Deep Listening, Trance, and the Srngara Rasa

It is no accident that the first *rasa* in Indian texts is always the *srngara rasa*, the erotic *rasa*. Erotic feelings are commonly aroused by musical listening and frequently reported by listeners in Western studies of music and emotions (Goldstein 1968; Crow 1984; Blood and Zatorre 2001). Sexual arousal while playing gamelan music is testified to in this excerpt from a nineteenth-century Javanese poem, *Serat Centhini:*

> The musicians played with skill and with the same feel for the piece.
> The tranquility of the rhythm vied with the melodic realizations in realizing desire.
> Their rendition was just the right length for a puppeteer's narration.
>
> They played so together that the *rasa* of the piece was obtained.
> So they played on and on.

They played the piece for a long time.
Then it sped up and moved into the second section.

The longer it lasted, the more intimate with one another the individual rendition became.
They seized the thrill of satisfaction.
The musicians were all sexually aroused, eager, and randy,
Feeling [*rasa-rasa*] as if they couldn't stand it any longer.

The quickened tempo could last no longer.
Then the final cadence came, followed by the *sendhon*.[9] (Soeradipoera et al. 1912–15)

Deep listening or trancing may incite sexual passion. Religious ecstasy is often described in explicitly sexual terminology. The similarities between trancing and states of sexual bliss or the invoking of sexual metaphors as a description of trance may be a problem for those whose beliefs systems place sexuality in the realm of the profane. As an orthodox Christian or Muslim, how is one to interpret the parallelism between religious ecstasy and sexual ecstasy?

Erotic imagery is an important part of many of the religious poems sung for a Sufi *sama'*. Below is an excerpt from a poem by the Indian Sufi, Amir Khusrau, whose tomb lies within the Nizamuddin shrine in New Delhi. The imagery of the poem is that of a lover longing for the beloved, a standard topos of Sufi mystic poetry.

I Don't Know Where I'm Going
(Poem in Persian by Amir Khusrau, 1254–1325 C.E., translated by Jeffrey Grice

A devoted suitor is approaching on horseback.
I was told tonight
That you were coming, my Love:
I lay down my head in sacrifice on the path
Which you will ride, my cavalier.
Without hesitation, I have laid the Jewel of my life as a carpet for your arrival.
I lay down my head in sacrifice on the path
Which you will ride, my cavalier!
Living only with your memory
Has brought me to the point of death.
O what use will your coming be,
Once I am dead?
The power of love is so strong
That its privileges cannot be taken away.
If you don't come to the funeral,
You will come to the grave!
In only coming once you stole
The heart, religion and patience of Khusrau.
Whatever will happen if you come in this way
Two or three times more?
I was told tonight

That you were coming, my Love! (Excerpted from Program Notes, concert of
Nusrat Fateh Ali Khan, Ann Arbor, Michigan, 1993)

Sufis stress the fact that they understand the imagery metaphorically, and
also that the Sufi path is always an individual one, entirely dependent on the
particular spiritual state of the devotee. One responds to any particular line of
poetry depending on one's own state of mind at the time.

> The name passion applied to other than Him is a pure metaphor, not a proper
> sense of the word, though he that has a lack, near in his lack to brute beasts some-
> times does not recognize in the expression passion anything but the seeking of
> sexual intercourse. And such a one as this is like a donkey-driver, with whom it is
> not fitting that one should use such terms as passion, union, longing, humane inter-
> course. (al-Ghazzali 1901–02: 233)

The problem of sexuality and ecstatic trance is not special to Islam. In Christianity it seems to have been compounded by the fact that it was more often
than not women who were overcome with spiritual ecstasy. The sensuality that
presented a problem in the Christian Middle Ages was not the eroticism of a
religious text but, specifically, the erotic dimensions of the trance experience
itself. The following passage is attributed to Angela of Foligno (died 1309 C.E.).

> And then the soul, participating in the highest one . . . desires to possess him, and
> embraces him, and squeezes him to herself, and conjoins herself with God, and
> God draws her to himself with the highest sweetness of love, and then the power
> of love transforms the beloved into the lover: that is, the soul, inflamed with divine
> love, transforms herself through the power of love into God, her beloved. (Caciola
> 1994: 41)

The metaphor of the lover and the beloved as representing the relationship
between the seeker and the Divine takes some of its power from this ambiguity,
from its association with sexuality. Because of its clear rootedness in bodily sensation, sexual imagery slides easily into powerful symbolism. The similarities
between divine love and human sensuality add color, emotion, and mystery to
the impact of trancing.

During the Barong/Rangda ceremonies, the trancing men who first attack
Rangda and then themselves often assume a stance and perform gestures similar
to coitus.

> The performer stands with legs apart and knees slightly bent. He holds the *kris*
> [dagger] with both hands down between his thighs, the point extending upward
> toward his breast. From this position, the performer may rear back, bringing his
> body into a position analogous to that of the other modes at the top of the thrust,
> or he may seem to fall forward upon it, so that the strong beat of the rhythmic
> motion comes on the forward and not on the backward bend. (Belo 1960: 21)

Eroticism in the secular trancing of *tarantismo* was attested to by many firsthand observers (Mora 1963: 418). The gestures of the women and some of the
lyrics indicate a strong sexual undertone to the dancing/trancing performance.

Where did it bite you, tell me, beloved, where it was.
Oh, if it was your leg, oh mamma! (Sigerist 1944: 220)

The semiotic, metaphoric relationship between trancing and the sexual act may be supported by a physiological relationship between the neural pathways of aroused musical listening and those of aroused sexuality. High arousal emotions can both precipitate trancing and the phenomenon known as "chills" in musical listening, a tingling at the back of the neck, down the spine, or the raising of "goosebumps." Trancing and "chills" may be linked to the circuits and chemicals of sexual arousal.

> We have shown here that music recruits neural systems of reward and emotion similar to those known to respond specifically to biologically relevant stimuli, such as food and sex, and those that are artificially activated by drugs of abuse. (Blood and Zatorre 2001: 11823)

This possible neural/chemical link has led Panksepp to label musically induced chills as a "skin orgasm."

> I chose to label the chill phenomenon as a "skin orgasm" on the basis of the assumption that there are underlying neurochemical similarities between the two phenomena. . . . many of the neurochemistries that underlie sexuality are the same as those that mediate other social processes. (Panksepp 1995: 203)

If the sadness of musical emotion is not necessarily depressive but may be stimulating, then, in musical/trancing situations, the sexuality of the longing Sufi, the longing of the victim of a tarantula bite, and the longing of the *bebuten* trancer may not be painful either. Or the sadness of the deep listener may be transformed into joy. Or the sexuality of a trancer may be a result of extreme joy or extreme arousal. If under conditions of extreme arousal the neural circuits and chemical reactions that are normally generated by sexual interest come into play for trancers and deep listeners, then that may only demonstrate the interconnectedness of our emotional circuits. Musical arousal and sexual arousal may share "underlying neurochemical similarities."

Panksepp goes further and links the "skin orgasm" reaction to particular types of musical stimuli.

> A certain kind of acoustic dynamic, with intrinsic emotion-activating properties (e.g. "piercing" crescendos) . . . may be essential for the phenomenon to be triggered, but a background mood of bittersweet, melancholy, and sadness may also be important for the responses to occur with any consistency. It also seems evident that certain types of sustained high-frequency notes, often presented by a solo performer, are an optimal stimulus for activating the response. (Panksepp 1995: 195–96)

His description of those stimuli could just as easily be descriptive of north Indian/Pakistani Chishti Sufi musical traditions as can be heard in the CDs of the late Nusrat Fateh Ali Khan or the Sabri Brothers. The performance tran-

Figure 2-6. Transcription of one verse of "*Shamas-ud-doha, badar-ud-doja*" sung by Nusrat Fateh Ali Khan and party. Reproduced with permission of Joshua Penman.

Figure 2-6. *Continued on the next page*

Figure 2-6. *Continued*

scribed in Figure 2-6 is played with heavy accents on downbeats, at high volume and with a penetrating voice quality.[10]

Unlike meditation, where strong emotions are to be eliminated or set aside or transcended, trancing in religious contexts draws on emotion, depends on emotion, and stimulates emotion through sensual overload: visual, tactile and aural. In trancing contexts, the ANS seems in overdrive, propelling the trancer to physical feats not normally possible, and to the feeling of numinous luminosity that encapsulates special knowledge not accessible during normal consciousness. In trance, all sensations become intense: hot or cold, smooth or rough, light or dark. Arousal and speed, arousal and dynamism, arousal and dancing, arousal and sex are all natural pairs. Although any kind of music can be associated with trance, it remains significant that much trance music is rhythmically vibrant and somewhat loud, or at least with a piercing tone quality. ANS arousal seems to be a central factor in precipitating trance, often dependent on enlivening musical accompaniment facilitating a sense of divinity, of the sacred realm. There is a joy in the pure bodily experience of strong arousal, a life-affirming quality of feeling truly alive that both deep listening and trancing can enhance. Both are affectively akin to sexual arousal.

Conclusion: Controlling the Uncontrollable

The generation of the initiating physiological responses to primary emotions generally are not under conscious control. We do not will ourselves to feel anger, or sadness, or elation. Damasio cites the one exception he found, which he believes to be rare, of the pianist Maria Joao Pires, who claims to be able to either hold back or enhance her emotional involvement while listening to music or playing music. Damasio was skeptical and submitted her to a test including skin conductance response and rate of heartbeat. One listening test was a "hold-back emotion" listening, the other was an "emotional release" listening. She not only demonstrated her conscious control over bodily reactions believed to be autonomic but also repeated the experiment and with the same results for a colleague who was sure someone had erred in the first experiment (Damasio 1999: 50).

One of the startling aspects of religious trancing worldwide is its stereotypicity. Trancers behave exactly the way in which they have learned to behave, and trance behavior is narrowly circumscribed by time and place. In my hometown, Pentecostal trancing can be witnessed each Sunday morning sometime between 11:30 A.M. and 1:30 P.M., in a particular church, with all trancers following basically the same gestural script. Likewise in the Rangda/Barong ceremony, the trancers who attack Rangda and then turn their knives against themselves do so on cue, so to speak. Very rarely do they enter trance before the proper narrative moment. Precisely at the point in the drama at which they begin trancing, their actions, gestures, and the duration of the trancing are predictable. Trance behavior is much more circumscribed, more stereotypical than everyday behavior. Trancers follow a script that determines the time of the onset of trance, the duration of trance, behavior during trance, and the style of withdrawal from trance.

How do they do it?

I believe they do it in part by control over the physiology of emotional arousal. To use the vernacular, they are able to turn on strong emotions at will. The case of the pianist Maria Joao Pires may not be as exceptional as it at first appears. Control over what are believed to be involuntary bodily states and reactions may be more widespread than is normally believed. We have all heard stories about Indian yogis who can control their metabolic rates and respiration rate to the degree that they can be buried alive for several hours or even days and yet survive. I suspect that less spectacular cases may be occurring regularly or occasionally with persons who are not, like yogis, professionals. One clear example is the ability of some patients with severe headaches to ease their pain by learning to redirect or redistribute their blood flow from their head to their hands or legs, called biofeedback (Green and Green 1989: 213). The headache sufferer is linked to a machine whose dials indicate hand temperature. The patient learns to redistribute blood flow not by watching the dial on the machine but by *imagination,* by visualizing her hands on a summers' day in full sunlight. I suspect that deep listeners, performers like Maria Joao Pires, and trancers also learn to control emotional arousal. Like al-Ghazzali's Qur'an listeners, they turn effort into effortlessness, force into habit.

> And therefore the Apostle of God commanded him who did not weep at the reading of the Qur'an that he should force weeping and mourning; for the beginning of these States is sometimes forced while their ends thereafter are true. (al-Ghazzali 1901: 731)

Trancers and deep listeners are not able to describe this process anymore than the pianist Maria Joao Pires could describe the opening and closing of her floodgates of emotion. Like riding a bike, or learning via biofeedback, once you learn you don't forget. You know that you know, but cannot describe the knowing to another.

> In learning voluntary control of normally unconscious processes, we do not become directly aware of the neural pathways and muscle fibers involved, any more than we become aware of what cerebral and subcerebral nerves are involved in playing tennis. . . . Everything that is learned, without exception, is learned with feedback of some kind, whether it involves the corticostriate system or the corticosubcortica-autonomic system. (Green and Green 1989: 211)

The trancers at a Barong/Rangda ritual "permit" emotional arousal on hearing music and finding themselves players in a religious drama. In the words of Merleau-Ponty, they "offer" themselves to "actions from outside." I suspect that strong emotional arousal stimulated by listening helps precipitate the onset of a trancing consciousness characterized by focus, by duration, by limiting the sense of self, and by the surety of special knowledge—the gnosis of trancing. Control of the autonomic bodily responses of emotion and the ability to affect the intensity of those physiological responses is one definition of a trancer.

How else can one reconcile the fact that within a society *who* trances, *when* they trance, and *where* they trance is so predictable? This predictability might lead one to suspect fakery, which surely sometimes happens, but not nearly so often as most nonbelievers suspect. The predictability of trancing and the stereotypicity of trancing, conforming to community expectations, is not, I am convinced, a result of fraudulence, of chicanery, but of skill. Trancers and deep listeners have more control over the activities of their minds and bodies than most of us. They are not "out-of-control" but, rather, more fully able to modulate and enhance what are normally autonomic bodily responses than most people. They are profoundly in control of themselves.

3   *Habitus of Listening*

Experimental studies on music and emotion conducted by Western scholars and scientists nearly always presume a particular image of musical listeners: silent, still listeners, paying close attention to a piece of music about which they name the type of emotion evoked by the piece to an attendant researcher. Naming of the emotion may be immediate in a laboratory setting, or retrospective, recalling the emotion after the musical event.

What is wrong with this image?

Nothing, if the intent is to describe the affective responses to decontextualized performances by middle-class American or European listeners to music while seated quietly in a concert hall or in a laboratory. The laboratory situation may reflect the habit of many current Western listeners, possibly even more so now than in the past as so much musical listening takes place attached to headphones rather than at live performances. Silent, still, focused listening is also the habit in some other musical traditions, notably the north Indian Hindustani tradition, where one sits quietly, introspectively listening to the gradual developing filigree of the musical structure of a *raga,* played, perhaps, on a *sitar.* Thoughts and feelings are turned inward. The setting is intimate, conducive to introspection and a distancing from one's fellow listeners.

But if the intent is to delineate something more general about the relationships between musical event and musical affect, the image of an inwardly focused, isolated listener is inadequate. This portrayal of listener and listening presents a set of unexamined ideologies and presuppositions that would not apply for most of the world. The unasked questions include: What constitutes "listening" to music? What are the appropriate kinds of emotions to feel? Who is it that is "having" the emotions?

A group of listeners develops a "community of interpretation" (Fish 1980), not necessarily uniform but overlapping in some salient features. This community of listeners will approach the music with a pregiven set of expectations, a "forestructure of understandings" (Gergen 1991: 104). Every hearer occupies a position in a cultural field not of his or her own making: Every hearing is situated.

We accumulate our listening habits and expectations largely unawares; only when confronted with an alternate kind of listening are we likely to reflect on our own conventionalized mode. Listeners can shift modes in different contexts, such as the ways in which one listens to music at a chamber music recital, or at

---

Portions of this chapter have been previously published in Becker 2001.

a rock concert, or a jazz club, or a movie, or at a salsa club (J. Becker 1983). Cross-culturally, modes of listening may add features not shared by us, or may not involve features that we take for granted. What is appropriate to say about musical affect, what is *not* appropriate to say, what one feels and what one does *not* feel may reveal underlying assumptions surrounding musical listening. What is *not* assumed in one mode (such as bodily movement in Western classical listening) may become central in another mode (such as dancing while listening to a salsa band). To sit quietly focused on musical structure at a salsa concert is as inappropriate as break dancing to a Schubert quintet.

We need a term to express the temporal and spatial situatedness of the hearer which is the aural equivalent of the visual term for modes of seeing, that is, *the gaze*. Frequently a feminist challenge to the dominance of "the male gaze" in literature (Kern 1996), film (Žižek 1991: 88), painting (Hebdige 1995), photography (Slater 1995), television (Morley 1995), psychoanalysis (Žižek 1996: 90), medicine (O'Neill 1995), and advertising (Barnard 1995), the term "gaze" is now used in a wide variety of contexts to exemplify the situatedness of looking, the historical and psychological specificity of any one visual approach, and the complex imbrication of modes of seeing with rhetorical and institutional structures and beliefs (Gamman and Marshment 1988; Jenks 1995; Brennan and Jay 1996). Modes of *looking* imply habits of seeing that change not only across space (Mitchell 1986), but also at different historical periods within a single culture (Baxandall 1974; Goldhill 1996). Similarly, modes of *listening* vary according to the kind of music being played, the expectations of the musical situation, and the kind of subjectivity that a particular culture has fostered in relation to musical events (J. Johnson 1995). Even more than modes of looking, modes of listening implicate not only structures of knowledge and beliefs but also intimate notions of personhood and identity. Listening addresses interiors; listening provides access to what is hidden from sight.

We need a word like Bourdieu's *habitus* (1977), coined as an alternative to terms such as "culture" which seemed too static, and sometimes seemed to imply a rigidity, an all-inclusiveness that obscured individual, idiosyncratic, or innovative modes of thought and behavior. Still left with the need to refer to the ways in which beliefs and behaviors seem relatively stereotypical within a given society, Bourdieu proposed the term *habitus* to do the theoretical work formerly carried by the word "culture."

> The structures constitutive of a particular type of environment (e.g. the material conditions of existence characteristic of a class condition) produce *habitus*, systems of durable, transposable *dispositions*, . . . that is, as principles of the generation and structuring of practices and representations which can be objectively "regulated" and "regular" without in any way being the product of obedience to rules, objectively adapted to their goals without presupposing a conscious aiming at ends or an express mastery of the operations necessary to attain them and, being all this, collectively orchestrated without being the product of the orchestrating action of a conductor. (Bourdieu 1977: 72)

Bourdieu goes on to define what he means by "dispositions":

The word *disposition* seems particularly suited to express what is covered by the concept of *habitus* defined as a system of dispositions. It expresses first the *result of an organizing action*, with a meaning close to that of words such as structure; it also designates a *way of being, a habitual state* (especially of the body) and, in particular, a *predisposition, tendency, propensity*, or *inclination*. (Bourdieu 1977: 214, f.1)

Habitus is an embodied pattern of action and reaction, in which we are not fully conscious of why we do what we do; not totally determined, but a *tendency* to behave in a certain way. Our "*habitus of listening*" is tacit, unexamined, seemingly completely "natural." We listen in a *particular* way without thinking about it, and without realizing that it even is a particular way of listening. Most of our styles of listening have been learned through unconscious imitation of those who surround us and with whom we continually interact. A "*habitus of listening*" suggests, not a necessity nor a rule, but an inclination, a disposition to listen with a particular kind of focus, to expect to experience particular kinds of emotion, to move with certain stylized gestures, and to interpret the meaning of the sounds and one's emotional responses to the musical event in somewhat (never totally) predictable ways. The stance of the listener is not a given, not *natural*, but necessarily influenced by place, time, the shared context of culture, and the intricate and irreproducible details of one's personal biography.

The term I have adapted from Bourdieu, *habitus of listening*, underlines the interrelatedness of the perception of musical emotion and learned interactions with our surroundings. Our perceptions operate within a set of habits gradually established throughout our lives and developed through our continual interaction with the world beyond our bodies, the evolving situation of being-in-the-world.

Emotion as a Cultural Construct

But recognition of the fact that thought is always culturally patterned and infused with feelings, which themselves reflect a culturally ordered past, suggests that just as thought does not exist in isolation from affective life, so affect is culturally ordered and does not exist apart from thought. (Rosaldo 1984: 137)

This view, while in the ascendancy among cultural anthropologists and ethnomusicologists, has not gone unchallenged within the discipline of anthropology.

I can make no sense of a line of thought which claims that "passions" are culturally defined. From my prejudiced position as a social anthropologist this passage reveals with startling clarity the ultimately radical weakness of the basic assumption of cultural anthropology, namely, that not only are cultural systems infinitely variable, but that human individuals are products of their culture rather than of their genetic predisposition. (Leach 1981: 16)

These two quotations, starkly put and differentiated by nationality, gender, and perspective—the American, female, cultural anthropologist and the British, male, social anthropologist—state baldly the issue at hand: the cultural relativism of emotion and thought, or the universality of emotion and thought. (Leach was not a racist but, rather, a believer in the commonality of mankind. See also Lévi-Strauss 1962: 161; Goodenough 1970: 122; Turner 1983; Spiro 1984; and Brown 1991). These contesting views have elicited penetrating dialogues on both sides of the divide and continue to evoke considerable emotion in their defenders. There are good reasons for these passions: Much is at stake.

Informing our beliefs about the universality or, conversely, the culturally conditioned aspects of music and emotion, the path of Western intellectual history leads in both directions; one direction taken by the sciences that stresses general laws and instances, the other taken by the humanities and cultural anthropology that stresses cases and interpretations (Geertz 1983a).

One way to understand the divide between the scientific and the cultural approach is to look at its development from the eighteenth-century Enlightenment onward. One of the great contributions of the Enlightenment was the propagation of the idea (already taught by religion, but little observed by society) that humankind shared a basic natural state, independent of geography, chronology, or personality ("We hold these truths to be self evident: that all men are created equal," Thomas Jefferson 1776). In its day, this doctrine was dazzlingly liberal and liberating. It led, in spite of all the detours to the contrary, to the end (almost) of institutionalized slavery in the Western world. A sentence from a history book of the eighteenth century vividly presents a theatrical metaphor for the belief in the commonality of human life and human nature.

> The stage-setting [in different periods of history] is, indeed, altered, the actors change their garb and their appearance; but their inward motions arise from the same desires and passions of men, and produce their effects in the vicissitudes of kingdoms and peoples. (J. J. Mascou, *Geschichte der Teutschen,* quoted in Lovejoy 1948: 173)

Although elegantly simple, and a vast improvement over earlier views concerning "The Great Chain of Being" (Lovejoy 1964), this view, in practice, led to the assumption that all peoples everywhere thought and felt like educated, male Europeans and Americans. Postcolonial studies (Spivak 1988; Appadurai 1996) and gender studies (McClary 1991; Solie 1993) have brought home the bias in such views. We have come to appreciate the nuanced differences of affect and emotion with different stage-settings, garbs, and appearances. The "desires and passions of men" have come to be seen as *not* producing identical "inward motions." Partly through the cumulative effects of works by cultural anthropologists writing in the 1970s (Geertz 1973a: 36; Myers 1979), the 1980s (Levy 1984; Rosaldo 1984; Shweder and Bourne 1984; Lutz 1986, 1988) and the 1990s (Irvine 1990; Lutz and Abu-Lughod 1990), scholars who championed the concept of the cultural construction of emotion, social scientists and psychologists have become increasingly sensitive to the cultural component in the categorizing of, the interpretation of, and the expression of emotion (Ekman 1980: 90; Ortony et al. 1988: 26; Russell 1991a, 1991b; Davidson 1992).

If we accept Leach's version of the uniformity of human passions, we condone the silences imposed on subalterns of all times and places whose feelings were assumed to be isomorphic with those of the persons who controlled the writing of history, and we ignore the developing body of data supporting the cultural inflection of the emotions. If we accept the idea of the social construction of knowledge, of morality, and emotion, we seem to be abandoning the idea of a *human* nature, a bond of mind, emotion, and meaning that enfolds us all, and binds us to one another. We may also be in danger of losing sight of the individual as he or she slips into the constructed conventionality of cultural appearance, behavior, beliefs, and desires, and disappears altogether. Persons may become exemplars, instances of this or that cultural model.

I would like to propose that both approaches have incontrovertible empirical support, and that, rather than choose sides, we need to accept the paradox that, in fact, we cannot do without either perspective (Needham 1981; Nettl 1983: 36; Solomon 1984; Shweder 1985). Cultural difference in the expression of, the motivation for, and the interpretation of emotion in relation to musical events has been persuasively demonstrated over and over again; for example, in South Africa (Blacking 1973: 68), Liberia (Stone 1982: 79), Brazil (Seeger 1987: 129), New Guinea (Feld 1982: 32), Peru (Turino 1993: 82), South India (Viswanathan and Cormack 1998: 225), Java (Benamou 1998), and Arabic music (Racy 1998: 99). Likewise, the fact that most of us can, with experience and empathy, come to understand differing expressive reactions to different kinds of music as reasonable and coherent, demonstrates some level of commonality and universality in relation to both music and emotion. It may be that we come into the world with the full range of human emotional expression available to us (H. Geertz 1974: 249). Through continual patterns of interaction with (primarily) close family members in the early years, we develop particular patterns of emotional feelings and expressions in relation to the events of our lives. For the most part, habituated responses and actions delimit the range and type of any one person's emotional responses. Yet, it would appear that we can imaginatively enter into a much wider palette of human emotional possibilities. We need to make a Hegelian move and transcend the dichotomy between scientific universalism and humanistic particularity and embrace both as necessary to the study of music and emotion.

Person and Emotion in the Habitus of Listening

The subjectivity of the listeners described in psychological studies, the proto-typical Western, middle-class listener is likely to be some variant of the following: an individual with a strong sense of separateness, of uniqueness from all other persons, an individual whose emotions and feelings are felt to be known in their entirety and complexity only to him or herself. Physical and psychic privacy is treasured. Emotional responses to a given piece of music are not felt to be in relation to anything outside of his or her own particular self history and personality: The emotion, for us, belongs to the individual, not to the situation or to relationships. Emotion is the authentic expression of one's being, and is, in some sense, natural and spontaneous. The emotion is interior, may or may not be shared with anyone else, and may be a guide to one's inner essence. Leo Treitler has written about one way in which this style of subjectivity can relate to listening to music.

> It is that interaction of the selves of the listener with those in the music—no, better put: the awareness of the self (selves) in the music through its (their) interaction with the listener's self—that interests me here; musical communication as a function of the interaction of identities. (Treitler 1993: 48)

The differing identities of the listening subject, and those projected by the music become the focus of interest and affect for Treitler. One common variant of this Western kind of subjectivity while listening to music is to identify with the different identity projected by the music. This interpretation segues into theories concerning one's fantasy life and seems to be a fruitful approach to the kind of emotion associated with music that one finds, for example, among adolescents (Frith 1987: 143; Shepherd and Giles-David 1991), and may help to explain their profound identification with the popular music of their times.

Being a Griot

How different is the subjectivity, the *habitus of listening* of the Wolof griots of Senegal and their listeners, as described by Judith Irvine (1990). Among the Wolof, the musical expression of emotion is dialogical and situational, not personal and interior. Griots, low-caste individuals, are believed to be highly expressive, highly excitable, "volatile and theatrical." The nobles are believed to be the opposite, composed, cool, detached, and somewhat bland in affect. It is the duty of the griots to stimulate the nobles to action, nobles who might otherwise be given over to lethargy. The highly expressive, emotional performances of the griots are intended, in part, to provide energy to the nobles so that they might carry out their governing duties. Irvine relates that a frequent image in Wolof oral poetry and epic narratives involves the playing of an ensemble of drums and iron clappers to awaken the king "lest his royal duties go unfulfilled" (Irvine 1990: 134). The emotion of the musicians and dancers is contrasted to the lack of emotion of their primary audience, the nobles. Both the emotion of the griots and its absence in the nobles are public, dialogical, and situational, not private and hidden. One of the primary manifestations of subjectivity among Europeans and Americans, emotions are not personal attributes for the Wolof griots and nobles in the same way. For us, emotional responses to music are not considered to be assigned by virtue of one's class and profession but to be an inalienable characteristic of a bounded, inviolate individual. This is not at all to say that Wolof nobles do not feel strong personal emotions, or that a griot is necessarily always highly extroverted and volatile. It is only to say that these are the *dispositions*, the *inclinations* that are likely to be fulfilled more often than not. The key participants in these musical events exhibit a *habitus of listening* and a type of subjectivity that largely conforms to Wolof cultural expectations.

The Habitus of Listening *to the* Sitar, Tambura, *and* Tabla

Earlier, I mentioned the similarity of the *habitus of listening* of the listener of Hindustani music and the Western middle-class listener in terms of physical stillness, focused attention, and inner withdrawal. Furthermore, both traditions would claim that music can *represent* emotion. In his autobiography, Ravi Shankar described his own subjectivity as a musician, a style of personhood that seems concordant with what I, or most readers of this book, might feel as performing musicians.

> A *raga* is an aesthetic projection of the artist's inner spirit; it is a representation of his most profound sentiments and sensibilities, set forth through tones and melodies.
> . . . I may play *Raga Malkauns*, whose principal mood [*rasa*] is *veera* [heroic], but I could begin by expressing *shanta* [serenity] and *karuna* [compassion] in the *alap* and develop into *veera* [heroic] and *adbhuta* [astonishment] or even *raudra* [anger] in playing the *jor* or *jhala*. (Shankar 1968: 23, 27)

The inner spirit of the artist, functioning within culturally constructed categories of affect, is made manifest in the outward expressions of his musical presentation. Bringing yet another dimension of similarity to the two listening situations is the fact that emotion (*rasa*) experienced in listening to Hindustani music is distanced and impersonal. One can feel the emotion without the troublesome immediacy and consequences of an emotion that compels action (Abhinavagupta in Gnoli 1968: 82–85; Masson and Patwardhan 1969: 46). June McDaniel, writing of *rasa* in the Indian province of Bengal, uses the metaphor of the glass window separating the experiencer from the emotion while still allowing a clear view.

> *Bhava* is a personal emotion; *rasa* is an impersonal or depersonalized emotion, in which the participant is distanced as an observer. Why is a depersonalized emotion considered superior to a personal one? Because the aesthete can experience a wide range of emotions yet be protected from their painful aspects. Emotion is appreciated through a glass window, which keeps out unpleasantness. Though the glass is clear, thus allowing a union of sorts with the observed object, the window is always present, thus maintaining the dualism. (McDaniel 1995: 48)

The following description is a Western mirror image of the way to experience *rasa*.

> When people listen, say, to "Questi i campi di Tracia" from Monteverdi's *Orfeo* . . . they do not directly perceive the anguish and guilt of the twice-widowed singer.

Listeners only hear a *representation* [italics mine] of the way his voice moves under the influence of his emotions. Nevertheless, this can give listeners important insights into a type of emotional response. Monteverdi skillfully displays the contortions through which Orpheus's voice goes. When listeners know how a voice moves under the influence of an affect, they are given (if they are familiar with the conventions of the music, and otherwise qualified) an immediate demonstration of something about the affect. A good performance of this aria immediately demonstrates to a sensitive audience something about what it is like to feel guilt, remorse, and despair. (Young 1999: 48)

In both the Hindustani and the Western classical listener, an emotion evoked by listening to music can be contemplated with a certain deliberation and calmness. But at some point the congruencies between the *habitus of listening* of each breaks down. The Western observer may well, as Treitler suggests, be involved with comparing identities, or with constructing a more glamorous self in relation to the music heard, or with contemplating "what it is like to feel guilt, remorse, and despair." The Indian, however, may be performing a very different act, a somewhat strenuous religious exercise, a kind of refining of emotional essence, a distillation of his or her emotion that will lead to a transformation of consciousness to a higher level of spirituality. Listening to music for the Hindustani music devotee should not be, according to canon, a passive act, but requires the active will and mind of the listener to carry consciousness to a higher plane, closer to the divine (Coomaraswamy 1957: 39). Western references to "inspiration" or "genius," which at one time perhaps indicated a holy possession, have become largely metaphoric rather than literal expressions of sacred connections between musical performance and musical listening. In Indian classical traditions, the pursuit of emotion, of *rasa*, in relation to listening to music, may be a path to greater awareness, leading one to cosmic insight. Dance can share as well in this configuration of emotion as a stepping-stone to a higher gnosis. One of India's most revered *Bharata Natyam* dancers has written:

> It is here that *Bharata Natyam*, the ancient and holy art of Indian dance, cuts deeply into the conscious and subconscious levels and revealingly brings to the forefront the fact that it is ultimately and intimately oriented to the nucleus, *atman* [the Universal Self]. It is a revelation not only to the performing artist, but in an equal measure to the audience as well. . . . By the inexplicable power born of the union of melody, lyric, rhythm and gesture, the emotions are released from their limited secular locus and are expanded to universal proportions where there is only pure spirit with nothing of the sensual. (Balasaraswati 1985: 2–3)

According to the contemporary Bengali version of *rasa* theory, and as in the ancient Indian theory of *rasa*, intense emotions, high arousal emotions, primary emotions are the appropriate vehicle to lead one to mystical knowledge of life's meaning and purpose. Emotions are compared to water that can best be understood by immersion in an ocean rather than by the delicate feel of a raindrop (McDaniel 1995: 51). What we might call emotional excesses become pregnant possibilities for greater spiritual attainment for an Indian music listener. Although the quiet stance and introverted demeanor of the listener in the proto-typical Western case and the Hindustani listener are similar, the understanding and interpretation of what is supposed to happen in each case differs. In one case, the listener may be exploring the affective nuances of his/her inner self or identifying with the affective interiors presented by the music: In the other, the listener is trying to bring about a kind of sea change, a different self altogether, one that comes closer to divinity.

Music and Ecstasy: The Sufis of the Nizamuddin Shrine, New Delhi

The knowledge of the cause why souls receive impressions through sounds belongs to the most subtle of the sciences of the Revelations which Sufis are granted, and the foolish, the frozen, the hard of heart, who are shut off from the pleasure of music and poetry, marvels how he that listens takes pleasure and at his ecstasy and state of emotion and change of colour, as a brute beast marvels at the pleasure of almond-candy and the impotent at the pleasure of sexual intercourse and the youth marvels at the pleasure of governing and at the pleasure that lies in breadth of reputation, and as the foolish marvels at the pleasure of the knowledge of God Most High and the knowledge of His majesty and might and the wonders of His creation. (al-Ghazzali 1901: 230)

The tomb of the Sufi saint Inayat Khan sits in the middle of a room off the second-story terrace of a square compound surrounding and opening onto a central garden courtyard at the Nizamuddin shrine in New Delhi. The architecture recreates the Mughal-Indian traditions though the building was constructed in the twentieth century. As one enters the spiritual sanctuary of the tomb, one first sees the tomb itself, raised about two feet off the ground, covered with a golden shawl and littered with flowers. Muslim devotees bow down before the tomb on entering the room, before moving to the side and sitting on the floor along the walls to await the beginning of a *sama'*, a concert of sung religious poetry. On three sides, latticed walls let the light filter through, illuminating the marble floor, the tomb itself and the one solid wall on which are inset green marble panels. This is a place of peace, of reverence, an *akasha* (lit., heaven) where "everything can find its place." The musicians, called *qawwals* in Pakistan and north India, assemble, and begin to sing their songs of devotion that may move some of the assembled devotees to a sense of communion with Allah, a deeply emotional experience called simply *hal*, "state". (See Plate 2.)

The leader of the small group of musicians plays the harmonium and is the lead singer. Although his voice has lost the power it had when he was younger, he is still a master of the old Farsi (Persian) texts, as well as knowing a large repertoire of Urdu and Hindu songs. His songs are supported by strongly articulated drum patterns played on the *dholak*. Five other singers form a chorus that joins him after each new line, repeating the line several times for emphasis; occasionally one of the other singers will assume the lead and introduce a new verse, or sing an extended *girah*, or inserted verse.

Perhaps the first line of the poem has some important spiritual association for the listener and he feels moved to rise from his seat, approach the presiding *pir* and make a money offering (Qureshi 1986: 201). Incipient arousal at hearing a personally pertinent line or verse may further move the devotee to strong swaying or head shaking. On seeing this, the lead *qawwal* will likely repeat that line over and over to further stimulate the worshipper to deeper levels of arousal. A more deeply aroused Sufi may raise his arms, weep, or shout. At this point, the *qawwals* may add intensifiers "such as extra weight on accented beats by drums or handclaps, clapping 'double' on half-beats, or gradually increasing tempo" (Qureshi 1986: 204). If emotional arousal continues to intensify and the worshipper reaches ecstasy, he will stand up, walk, or dance while the arousing musical verse will be repeated loudly in the upper range of the musicians' voice accompanied by maximum-volume clapping, singing, and drumming. In acknowledgment of the attaining of the ecstatic state by one of their fellow worshippers, first the *pir* and then all present will rise to their feet. The *qawwals* continue playing at high intensity until the ecstasy subsides, believing as they do that without musical support, the ecstatic might die.

> They call such a condition Hal. Hal means the same as condition; it is an appropriate term for it, because by hearing the drum they think of that condition and then they enter into it. They need not be very educated to go into that trance, nor very evolved; sometimes they are very ordinary people, but sound can have such effect upon them that they are moved to a higher ecstasy. (H. I. Khan 1994: 107)

Sufis are the mystics of Islam; they are expected to renounce worldly gain, the pursuit of power in favor of the development of an inner vision, a tuning of one's sensual and intellectual being to the gnosis of a higher power. For the saintly Sufi, death is the ultimate union with Allah. Thus it is the death date, the *urs'* that is the focus of celebration of a saint's final union with Allah. Around the final resting place of the body of the saint, a field of possibilities arises for similar seekers. Grave sites become favorite places for special intercessory prayers, for meditation, for Qur'anic readings, and for the spiritual concert *sama'.*

By the twelfth century, Sufism had become an integral part of Islamic societies. Orders of Sufi devotees grew around the tombs of saints, and missionary work established Sufi shrines and monasteries from Morocco to the Philippines. The emphasis on the power of music to help devotees attain transcendental states has always produced ambivalence or even opposition among more orthodox Muslim clerics. Al-Ghazzali's extended justification of the use of *sama'*, *The Alchemy of Happiness,* written in the early twelfth century, attests to the felt need of such an apologia. The same defensiveness is encountered today when speaking with the learned Sufi spiritual leader of the Nizamuddin shrine Khwaja Hasan Sani Nizami. The Khwaja likes to tell the story of Aisha, the wife of the Prophet, who wished to see and hear the musicians playing outside the wall of their compound. The Prophet himself lifted her up and held her so she could better enjoy the musical entertainment. Khwaja Hasan Sani Nizami has other stories, too—pointedly directed to those who oppose his musical religious practices. He tells of camel drivers who sing to their camels to help them keep traveling without food, water, or rest. With a smile, the saintly Khwaja Hasan Sani Nizami remarks that some camels have more sense than some people (interview with K. H. S. Nizami, January 1996).

Occupying the low rank of servants to the shrine, like those who sweep the premises, the *qawwals* sit farthest from the places of honor, the seat of the spiritual leader or the tomb of the saint. Devotees are not expected to look at the *qawwals* while they are playing but, rather, cast their eyes downward in deep concentration. When moved by a particular line of poetry, a money offering is made to the Sufi spiritual leader. Eventually the offering may go to the *qawwals*, but not directly. Offerings are indications of homage and love to the Sufi saint, not payment for musicians. Thus, while the music and poetry of the *qawwals* is revered, the *qawwal* himself is not. The *qawwals* remain poor and low cast, although their music may send others into flights of rapture.[1]

The strongest version of happiness in relation to musical listening and an example of extreme arousal is ecstasy. Usually associated with religious rituals, ecstasy, as extreme joy, almost by definition involves a sense of the sacred (although musical ecstasy can justly be claimed by some attendees at secular musical events such as rock concerts). The degree to which Muslim Sufi orders have formalized and institutionalized musical ecstasy has seldom been exceeded. The works of al-Ghazzali about music and ecstasy are still basic pedagogical texts for contemporary Sufis in Iran, Afghanistan, Pakistan, and north India.

> Lo! Hearts and inmost thoughts are treasuries of secrets and mines of jewels. . . . There is no way to the extracting of their hidden things save by the flint and steel of listening to music and singing, and there is no entrance to the heart save by the ante-chamber of the ears. So musical tones, measured and pleasing, bring forth what is in it and make evident its beauties and defects . . . and that it bears as fruit a state in the heart that is called ecstasy; and ecstasy bears as fruit a moving of the extremities of the body, either with a motion that is not measured and is called agitation or with a measured motion which is called clapping of the hands and swaying of the members. (al-Ghazzali 1901–02: 199)

Sufi doctrine interprets the music as supportive, as secondary to the all-important text, the religious poetry (Qureshi 1986: 83). Yet the question remains: To what degree is the arousal stimulated by the sensual overload of intensifying rhythms and soaring phrases sung over and over again at the top of the *qawwal*'s range?[2] If Western deep listeners feel that their secular listening experiences bring feelings of the sacred, they are likely to feel they have been blessed in some way. The holy feelings are experienced as a special bonus. If a listener from a community of believers feels blessed by the extraordinary beauty of the song and his emotional reaction to it, he may worry about the source of his pleasure: Is it the Holy Spirit or the consummate skill of the very human musician? The *habitus of listening* for the devout Sufi, as for the Christian Pentecostal, includes the hope that his emotion derives from spiritual communion, not simply from a terrific performance. This worry is at least as old as Plato

(*Timaeus* 28 A, B; *Republic* 401 D) and finds a poignant expression in the Confessions of St. Augustine (fourth century C.E.):

> I feel that when the sacred words are chanted well, our souls are moved and are more religiously and with a warmer devotion kindled to piety than if they are not so sung. All the diverse emotions of our spirit have their various modes in voice and chant appropriate in each case, and are stirred by a mysterious inner kinship. But my physical delight, which has to be checked from enervating the mind, often deceives me when the perception of the sense is unaccompanied by reason, and is not patiently content to be in a subordinate place. It tries to be first and to be in the leading role, though it deserves to be allowed only as secondary to reason. So in these matters I sin unawares, and only afterward become aware of it. (Chadwick 1991: 207–08)

Blurring the boundaries between secular and sacred, the pure aesthetic pleasure of melodiously sung poetry, the profoundly sensual appeal of soaring voices and captivating rhythms have been and remain a problem for Sufis. In a manual about Sufism, *Kashf-ul-Mahjub* "Unveiling the Hidden" written in Persian by Hazrat Ali Hujwiri (died 1072 C.E.), the author complains that there are two kinds of people who attend a *sama'*: "those who concentrate deeply upon the objective and moral lessons and the true meaning of Sufi poetry and those fond of musical concerts" (Siddiqui 1979: 54). The distinction Ali Hujwiri hoped to make may be problematic.

Between 1737 and 1741, a twenty-year-old nobleman, Dargah Quli Khan from Hyderabad, was stationed in Delhi as a representative of his home government. He wrote a diary in which he describes festivals at Muslim shrines as well as vivid sketches of many prominent musicians of his day. The language of the diary is Persian, the court language and the language of the Sufi nobles of the time, most of whom traced their ancestry to Persia. Writing of a festival at the Nizamuddin shrine, he indicates the juxtaposition of *qawwals* and nonreligious entertainers at such events. Figure 3-1 shows the public, central courtyard of the Nizamuddin shrine with *qawwals* playing in the midst of a milling crowd.

> Every Wednesday the nobles and plebians dress themselves [and gather here] for pilgrimage and the *qawwals* perform the ceremony of salutation with full traditions and regard. On the last Wednesday of the month of Safar an extraordinarily large gathering, having dressed their hair and adorned themselves, come here. After paying homage, they go wandering in the gardens in the surroundings of the blessed mausoleum. Artisans arrange their wares and all kinds of delicious eatables and other requisites are made available for the visitors. The excess of the melodies of the minstrels creates a cacophony of music. In every nook and corner are ventriloquists and dancers who perform to the best of their ability. (D. Q. Khan 1989: 9)

Dargah Khan also criticizes the musicians at a *sama'*, which he calls a *mehfils*, violating the Sufi injunction against an aesthetic approach to the *sama'* ceremony:

Figure 3-1. *Qawwals* at Nizamuddin shrine, New Delhi, 1996. Photo by J. Becker.

The author once attended one of these *mehfils*. The deafening and unrhythmic voice of Chalbal Dhadi sent shudders down the spine of those present, except the Sufis, who on reaching the state of ecstasy, became immune to the noise. (D. Q. Khan 1989: 85)

How is one to know if the thrill of a powerfully sung line comes from the spiritual message or the musical dimension? The message and its medium cannot easily be separated. Yet the distinction is crucial to the Sufis and they go to some lengths to delineate it experientially (Qureshi 1986: 121). The Sufi term *kaif*, "delight" or "pleasure," indicates an initial, preparatory state of spiritual arousal that may ultimately lead to the self-negating *fana-e-fana*, "the passing away of passing away" (J. Becker 1993: 94). For a devout Sufi, the distinction between *kaif* and *hal* is crucial; his musical delight may be a preview, a foretasting of his ultimate communion with Allah. For the medieval Tantric *rasa* theorists, knowing the distinction between aesthetic delight and the progress toward enlightenment also indicated a fine and necessary discrimination. The deep listener may not worry about the distinction. Although both may weep from excess joy, their interpretation of their emotions are not the same.

For a Sufi at a *sama'*, prepared readiness involves a special attentive listening. In the Muslim tradition, hearing is the most highly valued sense, the ear the way to spirituality and gnosis. One does not read scripture silently to oneself; one listens to it being recited by others, or recited aloud by oneself. The *habitus* of the Sufi listener at a *sama'* in New Delhi begins with the listener's understanding of the passages in the Qur'an that remind the faithful of the need to be a careful listener.

> And when the Qur'an is recited, give ear to it and harken, that you may obtain mercy. And remember thy Lord within thyself humbly and with awe, below thy breath, at morn and evening. And be not of the neglectful. (Qur'an 7: 204–05)

Sufis are concerned to bring about a transformation of ordinary consciousness to make receiving spiritual knowledge possible. Attentive listening is the path. One does not oneself play the music that will aid in this transformation, one listens to it being played by the *qawwals*. The tunes are vehicles for the all-important texts, which are not Qur'anic verses but which evoke the same kind of attentive listening as do Qur'anic verses. Sufis are waiting expectantly for that one verse that speaks to their condition, that affirms the importance of their presence at the *sama'* and that may lead them to a richer, fuller spirituality. The spiritual process of the listener is inseparable from what he hears and how he hears. Listening is a spiritual skill (Crow 1984: 33). (See Plate 3.)

> Lo! Hearts and inmost thought are treasuries of secrets and mines of jewels . . . For when the heart is moved there is made evident that only which it contains like as a vessel drips only what is in it. And listening to music and singing is for the heart a true touchstone and a speaking standard; . . . [K]now that the listening comes first, and that it bears as fruit a state in the heart that is called ecstasy. (al-Ghazzali 1901–02: 199)

A Sufi *habitus of listening* at a musical religious ceremony involves a sequence of emotion and feeling and action that could be called a "script" (Schank and Abelson 1977: 36–68; Russell 1991a, 1991b). Scripts are like liturgies in that they prescribe a more or less fixed sequence of events but the definition extends beyond liturgy to include as well the affective, phenomenological responses that tend to infuse the participants of the liturgy. Initially, while sitting quietly and reverently, the Sufi listener may hope that he or she will be touched by a particular line of text that seems directly applicable to his or her personal situation. If the lead *qawwal* catches the subtle indications of arousal in a listener, he will begin repeating the verse over and over again. The Sufi script then calls for swaying, weeping, rising up, moving to the center of the room and slowly turning in place. Musical emotion, musical feeling, and movement in the listener changes both its form and its intensity as the script progresses. The affect of the script, when fully acted out, is the ultimate joy of a direct and personal knowledge of Allah.

Music and Rage: Balinese Bebuten Trancing

The Rangda/Barong ritual of Bali, Indonesia, is an event invoked to restore the balance between the world of people and the "other" world of the

සූනියන්යක්ෂයා

Sooniyan Yakshaya, or Oddy.

Plate 1. Drawing of a *yakka*. From Callaway 1829: 10.

Plate 2. Meraj Ahmad Nizami (playing harmonium) and his troupe of *qawwal*s. Nizamuddin shrine, New Delhi, India. Photo by J. Becker.

Plate 3. Dancing Sufis, from the Kamseh by Djami, sixteenth-century miniature.
From *Persische Miniaturen* 1960: Plate 18.

Plate 4. Rangda, Balinese witch. Photo by J. Becker.

Plate 5. Barong, Balinese mythical beast. Photo by J. Becker.

Plate 6. Balinese *bebuten* trancers. Photo by J. Becker.

Plate 7. Balinese gamelan ensemble. Photo by J. Becker.

Plate 8. A *Bissu* priest, Puang La Sékké, from Sulawesi. From Hamonic 1987: frontspiece. Courtesy of the Centre National de la Recherche Scientifique, Paris.

deities, spirits, and demons. If some misfortune befalls a village, such as crop failure, pestilence, or frequent cases of mental illness, or the ritual calendar prescribes it, the village will stage an encounter opposing the great witch Rangda and her followers against the mythic beast Barong and his followers. Before the ceremony begins, all the participants are put into trance at the temple to the accompaniment of long lines of classical poetry sung slowly, in unison, by a chorus of women from the village. Rangda is fearsome to look at with her bulging eyes, long, flamed tongue, her mass of unruly flowing white hair, her pendulous, low-hanging breasts, and her skull necklace. Rangda is a death goddess, demonstrated by her Hindu names Durga and Kali. Although her form is monstrous she is not a monster; she is at once revered yet feared. If treated well, she becomes a protective goddess, and is sometimes even described as "beautiful" (Aryati, Ni Wayan, interview 1996). (See Plate 4.)

The elaborate mask of the witch Rangda will be brought from its storage place in the temple, blessed, and infused with spirit in a potent ceremony conducted by a priest. An exceptionally tall and spiritually strong man will be chosen to undergo the trance of *becoming* the witch. The sacred cloth that she carries draped over her arm like a waiter's napkin is an *anteng,* the sling in which Balinese mothers carry their babies. When attacked in the ritual by entranced men, she needs only to hold out the *anteng* to freeze the approaching attackers.

The cast of performers in this ritual may include up to twenty other minor demons, followers of the magical beast Barong, who may dance, cavort, or misbehave in amusing or threatening ways. A number of men, also for the moment followers of Barong, will volunteer to undergo a special kind of trance called *bebuten,* from the root *buta,* which means a creature of base instincts, low on the ladder of sentient beings, often translated as "demon." These men will confront the witch and with the help of the Barong ultimately neutralize her power. (See Plate 5.)

Bebuten trance is not ecstasy. It is a feeling of rage directed toward the witch Rangda, and may leave the trancer feeling embarrassed later by his behavior during the trance and with an exhaustion that may last for several days (Eiseman 1989: 153). Yet, the trancing is a social obligation that he fulfills voluntarily, surrendering his own comfort for the betterment of his community. He experiences a kind of homicidal rage (or, rather, "theo-cidal" rage).

> As for me, it is as if there were someone ordering me to stab. When it's like that, if I don't get hold of a *kris* [dagger], I should die, so strong is my anger. (Belo 1960: 128)

At the denouement of the drama, which may take several hours, the witch Rangda puts a curse on the human followers of Barong, whereupon they turn their daggers against themselves, pressing the blades against their sternum, or upper arm, or sometimes on their cheek, or just above the eyeball. (See Plate 6.)

Seldom do the trancers cut themselves.[3] Gregory Bateson theorized that the daggers were held in a tense state of perfect equilibrium between exerting enough pressure toward the body to puncture the skin and exerting enough pressure away from the body to remove the blade from the skin.[4] Gradually, as the force of their anger subsides, they fall to the ground in the classic "crisis" of trance (Rouget 1985: 38). They are then disarmed and removed to the inner courtyard of the temple where they are slowly brought out of trance. Throughout the public, theatrical part of the ceremony, the gamelan ensemble plays continuously. (See Plate 7.)

Different melodic motifs are associated with the numerous characters of the drama. At the point in the drama when the struggle between Rangda and the entranced human followers begins, the gamelan plays a short, loud, and furious ostinato pattern. The music does not *cause* the trance nor the self-stabbing. Members of the audience also hear the music but seldom go into trance. Sometimes a designated trancer will withdraw if his trance is shallow. And sometimes, contrary to expectations, an audience member may be overcome with rage and frustration and join the circle of trancers, be given a dagger by one of the attendants, and begin leaping about while stabbing himself.

The violent encounter between Rangda and Barong always ends in a standoff but somehow serves to restore cosmic balance. All the characters in this sacred drama are taken to the inner courtyard of the temple to be slowly brought back to everyday consciousness. (See Figure 3-2.) The young men come out of the trance feeling exhausted but relaxed, with faint memories of their spirit encounter.

In the Barong/Rangda ritual, the continuously playing gamelan creates the aura of a differing reality, a sound-mediated reality that renders plausible the appearance of deities and demons in the realm of humans. As one after another of the multitude of characters in the drama appear, the gamelan plays leitmotifs for each, both signaling their presence and making real their transition from the "other" world. The presence of these beings is in itself emotion-producing. One is not likely to be indifferent to the denizens of the "other" world who so strongly affect one's everyday life. Without their signature tunes, without the aural envelop of the myth-making music, their presence would not be nearly so affective. Music sets the stage, introduces the characters, fills the aural environment, and embraces all in its imaginary world.

Neither the trance, nor the ceremony, nor the pacification of the witch can happen without the gamelan music. The *habitus of listening* of the *bebuten* trancer on encountering Rangda would have to include not only the gamelan music and the presence of the witch but also a complex of beliefs about the negative forces of the cosmos, their effects on human communities, the embodiment of these forces in the divine witch Rangda, and the methods by which she may be contained and controlled. His own emotion, culturally constituted but felt interiorly, is a necessary component of the maintenance of community well-being. His murderous passion has little to do with an interiorized self, with his personal identity. His rage, in part musically induced, is in the service of his community. Like the Wolof griots, musical emotion for the trancer in a Balinese Rangda exorcism is public, situational, predictable, and culturally sanctioned.

The *habitus of listening* of a victim of the tarantula's bite, a *Yak Tovil* patient,

Figure 3-2. Rangda and *bebuten* trancers in the inner temple court after the Barong/Rangda ceremony. From deZoete and Spies 1938: 95. Courtesy of Faber and Faber, Limited.

the Wolof griot, an Indian *sitar* player, the Sufi listener, the Balinese *bebuten* trancer, and the Western concertgoer involve a scripted sequence of actions, emotions, and interpretations. Within each of these scripts, musical, behavioral, and emotional events will occur within a certain predictable frame. Simultaneously, each individual event will be unique and nonrepeatable. All have developed habits of mind and body in response to specific musical events. These habits are acquired throughout our life experiences of interaction with others in similar situations. The emotions are private *and* public, interior *and* exterior, individual *and* communal. Our *habitus of listening* as embodiment involves both embodiment as (2) personal, inner experience and as (3) involvement with the world, interaction with the world.

No *habitus of listening* is entirely stable nor entirely fluid. As interactions change, so do the interiors of those who are interacting. We may have developed a *habitus of listening* that inclines us to introspectively contemplate the colorful fluidity of changing emotional states in response to Bach's *Musical Offering*, but if it would not disturb the viability of our own structures, we could learn to dance ecstatically in The Spirit with the Pentecostals.

4   Trancing Selves

Inextricably linked with a *habitus of listening* is the particular configuration of the self who is doing the listening. Who are we when we listen to music or when we trance?

A transformed "self" is both a hallmark of trance and a phenomenon frequently associated with musical performance. Speculations concerning the ontological status of selves in or out of trance necessarily become important aspects of the study of music/trance relationships. With the rise of the theories of Sigmund Freud and psychoanalysis, and the development of the field of social psychology, concomitantly came an increase in the theories of "self" (Mead 1962; Lacan 1968; Taylor 1989).

Drawing on materials from evangelicals in colonial Virginia, contemporary Pentecostals, and transvestite priests in Sulawesi, Indonesia, in this chapter I will explore the idea that only certain kinds of selves, only certain constructions of selfhood are possible for one to participate in spirit possession. I suspect that certain other constructions of selfhood not only obstruct the possibility of spirit possession but also lead one to look down upon, even despise, the practice itself. I suspect that these different selves may affect one's openness to the emotional response elicited by the musical stimulation that accompanies spirit possession. Extreme emotions are the correlatives of spirit possession—emotions often attributed to the accompanying music. Like the obligatory roles of the spirit possession narrative, aroused emotions also must be acceptable components of one's sense of self.

The term "subjectivity" is often used among linguists and anthropologists to designate the area of study concerning one's sense of self, or personhood. To speak of subjectivity or one's sense of self, and to assume as I do that our sense of selfhood is culturally constrained, is, for one who has never thought of it, a profoundly anti-intuitive act. Our inner selves are felt to be so completely natural, so unique, so independent of the society around us that we may feel affronted by any suggestion that what we feel to be our sense of inner being is not our unique creation, and that selves can vary predictably across cultural boundaries.

> The "subjectivity" we are discussing here is the capacity of the speaker to posit himself as "subject." It is defined not by the feeling which everyone experiences of being himself (this feeling, to the degree that it can be taken note of, is only a reflection) but as the psychic unity that transcends the totality of the actual

---

1. This chapter is essentially the same as printed in Becker 2000.

experiences it assembles and that makes the permanence of the consciousness. (Benveniste 1971: 224)

Benveniste has argued that the sense of person, the sense of self, is a product of languaging, as have many others, including Buddhist philosophers. Although the sense of personhood seems inextricably tied to the development of language, one's sense of bodily boundaries, our sense of what (somatically) belongs to us and where our bodies end, seems to escape the linguistic formation of person and takes shape in areas of the brain not directly involved with languaging (Melzack 1992; Damasio 1999: 108). Starting in the 1970s, an influential group of anthropologists began to compile a series of articles and monographs that described senses of personhood around the globe that sometimes seemed far removed from Western understandings (Geertz 1973b; Myers 1979; Rosaldo 1980/1984; Errington 1983/1989; Shweder and Bourne 1984; Lutz 1988; Abu-Lughod 1986; A. L. Becker 1999). Notions of personhood do not reside in the mind as abstract entities, as disembodied, contextless images. They are imagined as situated within certain cultural narratives. We project ourselves imaginatively within a situation, acting in a particular way, responding verbally and gesturally to specific events and particular people. These imaginary narratives are, in broad outline, already present in the society into which we are born. Our subjectivities, our subject positions, our sense of personhood necessarily develops within cultural narratives that are preexistent.

The listening subject of a spirit possession ceremony, the self who may become entranced, enters into a special kind of narrative, not of his or her invention. The roles in these dramas are more specified, more particularly detailed, than the roles of either quotidian existence, or of the dramas into which we enter while listening to music as an activity in itself. The potential entrancee must be prepared to "receive the Holy Spirit," or to be willing to assume the role of a lower being in order to curb the power of a great witch (*bebuten* trance in Bali, Indonesia), or to become host to the "numinous energy of foreign peoples and wild animals" (a patient in a Tumbuka healing ceremony in Malawi), or to accept becoming a vehicle through which the spirits of the sky realm communicate with mankind (*bissu* priests in Sulawesi, Indonesia). Encounters with holy beings are, it seems, never easy, especially if one is expected to surrender (temporarily) a part of one's self as well. To participate in a ceremony of spirit possession is to enter into a narrative not constructed by oneself but a community narrative that gives moral purpose to the event. The narrative is both particular, (what happens for the duration of the ceremony, what might be called the "script") as well as broadly cosmological (the ultimate truths about humankind and the holy that are being enacted). Entering a spirit possession narrative means situating oneself as a certain kind of person—many ritual narratives may be precluded for us because we cannot imagine ourselves participating in that particular story. The story, the role, the emotional affect, and the moral purpose must be compatible with who we think we are.

Among my humanistic, academic peers, a discussion of the relationship between spirit possession and music will often, at some point, evoke a certain resistance. The reasons for our distrust of trance possession and of our distaste for it are multiple, involving, among many other historical developments, the history of the relationship of the Catholic Church and spirit possession throughout the Middle Ages. Although we have put aside many ancient fears and misunderstandings, there still remains a residue of misinformation and anxiety concerning trancing. We still do not easily accept the idea that someone who trances at a Pentecostal church on Sunday can function in a rational, controlled manner in a responsible job all week long. Yet, as an ethnomusicologist, my own experiences with people for whom trancing is an accepted, expected component of particular ceremonies, people who themselves may be skilled trancers and are simultaneously responsible, moral, orderly, even ordinary citizens sets up an incongruity between what I know of trancing and trancers and the unexamined beliefs of my academic peers.

The gentlemanly, well-educated director of the government Institute for Arts in Den Pasar, Bali, tells me, sitting in his modern air-conditioned office:

> When I come up to that tower, when the curtain opens like that, as soon as I step up to approach Rangda [the witch], I see a strong fire coming from her eyes. I just—"Oh! [slaps his hands together] I do this! I just jump! I feel myself just floating—because of the excitement, the aroma . . . whenever they pick up the music [sings *janga janga janga*], whenever you sing that song [sings a bit of a gamelan piece associated with trance] people just go crazy. I want to attack her!
> (I Wayan Dibia, interview, 1996)

There is, for him, no problem, no syncope, no epistemic gap between his trancing and his high-status, governmental administrative job. Why is there for us? Are we committed to the idea of a single model of personhood, that is, "the real me"? Do we resist the notion that more than one style of self may be available to us?

The Development of a Western "Self"

My hypothesis is that one style of Western self, the notion of a bounded, unique, inviolate self, may hinder the trance experience of the surrender of self and consequently the ability to imagine trance as a reasonable, natural phenotypic kind of consciousness. And that culturally defined and historically determined subjectivities may also influence one's openness to some ritual narratives and supporting musical expressions.

A classic definition of Western identity is that formulated by Clifford Geertz:

> The Western conception of the person as a bounded, unique, more or less integrated motivational and cognitive universe, a dynamic center of awareness, emotion, judgment, and action organized into a distinctive whole and set contrastively both against other such wholes and against its social and natural background, is, however incorrigible it may seem to us, a rather peculiar idea within the context of the world's cultures. (Geertz 1983b: 59)

It may be that one ingredient of the Western history of hostility to spirit possession, and of the reluctance of many to grant legitimacy to any kind of religious trancing in the United States concerns what are considered to be appropriate kinds of selves. Charles Taylor has written compellingly of the philosophical development of the Western self from its intellectual origins in Plato, through the decisive delineations of Descartes and Locke that led, through the Protestant Reformation and Romanticism, to our modern notions of self (Taylor 1988/1989). Two of the parameters concerning the modern self that Taylor has explored seem particularly relevant to the issue of spirit possession. One is the idea of personal will and control, while the other is the idea of the rational, disengaged self.

> Self-control is a basic theme of our whole moral tradition. Plato (*Republic*) speaks of the good man as being "master of himself." He remarks himself how paradoxical this can sound. Mastery is a two-place relation. So mastery of oneself must mean that something higher in one controls the lower, in fact, that reason controls the desire. From Plato through the Stoics, into the Renaissance, and right to the modern day, this mastery of reason remains a recognizable ideal—even though it is contested in modern civilization in a way it doesn't seem to have been among the ancients. (Taylor 1988: 303)

The rational mind, operating independently of body, an instrument of control, disengaged from the rest of the body was forcefully argued by Descartes (1596–1650). The trope of being one's own master, of being in control of one's own bodily appetites, thoughts, passions and desires sets up a sense of the disengaged self. We identify our "self" not with the body but with the governor of body, the mind. Our "self," this governor, seems in modern times to reside in the brain,[1] close to the eyes, near the frontal lobes associated with decision making and problem solving, with rationality. The detached, disengaged mind ideally rules the unruly, insistent body.

Rationality itself, for Descartes, assumes a new meaning with repercussions in both humanistic and scientific disciplines. Whereas for Plato and the Stoics, "reason" was attaining a clear vision of Goodness and Truth, Descartes abandons the "Order of Ideas in the Cosmos" and substitutes a procedural definition of rationality (Taylor 1989: 115–26). Descartes's aim was to promote a methodology that would lead to certainty, that is, a scientific methodology. The mental procedures that were equated with reason are the staple formula for rational thinking from Descartes's time to our own. Rationality is defined as the procedure in which one organizes thoughts, breaks a problem into its component parts, proceeds from simple to complex, and thereby reaches a true resolution, not influenced by the disturbance of messy emotions, desires, or fantasies (Taylor 1989: 144–51). To illustrate the different approaches to reality assumed by Cartesian thinkers or by fanciful Druidic thinkers, the phenomenologist Don Ihde has imagined the following drama

> Imagine two seers, a "cartesian" seer and a "druidic" seer. Both are assigned the task of observing a series of tree-appearances under a set of varying conditions

and reporting what the tree "really" is like. The cartesian seer returns with a very accurate description of the tree's color, the shape of its leaves, the texture of its bark and its characteristic overall shape. However, upon questioning him, we find that out of the conditions under which the tree appearances occurred, the cartesian seer chose as *normative* only appearances in the bright sun on a clear day. His clear and distinct tree, characterized as essentially an extended, shaped, colored configuration, is a cartesian tree, which appears best in the light of day, all other conditions being dismissed as less than ideal for observation.

The druidic seer returns with a quite different description. His tree emerges from an overwhelming nearness of presence and is eery, bespeaking its druid or spirit within. It waves and beckons, moans and groans, advances and retreats. Upon interrogation, it turns out that his *normative* conditions were misty nights and windy mornings in the half-light of dawn, when the tree appeared as a vague shape emerging from the fog or a writhing form in the wind. His tree is a druidic tree; a quiet sunny day fails to reveal the inner tree-reality. (Ihde 1977: 37)

The Druidic seer is more likely than the Cartesian seer to be a trancer.

The ideal enlightenment person is the broad-daylight, calm, dispassionate thinker-through of problems and philosophical issues. Mastery, self-control, and disengagement lead not only to success in strictly scientific endeavors but also in daily affairs as well. The world, the body, and the cosmos loose their enchantment and become objectified, objects of rational, scientific study. Descartes's self is the philosophically perfect correlative of the scientific revolution.

Mary Douglas also explores the Western roots of the modern problem of self and traces it to the Scottish Enlightenment philosopher and historian, David Hume (1711–76), who denied the existence of a "self-substance." Paraphrasing Hume, Douglas links the sense of self with autobiographical memory, an idea also developed by Antonio Damasio and explored in Chapter 6.

We are bundles of representations held together plausibly by the similarity of the experiences we have from moment to moment. There being no self-substance, our idea of our self arises out of the well-oiled grooves of mental associations; our remembered experiences, and the similarities between them, and other connections between them which we recognize, create relations between our ideas. These habits produce our idea of a continuous, rational, responsible self, which nothing else can justify. (Douglas 1992: 44)

While rejecting the idea of the existence of a unified "self-substance," Hume also felt the need to establish the single self for reasons of jurisprudence. We experience all our selves within one body. Only this justifies, according to Hume, the notion of a unified integrated self. Social order cannot easily be maintained within the Western system without a single personality with which the courts can deal. Douglas goes on to explore the necessity for the Western insistence on a unitary self based on notions of personal accountability. She believes that we would be better served to maintain two differing ideas about the self, one a unified self, the other a multiple self. Continuing in this vein, she argues:

Why can we not accept a number of self theories, involving multiple selves, passive selves, invaded and possessed selves, each serving different forensic purposes? Are we to conclude that all other civilizations are wrong if they encourage notions of transfers of the self between one body and another? (Douglas 1992: 49)

Both Hume and Douglas challenge deeply held "commonsense" notions of a Western self, notions that are also challenged by many trance traditions.

All cultures may have a reflexive pronoun to refer to the speaker, but not all have the nominalized, disengaged, objectified "self" commonplace in Western thought. Taylor links this objectified self to the Western emphasis on individuality and what he calls the "radical reflexivity" of modern Western conceptions of self.

> Radical reflexivity is central to this stance, because we have to focus on first-person experience in order so to transpose it. The point of the whole operation is to gain a kind of control. Instead of being swept along to error by the ordinary bent of our experience, we stand back from it, withdraw from it, reconstrue it objectively, and then learn to draw defensible conclusions from it. To wrest control from "our appetites and our preceptors," we have to practice a kind of radical reflexivity. We fix experience in order to deprive it of its power, a source of bewitchment and error. (Taylor 1989: 163)[2]

In this discussion, I have tried to outline some of the parameters of a modern Western sense of self and its historical antecedents in order to make the notion of personhood "visible" and available for inspection. In exploring the possibility of a correlation between the willingness and the ability to accept spirit possession and certain ideas concerning selfhood, we need to be able to imagine both what our ideas of selfhood are and what some other ideas might be. I believe that the notion of self that I have outlined has, throughout the history of the colonization of North America, worked to exclude the acceptability of spirit possession and trancing. The question comes to mind—but how many eighteenth-century Americans read Descartes, Hume, and Locke, much less Plato? Certainly most did not. Just as certainly, the social and spiritual elites did. But more than this, Descartes, Hume, and Locke were also imbued with the general cultural narratives of their times as well. Their doctrines were not totally original, nor were they without precedents. The idea of the controlled, disengaged self fell on fertile soil in eighteenth-century America, with a readership ready to accept these formulations of the world and one's proper relationship to it. Nonetheless, Cartesian views never gained anything near total hegemony. They were, and remain today, more internalized among certain groups and within certain individuals than others.

Trancers, it seems to me, must necessarily *not* experience their selves as disengaged. To feel oneself at one with the music and the religious narrative enacted there must be no distance at all between event and personhood: no aesthetic distance, no outside perspective, no objectivity, no irony. Later perhaps, the trancer may reflect on his or her experience, but to do so at the moment of trancing is to introduce the very disengaged subject that will break the enchantment. Likewise, a person whose integrity is severely challenged if he or she feels out of control cannot surrender his or her being to spirit possession.

In spite of the powerful influence of scientific thought on North American and North European notions of self, the disengaged self never completely subsumed other models. The conflict between different concepts of the self, and between trancers and nontrancers, is an old one in the United States.

Possession Trance in Colonial Virginia

From a journal entry written in Tidewater Virginia on May 10, 1771, comes the following entry:

> Brother Waller informed us . . . [that] about two weeks ago on the Sabbath Day down in Caroline County he introduced the worship of God by singing. While he was singing the Parson of the Parish [who had ridden up with his clerk, the sheriff, and some others] would keep running the end of his horsewhip in his mouth, laying his whip across the hymn book, etc. When done singing he proceeded to prayer. In it he was violently jerked off the stage; they caught him by the back part of his neck, beat his head against the ground, sometimes up, sometimes down, they carried him through a gate that stood some considerable distance, where a gentleman [the sheriff] gave him something not much less than twenty lashes with his horsewhip. . . . Then Bro Waller was released, went back to singing praise to God, mounted the stage and preached with a great deal of liberty. He was asked by one of us if his nature did not interfere in the time of violent persecution, when whipped, etc. He answered that the Lord stood by him of a truth and poured his love into his soul without measure, and the brethren and sisters about him singing praises to Jehovah, so that he could scarcely feel the stripes for the love of God, rejoicing with Paul that he was worthy to suffer for his dear Lord and Master. (Isaac 1974: 347; Little 1938: 230–31)

The attackers in this episode were Church of England gentry or near-gentry who represented governmental authority and established social values (Isaac 1974). The attacked were Separate Baptists, an evangelical group without a church, only a stage, a mixed-race, lower-class congregation who continued singing while their pastor was beaten and whipped (Thomas 1774). The revivalist movement called the "Great Awakening" swept over the colonies in the 1740s, but the most bitter conflicts between the evangelists and those of the Established Church in Virginia occurred after 1765 (Isaac 1974).

The Baptists provoked members of the Established Church on many levels. They were a clear challenge to the hierarchical order of the Established Church; any male could become a Baptist preacher if he felt the call. Their doctrine encouraged a direct, personal relationship with their God, emotional, intense, and without any sacramental mediation. Evangelist preachers were believed to be leading their followers into false doctrine that would lead to the breakdown of civilized society. Underlying these causes was a clash of social classes and the affront to the aesthetics of the Church of England followers posed by the Baptists. The Baptists were mostly poor, uneducated, and given to noisy expressions of their piety (Gewehr 1930: 128–33).[3] Included among their religious practices, little understood and maligned by their opponents, was spirit possession (D. Lovejoy 1969: 58; Weisberger 1958: 34).

> Personal testimonies of the experience of simple folk have not come down to us . . . but the central importance of . . . the common experience of ecstatic conversion is powerfully evoked by such recurrent phrases in the church books as "and a dore [sic] was opened to experience." (Isaac 1974: 354)[4]

One writer tells of a meeting of "multitudes, some roaring on the ground, some wringing their hands, some in extacies, some praying, some weeping . . . I saw strange things today" (Gewehr 1930:110, n. 23). Strong emotions forcefully presented in very public contexts, enthusiastic singing of hymns and spirit possession were not only unseemly to the gentry but ungodly as well. Physical violence against the Separate Baptists was fairly common.

One model of personhood among educated males in colonial Virginia was an enlightenment "rational" man who also was a person with an impressive bearing. Beneath a formality of manners, self-assertion, competitiveness, and proud self-presentation were admired. Horseracing, cockfighting, dancing, and card games offered venues for the display of this style of self (Isaac 1974: 348). The gentry set the tone that was emulated all the way down the social ladder. The Baptists, however, set themselves against the pastimes of the gentry, called each other Brother and Sister, and proclaimed a democracy of religion as well as of society.

Baptists were trancers, Church of England worshippers were not. The ideal of personhood, of self, of the Baptists allowed for the kind of surrender that all spirit possession involves. A trancer must be willing to accept a certain amount of insult to his or her bodily frame and to his or her external decorum. Trancers nearly always, at some point, end up on the ground. And they often utter strange cries or make guttural noises. Figure 4-1, a drawing of a nineteenth-century evangelist meeting, shows women dancing, on their knees, and collapsing. All this demands a surrender of impressive bearing and grand self-presentation. The price of ecstasy may be a loss of dignity. Little wonder that for the gentry of Virginia religious ecstasy was not an ideal; they ridiculed, despised, and feared the trancing Baptists.

Early in their history, the Separate Baptist preachers established the practice of spontaneity. They used no written texts but preferred to rely on the "gift of the spirit" (Downey 1968: 93). Unlike other evangelist groups, they produced few songbooks and those that did appear were from the urban north, not Virginia (Downey 1968: 93–95). Separate Baptists took current popular songs and ballads and changed the words to reflect their spiritual beliefs. The notation in Figure 4-2, published in 1805, illustrates the use of a popular Irish song as the basis for an evangelical tune. The text suggests the narrative drama invoked by the evangelical Baptists. Hell awaits those who are not yet free from sin. The Baptists were on a lifelong journey that would culminate in their death and unification with Christ.

"Wondrous Love" (Figure 4-3), a Baptist tune that possibly dates from the

Figure 4-1. Evangelist meeting. Courtesy of Library of Congress, LC-USZC4-44554.

beginning of the eighteenth century and could have been sung at Brother Waller's meeting, outlines the same eschatological Christian narrative. (Needless to say, the evangelicals would not have been concerned with either key signature or mode.) These songs were most likely sung unaccompanied with straight-on, untutored voices (possibly like the tone quality of Sacred Harp singers) with only the pastor as the lead singer.

Some evangelical songs, like this one, hint at the practice of trance and possession with new, sometimes mildly heretical, messages:

> Down from above the blessed Dove
> Is come into my Breast,
> To witness God's eternal Love;
> This is my heavenly Feast.
> This makes me *Abba Father* cry,
> With Confidence of Soul;
> It makes me cry, My Lord, my God,
> And that without Control. (Heimert and Miller 1967: 202)

The Separate Baptists were proclaiming a new relationship between themselves and their God, and a democratic church of equals. New music, new texts were iconic of their new mission and new faith. By taking old songs and placing them into the context of an emotional, fervent, passionate religious practice, the old songs took on a new urgency and were fitting catalysts for the dancing and trancing of the congregants. Over and over again the texts reiterated the evangelical Christian narrative, the drama into which the entranced congregants en-

Figure 4-2. "Johnny from Gandsey." From Jackson 1975: 72.

Figure 4-3. "Wondrous Love." From Jackson 1964: 114–115.

tered. Evangelical hymns were catalysts for the powerful emotions of Baptist trancing.

The deep difference in the sense of personhood between the Separate Baptists and their better-educated adversaries (Isaac 1974: 348) was an idea that neither may have formulated. At least in the extant literature, their arguments were on theological grounds (Heimert and Miller 1967). Institutionalized emotionalism, reflected in and undoubtedly inspired by the singing of newly composed hymns "opened a door to experience," an ecstatic experience of possession trance. Cartesian rationalism, disengagement, and self-control give way to acceptance and surrender. A disengaged, rational self would seem unlikely to cry out "*abba* Father," nor imagine the blessed Dove to enter her breast.

Possession Trance among Contemporary Pentecostals

Pentecostal religions, one of the modern-day descendents of eighteenth-century evangelism, were formally constituted at the beginning of the twentieth century. Contemporary Pentecostals seek a direct, unmediated, personal, and deeply emotional experience of the divine. They also are tolerant of trancing and dancing within religious services. Pentecostalism constitutes a faith that is dependent on music to structure its religious services and to validate its system of beliefs by provoking intense emotional reactions within its most devout practitioners, leading them to "testify." To dance in The Spirit, to be possessed by the Holy Ghost, is demonstration that one is accepted into the congregation of those blessed beings who will experience the final act of history, the reappearance of Jesus Christ and the establishment of the Kingdom of God on earth. Music is the driving force for this emotional apotheosis. From softly played passages underlining a sermon or a prayer, to swinging, driving choruses sustaining a wave of religious emotionalism, music is rarely absent from the hours-long services.

Pentecostal churches use a wide variety of musical instruments, often including piano, electric organ, synthesizer, guitars, and drum set, to back up their driving, repetitive gospel hymns. Just as eclectic as their instruments is their selection of musical repertoire. Old evangelical hymns are mixed with current popular gospel styles in a musical mélange that draws from diverse sources. The hymn "Leaning on the Everlasting Arms" (Figure 4-4), still heard today, appears in a book published in 1894. Harmony is now standard, as are the presence of trained musicians in the bands. But the emphasis remains on total participation, total commitment, and loud, strongly emotional delivery.

As with the eighteenth-century evangelists, hymnbooks are seldom used. Lowering one's head and reading from a written text would be gestures of alienation and separation from the communal immediacy of a Pentecostal service. Songs are learned by rote and all participate. Sometimes words will be projected on a screen, a concession to nonregulars and visitors that maintains the attentive focus of the congregation on the leader and on each other.

Pentecostal musical offerings shape a musical/emotional/ religious arc that carries the congregation along with it. A service may begin with quiet, slow, soothing music: "Music gets people in the attitude of worship. It helps them to forget outside influences and to focus on the Lord" (Jerry Trent, Church of God, Willow Run, Michigan, 1996). As the music becomes louder, more rhythmic, more repetitive, its driving quality supports, propels, and sustains the hand-

40 Leaning on the Everlasting Arms.

Figure 4-4. "Leaning on the Everlasting Arms." From Date 1894: 40.

waving, hand-clapping, foot-stomping choruses of "Amen!" High on the trajectory of the musical, emotional arc, worshippers may come forward to the altar to pray, and some may dance or trance. The musical support will continue at a high intensity until all worshippers have worked through their transport. Religious ecstasy is a confirmation of the salvation of the worshippers. He or she has become a part of the historical narrative of millenarian Christianity and will join fellow believers at the right hand of Jesus at the last day. The music never flags as some members are moved to tears, to dance, to quiver and jerk in the uncoordinated gestures of some religious trances. As religious passions subside, so does the music, until every last ecstatic has become quiet—exhausted and joyful.

> "And it was terrific," exclaimed one worshipper at a service marked by intense, sustained, high-energy music, dancing and trancing: "and we really *got down* here. I mean we really *had church*." (Cox 1995: 268)

If a certain readiness, a certain kind of subjectivity is a precondition for trancing, then it is not surprising that the doctrines or practices of churches in which trancing is institutionalized includes overt or covert instruction concerning that state of readiness. "Tarrying" is a technical term for Pentecostals. "Tarrying at the altar" means waiting on bended knee at the altar in front of the church in prayerful, hopeful anticipation that one will be entered by the Holy Spirit. One waits, one listens, one hopes. All is openness, all is readiness. Maybe the Holy Spirit will come, maybe not. There can be no coercion and no premature possession. It is like the Sufi metaphor of the lover awaiting the beloved. One must become a prepared, anticipatory, open, and empty vessel.

> Her mother had taught her that the way to pray was to forget everything and everyone but Jesus; to pour out of the heart, like water from a bucket, all evil thoughts, all thoughts of self, all malice for one's enemies; to come boldly, and yet more humbly than a little child, before the Giver of all good things. (James Baldwin, *Go Tell It on the Mountain*)

"Baptism in the Holy Spirit" is the third stage of spiritual development among Pentecostals and the sign of one's acceptance among God's chosen people. The first stage, salvation, happens when an individual seeks acceptance and forgiveness from God. Sanctification, the second stage, happens when the petitioner is cleansed by God of weakness and inclination to evil. The third stage, Baptism in the Holy Spirit, is usually signified by the spontaneous practice of glossolalia by the worshipper, the utterance of a string of sentence-like vocables that are not immediately, or not to an outsider, decipherable. Thus to "speak in tongues" is a kind of spiritual legitimization, a sign of one's own acceptance into the realm of those who will, at the last day, see Jesus face-to-face. Spirit baptism is also a sign of holy approval for the whole congregation; ethical behavior and close personal relationships are the precondition for activity of the Holy Spirit within a religious community (Wood 1965: 23). The emotional and intellectual rewards are enormous.

After being saved I still felt blue and doubted. I couldn't really tell when I was sanctified, but I must have been, for I went on and got the baptism of the Holy Ghost. I didn't really know what I wanted but I sought it and all of a sudden it was there. It was really a matter of my putting aside my resistances and receiving what God had for me. It was really simple. I felt so happy I couldn't control my speech. I spoke in tongues . . . I felt, after the baptism of the Holy Spirit, that I loved everyone. I felt that God loved everyone—sinner as well as others. . . . After one has had the baptism of the Holy Ghost one will never be satisfied with another religion. (Wood 1965: 26)

The stance of prepared readiness emphasized by the Pentecostals is probably a necessary component of all religious trancing. Sometimes trancing appears to strike one unawares; I've seen such apparently unprepared tracing in Bali, where a member of the "audience" unexpectedly begins to trance and joins the cosmic narrative with all the other prepared performers. But usually the trancer is awaiting the trance and is not surprised. An essential part of the awaiting is self-surrender and submitting to the penetration of one's bodily boundaries by a spirit more powerful than one's own.

We must fully surrender the tongue to [the Holy Spirit's] control. . . . It takes some time for most people to learn how to do this. (Wacker 2001: 56)

Eighteenth-century Separate Baptists and contemporary Pentecostals demonstrate resistance to the internalization of the Enlightenment ideal of the detached, objectified self. Pentecostal immediacy and union replace objectivity and distance. A Cartesian method for attaining knowledge is challenged by direct gnosis. Pentecostal certainty in emotional revelation replaces careful, rational procedures. Evangelicals in eighteenth-century Virginia and contemporary Pentecostals live in an enchanted universe in which music provides the milieu for the drama of millenarianism; music sustains the transport into that drama of the moment.

Possession Trance in Sulawesi, Indonesia

In Eastern Indonesia on the southwestern peninsula of the island of Sulawesi live the Bugis, a people famous for their navigational skills and trading prowess. Beginning in the seventeenth century, the Bugis were gradually converted to Islam and are now among the most devout of Indonesia's many ethnic groups who follow Islam (Pelras 1996: 83–85). Nonetheless, they maintain the mythic stories of the origins of the Bugis people and Bugis society, predating Islam, that underline the importance of maintaining ties with their spiritual progenitors. From the sacred text *I La Galigo* comes the story of the founding of one of the main Buginese dynasties, the kingdom of Luwu, and the peopling of the province. The oldest son of the principal deity of the sky, or upper realm, descends to earth (the middle realm) encased in a sheath of bamboo, sliding from sky to earth along the length of the arc of a rainbow (Hamonic 1975: 129). This spiritual son of the sky, named *Batara Guru*,[5] then marries the daughter of the lower realm (the sea or sometimes beneath the earth) and brings order to the chaotic middle realm (the realm on the surface of the earth, the realm of humankind). Sky realm and sea realm, with their myriad of spiritual beings, are thus the progenitors of the Buginese nobility and the protectors of the land and its people. Over the centuries, a process of assimilation and adjustment has gradually taken place as the old beliefs of the Bugis concerning sky realm, earth realm, and sea realm have been absorbed into Islamic doctrines or exist uncomfortably beside them (Pelras 1996: 196; Hamonic 1975: 122; Sutton 1995: 685).

The Bugis language, as do all languages, has a full set of first-person, reflexive pronouns that relate what is being said to an "I" (Tupa 1997), but the lexicon does not include the noun "self" (Errington 1989: 132). While not having a nominalized "self" in their language as does English, the Bugis hold clear ideas about how people are constituted—emotionally, physically, and spiritually—and of the location of the sources of human effectiveness. The nearest Bugis equivalent of the English-language "self" seems to be the body itself. Various parts of the body are believed to control functions we ascribe to the brain. Memory and thinking are located in the chest; emotions are associated with areas of the abdomen, especially the liver (Errington 1989: 78–79). A central metaphor within a complex of beliefs about the nature of human beings is the term *sumange'*, a kind of life force which is attached at the navel. The head is the location of the senses, and thus the means by which we communicate with the world and the world communicates with us. The importance of the head lies in the fact that it is the highest part of the body (vertical relations are meaningful in all spheres) and is also the location of many openings of the body to the outside world (Errington 1989: 76–78). The world can "enter" us through our eyes, our ears, our noses, our mouths. The whole body or at least the whole trunk and head share the seats of intellect, emotion, and spirituality.

Sumange' describes a kind of spirit-energy that animates the material universe. *Sumange'* is a linguistic cognate and overlaps semantically with similar terms widely found in island Southeast Asia such as *semangat* (Malay and Indonesian) meaning "vital spirit," "consciousness," or sometimes "enthusiasm." *Sumange'* is a morally neutral force in the universe and in human beings supports health, consciousness and effective action. All persons contain *sumange'* but not to the same degree. Persons of noble ancestry inherit more *sumange'* than do commoners. One can lose *sumange'* through uncontrolled actions or gain *sumange'* through meditation. *Sumange'* is invisible and intangible but can be recognized through its results. A person with much *sumange'* will be calm, under control, effective in her actions, and exhibit total awareness of the situations in which she finds herself. People with a fullness of *sumange'* are able to protect others with less *sumange'* from ill health, accidents, or destructive forces (Errington 1983).

Sumange' is embodied, collected around the energy center of the body, that is, the navel. In South Sulawesi, as in Indonesia as a whole, the navel becomes, metaphorically, the term for a center of power or potency. The capital of the country, Jakarta, is the "navel" of the country. A center of cultural or religious activity is called the "navel" of that activity. Likewise, the center of spirit energy, of consciousness and effectiveness is not the head of a person but the navel. *Sumange'* may fluctuate in intensity through different periods of one's life, may be loosely or tightly attached, and must at all times be closely guarded. One of the ways in which one may loose *sumange'* is through the openings in the body. *Sumange'* may escape if one carelessly lets one's mouth hang open. One keeps or increases *sumange'* by concentration, awareness, carefulness, and by control of emotions and actions. Anger causes one to loose *sumange'* just as controlled action may increase it. Health is also tied to one's state of embodied *sumange'*. A sick person needs attention from others to help coax back his or her *sumange'*.

Fear of the penetration of the body is an abiding concern for the Buginese. To be penetrated by a spirit or by a dagger not only diminishes one's *sumange'* but also is evidence of a certain lack of *sumange'* in the first place. Persons of aristocratic heritage or persons in high office must, to be effective, have an abundance of *sumange'* and must also guard against its loss. The ordinary person also, if he or she wishes to have control over his or her destiny and avoid misfortune, must take care not to allow a thoughtless dispersion of *sumange'* (Errington 1989: 51–57). One would expect that persons in high positions or persons from aristocratic families do not become possessed in South Sulawesi. Indeed, that is the case (Errington, personal communication). Because belief in the spirit energy of the world and the ways in which a person may tap into it or loose it are shared across the social hierarchies of the Bugis peoples (Errington 1983: 568), one might further expect there to be no institutionalized trancing, especially among an intensely Muslim population in which spirit beliefs are strongly discouraged.

An extraordinary exception remains, if only marginally. These are the *bissu,* a group of transvestite priests who may still officiate at rural weddings and funerals. *Bissu* are healers and in religious ceremonies may enter into trance possession, flaunting all the injunctions against penetration. *Bissu* may or may not be homosexuals, but they are always transvestites and exhibit feminine traits in gestures and movements. In order to become a *bissu,* a young man has to be "called" by a supernatural being who then becomes the spirit spouse of the *bissu* (Pelras 1996: 83). Indications of a call may be some trauma such as an illness or sudden mutism, episodes that are followed by apprenticeship to a *bissu* master into the metaphysics of the *bissu* worldview, and the procedures of *bissu* rituals (Lathief 1983: 23–24).

The *bissu* live within a hierarchy of their own led by an elder called the *pua matoa.* When the *pua matoa* goes into trance, he speaks the language of the deities (Hamonic 1975: 126), a kind of Buginese "speaking in tongues" incomprehensible to ordinary Bugis. The *bissu* are intermediaries between the spirits/ deities (*dewata*) of the upper world and the human world. (See Plate 8.)

All *bissu* rituals contain two sequences, the first directed toward the lower realm and involving water, such as a procession toward the sea during which the *bissu* will make offerings. The second sequence is directed toward the upper

Figure 4-5. *Bissu* priests holding *lalosu* rattles. From Kaudern 1927: 466.

realm, involving bamboo, such as a bamboo tree trunk erected before the house of a sick person (Hamonic 1975: 128). The dress of the *bissu* during rituals also includes paraphernalia associated with the lower and upper realms such as a dagger (*kris*) made of elements of the earth, and the rattle (*lalosu*) which they carry while dancing made of bamboo and shaped to resemble a hornbill, the bird particularly linked to the sky realm. The name of the rattle, *lalosu*, has two etymologies. One claims that *lalosu* comes from the root *lao-lisu*, meaning "to go back and forth," indicating the right/left motions of the *lalosu* in the hands of the dancing *bissu*. The other etymology relates the term to *alusu*, a word meaning intangible, that which cannot be seen, touched, heard, smelled, or tasted (Errington 1983: 555). *Alusu* is an adjective tied to spiritual things such as Allah as well as the deities of the other realms. *Alusu* can also be a description of *sumange'*.

The songs of the *bissu*, long "recitatives" or "psalmodies" according to Hamonic (1975: 128), along with the dances of the *bissu*, bring to the middle world the spirits from the upper world and drive out the possibly malevolent spirits of the lower world. A section from part of the liturgy chanted by the *bissu* imploring the deities to descend, to possess their "disciples," illustrates the close relationship between *bissu* and the spirits of the upper world:

> Children of the deities, travel to here!
> Children unrivalled in the sky, travel to here!
> Appear here, as a quickening revelation,
> Envelop the disciple,
> To be perfect, like you.
> And the offering cloth ornamented with the Moon-Dragon

That makes the clouds rise in tiers,
That shakes the edges of the sea.
Coconut-palm, agitated, from the beginning,
Sparks that increase
Like spurting flashes of lightening,
Claps of thunder
Expand boldly!
Celestial beings without equal, come here!
You who quicken the possessed. (Hamonic 1987: 56)[6]

During rituals, *bissu* wear special clothing, carry a sacred dagger and rattle, and perform a slow, undulating dance to the accompaniment of drums (*gendang*), gong, metal plates (*suji kama*), sometimes an oboe (*pui-pui*), bamboo spring-clappers (*lae-lae*), and a small hand cymbal (*kancing*) (Lathief 1983: 25; Pelras 1976). The music that accompanies the *bissu* dance is a variant of the drum/gong ensemble music found throughout island Southeast Asia, a cyclic structure marked at the end/beginning by a stroke on a gong. These musical forms have been/are used for contacting spirit beings from time immemorial (J. Becker 1979: 202). The more popular genres of Buginese music today such as *dangdut* or brass band music (Sutton 1995: 673) would be inappropriate to invoke the deities of the upper world, or to accompany the dancing of transvestite priests. The largely tone-less, cyclic pattern of the gong/drum ensemble becomes iconic for the power of other worlds, other beings, and unseen forces. Gongs, iron plates, and cymbals forged from the earth express chthonic powers (J. Becker 1988).

Repeated, end-stressed beat pattern:

Figure 4-6. Diagram of musical accompaniment for *bissu* dancers by Joshua Penman.

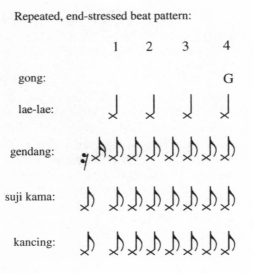

The pattern in Figure 4-6 repeats several times, alternating with a drum and rattle roll punctuated at the end by a stroke on the gong.

At the climax of the ceremony, the entranced *bissu* draw their daggers from scabbards attached at their waist and commence self-stabbing (Hamonic 1975: 121). The initial penetration of possession is reiterated in the act of self-stabbing. Like the famous self-stabbing trancers of the Barong/Rangda ritual in Bali, *bissu* aim their daggers at vulnerable parts of the body such as the neck or the temple. And, like the Balinese self-stabbers, they emerge unharmed.[7]

This is an extravagant display of *sumange'*. Only someone "full" of *sumange'* could risk and survive the double penetration of spirit and sword and not die, nor fall ill, nor go mad. In their asexual, androgynous selves, the *bissu* are believed to represent a sacred unity that existed before the disunity and bifurcation of human sexuality. Closer to heavenly beings, the *bissu* are more *alusu* than ordinary mortals. The implication seems to be that their *sumange'* so far exceeds that of ordinary persons that they are able to transgress recklessly the usual precautions against *sumange'* loss, and that these special powers are a part of their sacrality and their ability to communicate directly with spirit beings.

The narrative into which the *bissu* propel themselves and their listeners is the origin myth of the Bugis, a time before time when the deities of the upper realm were the guardians and ancestors of the Bugis. The musical accompaniment enhances the presence and immediacy of the narrative of spirit beings descending from the sky and speaking to their earthly children. To become possessed by the deities, there must be no ironic distance between *bissu* selves and the origin myth they enact. Music, story, *bissu,* and deities become one.

Conclusion

Trancing evangelicals and trancing *bissu* share certain characteristics that differentiate them from many of their contemporaries, such as senses of self that are not entirely orthodox within their respective societies. Eighteenth-century Virginia evangelicals and contemporary Pentecostals show an openness to experience, a willingness to give up control and to surrender their selves to a more abiding, more powerful "Holy Spirit." They willingly accept being swept away by strong emotional reactions to the gospel hymns and the millenarian narratives that are overwhelmingly present in their services.

Bissu present a different picture. They, too, transgress cultural norms of protecting and striving to increase *sumange'* by avoiding emotional excess and bodily penetration. But, in so doing, they assert their own special potency and nearness to the divine. *Bissu* must believe in their special selves as intermediaries between ordinary humans and deities in order to be able to perform their rituals. Only if other Bugis also believe both in the mythic narratives and in the *bissu*'s trance persona can the *bissu* maintain their traditions and their music. *Bissu* and Pentecostals inhabit a world narrative that may seem full of error to their more orthodox Muslim and Christian contemporaries.[8]

Notions of self are not immutable, but may in special circumstances become permeable, changeable in surprising ways. Situations of extreme stress, illness, or drug use may alter one's sense of personhood. Living among people who hold very different senses of self may also precipitate a change in one's own subjectivity. Friedson, anthropologist and ethnomusicologist, describes movingly his own experience of spirit possession among the Tumbuka of Malawi and the changing sense of self that he experienced. He speaks of the experience of spirit possession as a new way of being-in-the-world (Friedson 1996: 14) and as a transformation of his usual, Cartesian self. After he had been "dancing a spirit" for a considerable time, was so exhausted he could no longer stand, and his accustomed self was regaining ascendancy, he began to reflect on what had just happened to him.

> It seems that my physical body had experienced *vimbuza* [spirit possession] as much as my thinking self had, if not more. But this is a way of interpreting experience which assumes that the mind and body are somehow separate entities, and implicit in this assumption is the priority of the mind over the body. . . . Nevertheless, for those of us inculcated in the metaphysics of a split between mind and body, it is hard *not* to interpret experience in these terms. I often—though not always—experience myself as a thinking subject. On the night I dance *vimbuza,* however, I experienced not so much the absence of this phenomenon but its transformation. (Friedson 1996: 19–20)

The *habitus of listening* of a trancer and the self who is listening are indivisible: One includes the other. The listening self at a spirit possession ceremony is a self who waits and listens for clear signs of intervening holy spirits, signs that he/she is about to become a different self. The ears become the valorized sense, music the vehicle for transformation. Just as the spirit powers are invisible and intangible, the music that summons them invokes a realm of unseen power and limitless extension. Music makes real, somatically, the narrative of millenarian Christianity or the Buginese story of *Batara Guru's* sliding descent to earth on the arc of a rainbow. What seems impossible becomes a felt certainty as the Pentecostal worshipper or the *bissu* comes to know an indwelling spirit. The listening self in these ceremonies may be the same body but may not be the same self as that inhabited in more commonplace life activities. Music, for many deep listeners, opens pathways of being not ordinarily experienced in everyday life. How much more intensely is this the case for the receptive, alert, and expectant self who is literally entranced by the music at a spirit possession ceremony?

I have emphasized certain ideas of self held by Pentecostals and Indonesian *bissu* priests in order to delineate the ways in which trancing individuals transgress culturally hegemonic notions of self. The examples chosen, however, illustrate another thesis: all of us have more than one model of selfhood pregiven in our cultures and languages, and more than one option for selfhood when immersed in a musical, mythologized, religious service. We, too, may surrender control, "rationality," and distance and become Druids when the music begins.

The definition of embodiment stressed in this chapter is embodiment (2), the body as the venue of inner life. The next chapter more clearly includes the sense of embodiment (3), the body in interaction with other bodies.

5 Being-in-the-World: Culture and Biology

> The world is inseparable from the subject, but from a subject which is nothing but a project of the world, and the subject is inseparable from the world, but from a world which the subject itself projects.
>
> —Maurice Merleau-Ponty [1962] *Phenomenology of Perception*

Part 1. Rethinking Perception

Integrating the insights of phenomenology and those of neuroscience means reexamining two ideas with profound roots in Western intellectual history; ideas that have provided us with a bedrock of stability for both science and religion; ideas that have spawned spectacular scientific discoveries and sustained profound religious values. Nonetheless, some concepts central to our world understanding may have inhibited our search for the ways that we can be transformed by music and by trancing.

These two related ideas are so much a part of our intellectual heritage that they are not considered to be concepts or theories but "facts."

1. There is an objective world outside of myself that has definable properties and
2. I am a single, bounded, unitary consciousness that rationally perceives that objective world and thinks and acts on the basis of "correct" perceptions or representations of that world.

Musical experience can be deeply subversive to both views. How we perceive a piece of music has everything to do with our own histories, our own set of experiences relating to that particular piece of music, our "manner of offering ourselves" to an external stimulus. Different musics can evoke within us very different "selves" with changing ways in which we present our being to receive the enveloping sounds.

Trancing is even more of a challenge to the objective worldview and the belief in a unitary consciousness, so much so that for many it cannot even be considered a serious event. The trancer's world outside of herself does not necessarily resemble our factual world, and the trancer's consciousness seems often not to be single, bounded, or unitary.

Questioning the assumption of a pregiven world independent of our perceptual/cognitive understanding of that world, is, at first blush, so outrageous as to be absurd. Yet there is accumulating evidence that our world and our sensori-motor interactions with it are coupled. To contemplate a world that is not pre-given, not *represented* in the mind, but tied to our interactions with all beyond the boundaries of our skins conjures up the impossible idealistic alternative that "it's all in our minds." We feel as if presented with what Varela, Thompson, and Rosch have dubbed the "chicken and egg position."

> *Chicken position:* The world out there has pregiven properties. These exist prior to the image that is cast on the cognitive system, whose task is to recover them appropriately (whether through symbols or global subsymbolic states).
> Notice how very reasonable this position sounds and how difficult it is to imagine that things could be otherwise. We tend to think that the only alternative is the *egg position:*
> *Egg position:* The cognitive system projects its own world, and the apparent reality of this world is merely a reflection of internal laws of the system. (Varela, Thompson, and Rosch 1991: 172)

These authors and many others (M. Johnson 1987; Lakoff 1987; Edelman 1992; Nuñez 1997; Benzon 2001) are trying to pry us loose from the *chicken position* and to suggest a middle way in which our mental mappings of the world emerge from our sensorimotor interactions with our milieu; "sensorimotor" means perceptions plus actions. The following three case studies illustrate the accumulating evidence of the embeddedness of perception and cognition in embodied action.

> In a classic study, Held and Hein raised kittens in the dark and exposed them to light only under controlled conditions. A first group of animals was allowed to move around normally, but each of them was harnessed to a simple carriage and basket that contained a member of the second group of animals. The two groups therefore shared the same visual experience, but the second group was entirely passive. When the animals were released after a few weeks of this treatment, the first group of kittens behaved normally, but those who had been carried around behaved as if they were blind: they bumped into objects and fell over edges. This beautiful study supports the enactive view that objects are not seen by the visual extraction of features but rather by the visual guidance of action. (Varela, Thompson, and Rosch 1991: 174–75)

If we think about it for a moment, we all know that round tables present themselves to us as ellipses and that rectangular desktops present themselves to us as trapezoids, yet we usually "see" tables as round and desktops as rectangles. In an old study that challenges our normally adjusted perceptions, subjects are presented with a model of what seems to be a rectangular room, looking "normal" from the position of the seated subject who is given only a monocular view. (See Figure 5-1.) But in fact the room is distorted with the left wall about twice the size of the right wall and with the floor, the ceiling, and the back wall slanted so as to become narrow at the right side. A tiny bug is painted on the left wall far toward the back. The subject is given a pointer and asked to touch the bug. The subject has to keep reaching farther and farther back to touch the bug and

Figure 5-1. Distorted room. Courtesy of Eric Schaal/TimePix.

comes to realize the error of her initial perception. Eventually, her perception of the room will change and she will be able to immediately touch the bug. The point is that we perceive according to our past bodily experiences and in order to change an ingrained perception, we need to physically interact with the novel environment (Livingston 1978: 39). Behavior shapes sensory processing.

A third case study relates similar, parallel findings that further challenge objectivist views concerning perception.

> Bach y Rita has designed a video camera for blind persons that can stimulate multiple points in the skin by electrically activated vibration. Using this technique, images formed with the camera were made to correspond to patterns of skin stimulation, thereby substituting for the visual loss. Patterns projected onto the skin have no "visual" content unless the individual is behaviorally active by directing the video camera using head, hand, or body movements. When the blind person does actively behave in this way, after a few hours of experience a remarkable emergence takes place: the person no longer interprets the skin sensations as body related but as images projected into the space being explored by the bodily directed "gaze" of the video camera. Thus to experience "real objects out there," the person must actively direct the camera (by head or hand). (Varela, Thompson, and Rosch 1991: 175)

Persons who have been blind from birth learn the shape of objects exclusively through touch, through bodily movement. Thus they are never required to make the automatic adjustments that seeing persons make in their visual perception of round objects or rectangular objects, nor do they need to adjust for the influence of visual distance from the object. Blind persons who are provided with cutaneous substitution for visual perception (as above) have to learn to make these adjustments just as seeing people do. One of Bach y Rita's blind patients, on beginning to understand how visual images are non-conformant to the touched shape of things, exclaimed that seeing persons "live in a very distorted world" (Livingston 1978: 37).

These studies locate cognition as interaction with a world through perception and action, a biological process that is continually shaped by its milieu. Our interactions continually reshape, reconfigure our brains. The outside world is not represented in the brain but is interpreted and given meaning by the brain.

> A stimulus excites the sensory receptors, so that they send a message to the brain. That input triggers a reaction in the brain, by which the brain constructs a pattern of neural activity. The sensory activity that triggered the construction is then washed away, leaving only the construct. That pattern does not "represent" the stimulus. It constitutes the meaning of the stimulus for the person receiving it. (Freeman 1997: 69)

More recently, Freeman has explained how reactions of sensory receptors and cortices within the same animal to the same stimulus are never identical. The activated pattern of neural activity to a given sensory stimulus constantly changes. He maintains that all the evidence leads one to conclude that the same phenomenon is true of humans. The pattern of neural activity in the brain of the receiver represents not the pure stimulus, but the *meaning* of the stimulus and that meaning is always and ever fluid (Freeman 2000: 413–14).

Damasio (1999) addresses the same issue in defining what he means by "representation," a central part of his theory of consciousness (addressed in the Chapter 6):

> I use representation either as a synonym of mental image or as a synonym of neural pattern. . . . The problem with the term representation is not its ambiguity, since everyone can guess what it means, but the implication that, somehow, the mental image or the neural pattern *represent*, in mind and in brain, with some degree of fidelity, the object to which the representation refers, as if the structure of the object were replicated in the representation. When I use the word representation, I make no such suggestion. (Damasio 1999: 320)

It takes some adjustment to be able to accept the anti-intuitive idea that the tree that I look at, the tree that I "see," is not a straightforward mental representation of that tree out there. It is easier, I think, to imagine how we construct the images of other people in our minds. Seeing particular persons can infuse us with warmth or fill us with dread—neither our warmth nor our dread are intrinsic to the person we are looking at. Or, think of how differently two equally intelligent and sensitive persons may react to hip-hop music. Or, imagine the sights, sounds, smells that happen within the mind of a participant in a rousing religious ceremony, in a situation of sensory overload replete with cosmological import. How do those "image-meanings" translate into action, interaction, and reaction?

When I witness a Rangda/Barong ceremony, I see Rangda as a Balinese man dressed in a witch's costume. How is it that my educated, sophisticated, world-traveled friend sees a powerful being from the other world whose malevolence must be curbed? He may have come to believe it because his community believes it, but surely the fact that he has been a *bebuten* trancer interacting physically with Rangda is a factor. He has attacked her with his dagger and found himself irresistibly stabbing himself instead. Like the Pentecostal who feels as if he were "knocked about" and who "didn't know what was going on," the Balinese *bebuten* trancer has felt the power of Rangda in his own body.

Until we can accept that to a large extent we construct our own world and act within that world on the basis of our own constructions and that those actions become a part of the meaning of the world and of all subsequent constructions, we are precluded from gaining insight into the phenomenology of either deep listeners or trancers.

Edelman and the Theory of Neuronal Group Selection

Gerald Edelman (1992) spells out for the nonscientist a biological theory of the brain that helps in understanding how a *bebuten* trancer comes to see fire coming from the eyes of Rangda or a deep listener thinks he is soaring above the audience. Edelman's theory (Theory of Neuronal Group Selection, or TNGS) allows one to begin to imagine just what happens at the neurological level to persons involved in musical religious ceremonies who are simultaneously trancing. The theory is dense and complex and cannot be reduced to a few sentences. Nonetheless, his central thesis maintains that perceptions/actions stimulate the brain through neuronal activity that groups bundles of neurons together into an operational unit. It is not individual neurons that determine thought and behavior but, rather, neuronal groupings, and groups of groupings, called "maps." These maps are located in specific areas of the brain and become linked through past behavior, by what are called reentrant processes. Separate groups or maps are massively connected by neuronal circuits and neuronal loopings (Edelman 1992: 83–85). Through repeated behavior (or repeated learning), certain linkages are habituated so that the stimulation of one map—say, the perception/hearing of a particular piece of music (stimulating the auditory cortex and the right frontal lobe) almost simultaneously stimulates many other maps as well. These bundles interact with other bundles of neurons that also have become an operational unit through groupings stimulated by perception, action, or by other neuronal groupings. In this cumulative way, the brain develops "classification couples," that is, different groups of neurons that will tend to be activated together given the same stimulus (perception or action or both) that originally initiated their connectivity. The initial perceptual stimulus comes, through structural coupling in a ritual context, to excite large areas of the brain with no necessary connection with the original perception. Seeing Rangda activates fear and rage in the *bebuten* trancer, strong emotions that facilitate the transition into trancing. At some point in his life, the *bebuten* trancer may have heard tell of, may dreamed of, or saw a drawing of Rangda with fire coming from her eyes. The representation of Rangda and her fire-propelling eyes becomes indistinguishable, in his excitement, from the sight of his neighbor dressed in a witch's costume. The communal emotion of the ritual itself activates the multiple bundles of neurons, the groups of groups, that ultimately lead to his trancing and his visions.

Edelman proposes an open-ended theory in which the structure of the brain, the connections between massive bundles of neurons, are not permanently "hard-wired" except in a gross sense. The brain continually reconfigures its connections according to interactions with the outside world and with interactions with other parts of the brain according to its own internal needs. In other words, change, adjustment, "creativity" are basic elements of the biological structure of our brains.

> The intricacy and numerosity of brain connections are extraordinary. The maps that "speak" back and forth are massively parallel and have statistical as well as precise features. Furthermore, the matter of the mind interacts with itself at all times. I have not yet mentioned that the dynamic arrangements of the brain show the system property of memory: previous changes alter successive changes in specified and special ways. Nervous system behavior is to some extent self-generated in loops: brain activity leads to movement, which leads to further sensation and perception and still further movement. The layers and the loops between them are the most intricate of any object we know, and they are dynamic; they continually change. (Edelman 1992: 29)

A continually changing brain in bodily interaction with a milieu becomes a linchpin for proposing the thesis of a continually evolving body as being-in-the-world. With the prior condition of mental malleability in interaction with sights, sounds, smells—the whole atmosphere of a ritual—a changing consciousness becomes not only plausible but expected.

Because the neurology of the visual system is better known than that of any of the other senses, the visual system is often the focus for sophisticated research into cognition and perception. A visual perception consists of at least thirty separate sets of neuronal groupings, each responding to a feature of the stimulus such as boundary, edges, light or darkness, movement, and so on. All are linked by reentrant processes. What we "see" is a composite instantaneously constructed by millions of neurons in separate groupings all firing in response to a visual perturbation.

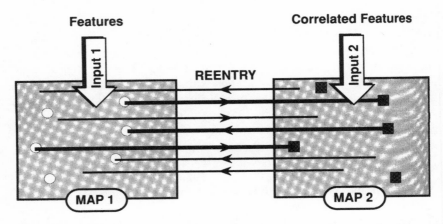

Figure 5-2. Reentry. From Edelman 1992: 90. Copyright © 1992 by Basic Books, Inc. Reprinted by permission of Basic Books, a member of Perseus Books, L.L.C.

The two maps receive independent inputs. Say, for example, Input 1 consists of visually detected angles, while Input 2 consists of an object's overall movement. The two maps are connected by numerous, dense fibers that "map the maps" to each other. If at some point a circle in Map 1 becomes associated with a square in Map 2, this connection may become a "classification couple" and may be triggered by a related image whether or not that particular feature is "really" there or not. The person viewing the object may see the feature as a result of the prior established visual coupling. Fire does not have to be coming from the eyes of the Balinese peasant playing Rangda for the *bebuten* trancer to see fire coming from her eyes.

Although the auditory system in the temporal lobe is less well understood, it, too, consists of neuronal groupings, each responding to a different aspect of the incoming signal, that is, timbre, pitch, loudness, melody, rhythm, harmony, stress, and so on. Through reentrant or looping processes, that is, synaptic connections going to many other parts of the brain, we are simultaneously, or so it seems, aware of the last time we heard this piece, or one like it, as well as concomitant feelings of joy, sadness or even fear—involving many billions of other neuronal firings in other neuronal groupings in other distant parts of the brain. We may start to dance—involving motor activities located in the parietal lobes and the central nervous system down our spines and out to our toes. All the studies which locate the reception of music in special areas of the frontal lobe, that is, melody in the right, harmony in the right, rhythm, singing, and syntactic sequences in the left ignore the massive reentrant linkages which trigger neuronal activity in many specialized and distant brain areas.

An important aspect of Edelman's theory is that "reentry," the interaction between neuronal bundles or groupings, is not just a one-way interaction, but operates both ways. Groups of groups also come to be interactively connected so that a single stimulus such as a sight or a sound may trigger multiple connectivities of bundles of neurons throughout the brain, resulting in what he calls "a global mapping." If a particular sound or sight results in the excitation of a global mapping, the individual may be associating the sound with a complex set of memories, emotions, inspirations to actions, beliefs, and even the experience of another realm of being.

Hearing the musical theme alone, a Balinese trancer would be able to imagine the witch, know that she has come from another realm, realize the threat she poses to his community, envision the scene in which she is to be attacked, and feel the rage and terror which she inspires. Minimally, this act of hearing involves not only the auditory cortex but also frontal lobe areas where the association of Rangda with evil acts occurs, plus the lower limbic areas of the brain where emotions such as fear and hate are activated. In this way, a particular sensory stimulus acts as physiological metonym—one part (music) invokes the whole mythology and its accompanying behavior and emotional feel. A "global mapping" is not just the registering of an impression, a representation of a scene outside the individual but also a restructuring of the sensorimotor system of the individual.

This metonymic action of the involvement of many brain areas in response to a single auditory stimulus is a familiar one. We all know that listening to a particular piece invokes thoughts, memories, and feelings that are in no way intrinsic to the musical signal itself. All this implies the excitatory aspects of the firing of neuronal groups, linked by massive reentrant processes. These studies reinforce what we already know concerning listening to music and trancing. That is, that many areas of the brain become active—not only the specialized acoustic areas in the temporal lobes, or the emotion producing areas of the brain stem and limbic systems.

Perception and action may become linked in a conjoining of sound with a cosmology that transforms the bodily/self experience of the individual. Edelman's diagram of a global mapping conjoins perception ("sensory sampling"/ "sensory sheets") in linked classification couples with many brain areas including those involved with emotion, memory, and the frontal lobes associated with complex intellectual processes (such as those necessary to construct cosmologies). Muscles, bodily movement are involved at both beginnings and endings of the circuit. Edelman is proposing a theory that connects perception, emotion, cognition, and action through multiple neuronal groups involved in multiple reentries, that is, two-way connections.

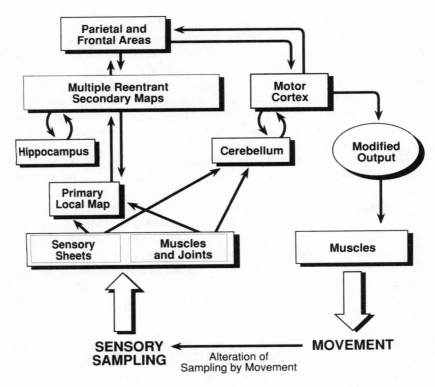

Figure 5-3. Global mapping. From Edelman 1992: 91. Copyright © 1992 by Basic Books, Inc. Reprinted by permission of Basic Books, a member of Perseus Books, L.L.C.

In this figure, Edelman is attempting to show how the coordination of input and output from neuronal bundles, immensely interconnected with other neuronal bundles and "bundles of bundles," interact in relation to sensory input. Bodily involvement, "muscles and joints," is not simply an end result but a beginning as well. "Global mapping" of a perceptual stimulus is always a dynamic, ever-changing process. We do not always "see" or "hear" the same thing when presented with a stimulus nearly identical to one seen or heard before. "Perturbations at different levels cause a global mapping to rearrange, to collapse, or to be replaced by another global mapping" (Edelman 1992: 91).

Persons who are trancing and hearing ceremony-specific music may experience a dramatic reconnection of neuronal groups that allows for a new kind of experiencing and knowing of the phenomenal world. The visual, aural, imaginative world of the trancer is as real as any everyday imaginative world. Special neuronal connections have been established in relation to the ritual world that allows the trancer to see extraordinary sights, to hear more intensely than one normally would, and to experience emotions that stimulate feelings of closeness to the holy. The reconnections are not long-lived but can often have effects long after the trancer has returned to a more "normal" connectivity of neuronal groups. Trance can transform, and the creative flexibility of Edelman's model of the continually reconfiguring brain makes it possible to imagine what might be happening during that special, ecstatic experience.

Part 2. Biological Phenomenology

Bridging the gap between traditional phenomenology and contemporary neuroscience and biology may be the ardent pursuit of some humanists, but its realization is difficult and may be troubling as well. Neuroscientific knowledge presents formidable barriers to an outsider and its basis in empirical studies is not necessarily compatible with culturally based research. Thus it is with joy and relief to know that there are neuroscientists and biologists who are actively reaching out to humanistic scholars, making "hard science" both understandable and acceptable within a framework that values individual experience within cultural frames of reference. The trancer as constituted within cultural modes of expectation regarding ideas of selfhood and a socially sanctioned *habitus of listening* is also a trancer whose ANS system is aroused, whose brain stem and limbic system neurons are firing and whose hormonal systems are flooding her brain and body with chemicals that translate into high excitement and deep emotions—all resulting in trancing deeds, trancing gestures, trancing actions appropriate to the moment. Trancing is interacting with a world (embodiment #3).

An enactive approach to meaning and cognition influenced by phenomenology and based in biology, placed between phenomenology and scientific materialism that transcends the division between the cultural and the biological, has recently been proposed by a number of scholars including Maturana and Varela (1987), Varela, Thompson, and Rosch (1991), Edelman (1992), Nuñez (1997), Foley (1997), and Damasio (1994/1999): a group including biologists, neurologists, linguists, and psychologists; scholars who are focused not on trance or music but on the problem of consciousness itself. These scholars are not reductionist, do not discount purposeful, meaningful intentionality as outside the scientific realm, are able to "save the phenomenon," and are coming up with theories of astonishing complexity and persuasiveness. Resisting the tidal wave of objectivist cognition studies, they attempt to change the way we approach the problem of consciousness, believing as they do that until we reformulate both the problem and our approaches to the problem we will continue to find ourselves with a gulf between sophisticated functional studies of human neurobiology, more and more revelatory findings about the workings of the human brain (embodiment #1), and our existential, phenomenological experiences of our everyday lives (embodiment #2). The term "phenomenology" comes from the study of what have been called "phenomenal states," the subjective experiences, feelings, and sensations that constitute our awareness of being; our sense of ourselves as thinking, feeling persons. Our constantly shifting states of awareness, of emotion, of sensation, that is, of consciousness, the unique sense each of us has of our own being is the problem of phenomenology. Subjective experience has always been the privileged domain of philosophers, songwriters, actors, dancers, musicians, composers, novelists, diarists, and, most especially, poets.

Within the current dominant objectivist epistemology there is no way to bridge the epistemic gap between the firing of the neurons that result in the release of the neurotransmitter serotonin which contributes to a mood of happiness and the experiential ecstasy of the Pentecostal. The impasse that has developed between these two perspectives on human behavior has led scholars in the field of consciousness studies to split the field into what are called the "easy" problems and the "hard" problem (Chalmers 1995: 200). The easy problem is the one that is believed to be ultimately solvable with the research tools and the epistemology we now have, that is, the ability to find out which brain structures, what neuronal groupings, and what chemical neurotransmitters need to be activated to make one feel happy, or sad, or sexy, or powerful, or sleepy. These are the "easy" problems.

The hard problem is: Why do *Yak Tovil* patients, or Christian Pentecostals, or women bitten by a tarantula in south Italy, on hearing certain kinds of music, feel overwhelmed by emotion, compelled to moan, shake their heads, dance, and finally to collapse? Neurophysiology has opened up the "easy" problems; we have learned or are learning how to approach them. First-person experience is the hard problem. We don't yet know how to think about subjective human experience, called "qualia" in the scientific community, from a scientific perspective. Within the mainstream of scientific studies of consciousness, "qualia" have been considered as "accompanying" consciousness, rather than as constituent of it. Our perceptions are believed to be "represented" in the mind that then, through consciousness, works with those representations to decide on action or value. Inner consciousness uses outer perceptions as its fodder, so to speak. This understanding of consciousness as a processing box which receives input from a world but which is distinct from that world, is so much a part of our intellectual heritage as to be intuitively felt as "true." Reconceptualizing consciousness as constituted within experience, as interdependent with its world, as based on bodily involvement with a world, as constituted through action and interaction with a world owes much to European phenomenology, particularly to the works of Martin Heidegger (Dreyfus 1991) and Maurice Merleau-Ponty (1962, 1963, 1964). One of their central insights was that perception is dependent on the properties of the perceiver and her physical interaction with a world, that perception and action are fundamentally inseparable, and that together they are constitutive of a "world."

> The organism cannot properly be compared to a keyboard on which the external stimuli would play and in which their proper form would be delineated for the

simple reason that the organism contributes to the constitution of that form. . . .
The properties of the object and the intentions of the subject . . . are not only inter-
mingled; they also constitute a new whole. When the eye and the ear follow an animal in flight, it is impossible to say "which started first" in the exchange of stimuli
and responses. Since all the movements of the organism are always conditioned by
external influences, one can, if one wishes, readily treat behavior as an effect of the
milieu. But in the same way, since all the stimulations which the organism receives
have in turn been possible only by its preceding movements which have culmi-
nated in exposing the receptor organ to external influences, one could also say that
behavior is the first cause of all the stimulations.

Thus the form of the excitant is created by the organism itself, by its proper
manner of offering itself to actions from the outside. Doubtless, in order to be
able to subsist, it must encounter a certain number of physical and chemical agents
in its surroundings. But it is the organism itself—according to the proper nature of
its receptors, the thresholds of its nerve centers, and the movements of the or-
gans—which chooses the stimuli in the physical world to which it will be sensitive.
The environment emerges from the world through the actualization or the being
of the organism—[granted that] an organism can exist only if it succeeds in
finding in the world an adequate environment. This would be a keyboard which
moves itself in such a way as to offer—and according to variable rhythms—such or
such of its keys to the in itself monotonous action of an external hammer. (Merleau-Ponty 1963: 13)

Structural Coupling

Integrating the insights of phenomenology with those of contemporary
biology has brought forth fresh ways to think about human interaction, mutually constituting organisms, and the trancer saturated with music who feels herself participating in a cosmic drama. The interactions of groups of people in
communally shared situations is often called "communication," invoking the
image of something transferred intact from one person's mind to another person's mind, or vaguely referred to as "bonding" with no explanation of the
"how" by which bonding transpires. Wishing to imply something more fundamentally biological to talk about what are usually referred to as social or cultural
phenomenon, I use the term "structural coupling," developed by Maturana and
Varela (1987), to describe a process that encompasses single cell organisms up
to human social groups to help imagine what happens when groups of like-
minded people are involved in recurrent situations of shared music and trancing. Maturana and Varela's usage extends from interactions of single cells to
multicellular organisms, to groups of mammals, to include human communities. "Structural coupling" is a difficult concept but once mastered, provides a
new perspective on musical groups, on rhythmic entrainment and trancing.

One begins with the understanding that an organism's first task is to maintain the integrity of its own structure. Or, in the language of Maturana and
Varela, organisms are autonomous and autopoietic (self-creating); they will only
"accept" or integrate changes that do not disturb their structural integrity, their

internal homeostasis. Most of the activity of our bodies and our brains functions to maintain our physical stability, our internal coherence, our life. For the most part, this activity goes on with no conscious control or conscious awareness. The constant monitoring and adjusting of our internal milieu proceeds whether we are awake or asleep, and regardless of what we may be thinking about at the moment. Damasio (1999) calls this unconscious continual mapping of the body-state the "proto-self." Maturana and Varela diagram this self-monitoring activity of all living organisms as a closed circle with arrows going round and round.

Figure 5-4. Self-monitoring organism. From Maturana and Varela 1987: 74. Reprinted by arrangement with Shambhala Publications, Inc., Boston, <http://www.shambhala.com>.

If this were all there were to organic life, the result would be total solipsism. But all organisms live within an environment that includes organic and nonorganic components with which the organism is necessarily in continual interaction.

The organism, through its continual interaction with the environment, the

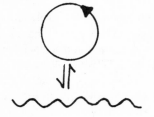

Figure 5-5. Organism in interaction with external milieu. From Maturana and Varela 1987: 74. Reprinted by arrangement with Shambhala Publications, Inc., Boston, <http://www.shambhala.com>.

external milieu, is constantly, inevitably, and subtly changing the environment and just as subtly being changed by it. The organism is not only interacting continuously with the environment which may be inert but also with other organisms like itself.

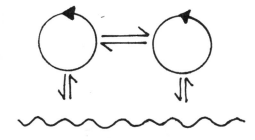

Figure 5-6. Organisms in interaction with external milieu and each other. From Maturana and Varela 1987: 74. Reprinted by arrangement with Shambhala Publications, Inc., Boston, <http://www.shambhala.com>.

Because of the autonomous nature of the organism, interactions between organisms or interactions between organism and inert environment, called "perturbations," never specify what changes may take place in the organism. The organism itself "determines" which perturbations are "allowed," how and to what degree a perturbation will be modified. Thus perturbations never cause the changes in an organism, they can only instigate or trigger change. The organism is "autopoietic," "self-creating," and the process of its changes are "autopoiesis," or "self-creation." It is not the environment or the interaction but the organism itself that "creates" itself.

If interaction between two organisms is recurrent, and if the changes in the two organisms are congruent, if they are similar, then the two organisms become involved in shared ontogenetic change—they change one another, together, and become complementary. Over time, cumulative change leads to "structural coupling" between two organisms as their internal milieu (including human brains and bodies) become linked through repeated interaction, "co-ontogenies with mutual involvement through their reciprocal structural coupling, each one conserving its adaptation and organization" (Maturana and Varela 1987: 180). Change through interaction with other beings and with the environment also can be called "learning" but differs from the dominant academic, scholarly, cognitive model that uses the metaphor "transmission of information." The metaphor of the mind as receiving information which is "represented" in the mind and which is then processed is not the orientation proposed here. I believe that the biological notion of structural coupling is more helpful than the model of traditional cognitive studies in understanding the phenomena of rhythmic entrainment, of the emotional affect of musical performance and musical listening, and trance.[1] The incipient trancer, through repeated participation in a religious ritual, comes to know the script of the ritual and gradually comes to enact that script herself. As belief is intensified through action, the incipient trancer allows internal physical changes in brain and body that may eventually also allow for trancing. The mind and body of the trancer becomes structurally coupled with the drama of the ritual. Her belief, imagination, sense of self and *habitus of listening* are coordinated with those of the other human participants and the projected presences of holy beings, the cosmic drama that all enact.

Supra-individual Biological Processes

From the early studies of music and the brain, such as Neher's early work in the 1960s analyzing the brain rhythms of subjects listening to drum beats in a laboratory, to the more recent works of Clynes (1986), Wallin (1991), and many others, musical scholars have adopted the scientific model and studied single brains in isolation. Studies in music cognition have largely followed the empirical models of cognitive studies in their efforts to model the algorithms of single brains processing music (Raffman 1993; Lerdahl and Jackendoff 1983). Neurophysiologists and psychologists of consciousness likewise follow the dictates of their scientific training, isolating and narrowing the problem as much as possible in order to have some control over the variables. In fact, some of the most exciting advances in the understanding of the mind have come from scientists and philosophers who have focused on single minds/brains (Churchland 1986; Dennett 1991; Edelman 1992). The development of technologies such as magnetic resonance imaging (MRI) and positron emission tomography (PET) scanning have reinforced the practice of the study of single minds in the attempt to unravel the mysteries of conscious experience. The choice of a single human brain as the unit of analysis has larger implications as well. The emphasis on the primacy of the self-contained individual has been a treasured credo of Western intellectual pursuits in all fields for many centuries. Contemporary examples include the cognitive sciences, music cognition, Piaget's genetic epistemology, and Freudian psychoanalysis.

Trancing and music underline the phenomenological necessity of understanding our experiences as including more than our bounded, unitary selves. Although only one person may be trancing, and only a few may be musicking, the total event is the unit of analysis, not just the trancer, not just the musicians. Whether in the language of Maturana and Varela we speak of "structural coupling," or in the language of Nuñez we talk of "supra-individual biological processes," or the language of Oughourlian (1991) as "interdividual" processes, the analysis of trancing and music benefits from thinking about the transformations as not happening solely inside a particular body, but happening across several, or many bodies. This approach is helpful in looking at any musical occurrence, and helps to nudge us away from our cultural/intuitive sense that what happens in trance events happens exclusively within a particular body, rather than across bodies, in which each individual may be playing a different role, but in which the trancing and musicking are not localized within one individual.

We are accustomed to thinking of biological processes as extending from a single cell, to multicellular organisms such as a tree, to animals and to a single human being. When groups of people act in some kind of accord, we tend to say that the phenomenon is social, or psychological, or political, not biological. Viewing musicking and emotions as supra-individual biological processes, one can describe the changes that occur in individuals and in groups of individuals as having evolved over time through an historical process of structural coupling, structural changes that occur within an organism as a result of interaction with other organisms and with a world; changes of one's being, one's ontology. These changes become new domains of knowledge, knowledge gained through interactive behaviors, through doing. Music listeners as well as musicians undergo a learning process in which they imitate physical and mental gestures that ultimately transform both their inner structures as well as their relations to everything beyond the boundaries of their skins. Music and emotion are part of a larger processual event that subsumes many other people doing many other things while the whole event unfolds as a unity organized and reorganized over time by small structural changes within the participants. Groups of people who are focused on a common event and who share a common history of that event, act, react, and to some extent think in concert, without sacrificing their bounded personal identities.

The advantages of this approach are that we are discouraged from trying to look inside a particular brain/body to find the answers to the special aura that such events have, but are looking rather at the aura of the whole. The event is not coded in the culture or even in an individual. It is an enactment, a performance by particular groups of persons who continually restructure each other and subsequent events.

Thus, the *habitus* of the devout Sufi prompts a specified sequence of actions, cognitions and emotions ultimately linked to, structurally coupled with an evolving musical and textual performance. A particular movement such as swaying in a Sufi devotee will evoke a particular response by the musicians which leads to another particular action by the Sufi and another particular reaction by the musicians. Both musicians and aroused worshipper are in a relationship in which the actions of the one directs the subsequent actions of the other. They are linked in a continuous, evolving event in which each directly conditions the next move of the other. A *sama'* script is never totally predictable. The *pir*, the worshipper, and the musicians have a degree of autonomy. They have the possibility of choice. Any one may break the sequence of repeated structural coupling if there is a reason to do so. Qureshi tells of the ecstatic embrace of an exalted spiritual leader by a devotee and the responsive musical crescendo by the musicians cut short by the presiding *pir* who felt that social norms of respect were being transgressed (Qureshi 1986: 205–06). But a successful *sama'* is one in which the gradual crescendo of spiritual arousal in the devotee and musical intensification are in sync, in which the structural coupling of Sufi and *qawwal*s is smooth and gradual, resulting in a feeling of satisfaction by all present, the vicarious pleasure of knowing that a fellow worshipper attained the desired union with Allah.

This type of analysis is aided by technologies such as film and video. One needs to be able to see everything at once, and to have the opportunity to replay the event. Regula Qureshi's skillful score-like transcriptions of the multiple events at a Sufi religious ceremony demonstrate one method of researching music, emotion, and trancing that does not focus on individual emotions but on individual actions within the context of many other individual actions (Qureshi 1986: 143–86). (See Figure 5-7.) One can study her scores and literally *see* how the musicians interact with the congregants, and one can imagine how the emotions of one listener may have stimulated the emotions of another, leading to the ultimate reaction, an enactment of trancing.

Nuñez uses the example of linguistic accents to help one think about this way of approaching human experience. A linguistic accent can be attributable to a particular individual, but it is not the creation of a particular individual but results from historical processes of language imitation and repetition. A person may "have" an accent, as a person may be "in trance," as a person may play a drum, but neither the language accent, nor the trancing, nor the playing of the drum need be isolated within an individual. Trancing events usually entail a number of individuals participating in fairly prescribed roles. The ritual practitioner may not be a musician, or a trancer may not be an audience member, or a ritual practitioner may not be a dancer. Everyone knows who are the appropriate musicians, ritual practitioners, and trancers; these boundaries are maintained. Yet, the phenomenon of trancing is transpersonal, does not take place in one particular mind alone, although it also takes place there. In Heideggerian terms, the trancing and musicking is a way for a group of people to be-in-the-world. And by their being-in-the-world they communally bring forth the world in which trancing is a natural, expected, unsensational occurrence. No one person is responsible, no one person is existentially alone, there is no solitary consciousness observing the world, or even a unitary self-contained being in a strongly communal event. The group acts as a unit. Ritual practitioners, patient (if there is one), trancer, musicians, onlookers, even hecklers in some situations become part of a larger, ongoing, largely predictably event. The world brought forth by all the participants makes possible the extraordinary moves of the ritual practitioner, or the endurance of the trancer, or the inspiration of the musicians; a world which may on another day seem strange but within the situation itself is coherent, reasonable, truthful, and authentic.

Emotions can usefully be viewed as being about an individual within a community rather than being exclusively about internal states. Emotions are about relationships. First-person descriptions of music and emotion are rife with tropes of interiority, yet the understanding of how music affects interiors takes place within consensual, shared views of what makes up "reality." Musical events set up an aural domain of coordination that envelops all those present. Even when couched as first person individual experience, trance descriptions implicitly include the community. Trancing, though experienced in a particular body, seems never to be bounded by that single body.

Friedson emphasizes the limitations of a semiotic approach to trancing and music, preferring to stress the noetic aspect of trancing in its ability to obscure

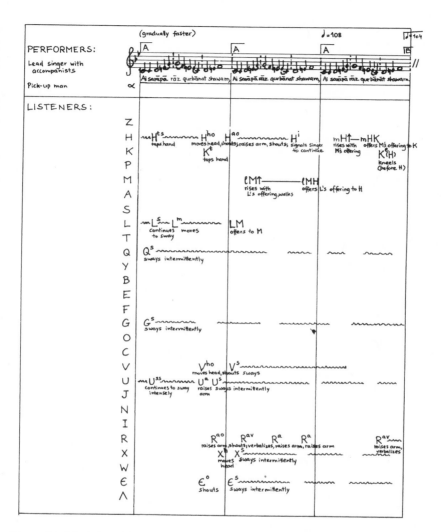

Figure 5-7. Music/participant interactions. From Qureshi 1986: 171. Reprinted with the permission of Cambridge University Press.

the boundaries between the knower and the known, subject and object, between music and self, while stressing the intersubjectivity of music and trancing.

Music is not given here as an object of reflection, something that points beyond itself. It is there in immediacy, before the distinctions—between act and content, subject and object,. . . . For Tumbuka gathered inside a temple, making music together is an intense, intersubjective experience that brings healer, patient, and spirit into an existential immediacy unparalleled in quotidian or ritual life. Through music, with its resultant trance, Tumbuka have the possibility of experiencing the present—and thus each other—in complete "fulfillness." (Friedson 1996: 6)

The early-twentieth-century ethnography of S. M. Shirokogoroff, who established the term "shaman" for a particular type of trancer, also provided vivid descriptions of the bodily experience of skilled shamanic healers, and the shared experience of "lightness" between patient and healer.

> According to the shamans, they feel an extreme lightness of the body during ecstasy. This feeling is seemingly also communicated to the sick persons, for the Manchus assert that when during the performance the shaman steps on the person lying on the ground, the shaman is felt to be very light. (Shirokogoroff 1935: 364)

Paul Stoller describes how the unseen world of Niger spirits is brought into the shared perceptions of musicians and congregants:

> The sound of the godji [fiddle] penetrates and makes us feel the presence of the ancestors, the ancients. We hear the sound and know that we are on the path of the ancestors. The sound is irresistible. We cannot be unaffected by it and neither can the spirits, for when they hear it "cry," it penetrates them. Then they become excited and swoop down to take the body of the medium. (Adam Jenitongo quoted in Stoller 1996: 174)

Abhinavagupta's twelfth-century text on *rasa* theory speaks to the unification of consciousness of the participants in a religious ritual (that he calls here a "spectacle").

> Just for this reason, in meetings of many people (at a spectacle of dancers, singers, etc.), fullness of joy occurs when every bystander, not only one of them, is identified with the spectacle. The consciousness, which, considered separately also, is innately made up of beatitude, reaches, in these circumstances—during the execution of the dancer, etc.—a state of unity, and so enters into a state of beatitude which is full and perfect. In virtue of the absence of any cause for contraction, jealousy, envy, etc. [the causes of contraction are the *vighna*, obstacles] the consciousness finds itself, in these circumstances, in a state of expansion, free of obstacles, and pervaded by beatitude. (Abhinavagupta quoted in Gnoli 1956: 70)

The linguist William Foley links a transpersonal, biological model of languaging to culture and to Bordieu's *habitus*. A trance and music event is also a cultural practice involved in on ongoing history of social structural coupling.

> This embodied understanding, including dispositions in the habitus, is tacit knowledge and hence one can only be subsidiarily aware of it; this accounts for why so much of the habitus is preconscious and unable to be reflected on or modified. This conservatism leads to the practices generated by the dispositions of the habitus being transmitted from generation to generation, in other words they are potentially *cultural practices*. Culture in this view is that transgenerational domain of practices through which human organisms in a social system communicate with

each other. These practices may be verbal or non-verbal, but they must be communicative in the sense that they occur as part of ongoing histories of social structural coupling and contribute to the viability of continued coupling. . . . Culture, then, consists of the things people do to communicate in ongoing transgenerational histories of social interaction. (Foley 1997: 14)

Like languaging, like emotion, like musicking, trancing is an enactment, not a representation in the mind. It is a way of being-in-the-world, not a way of thinking about the world.

> The experience of anything out there is validated in a special way by the human structure, which makes possible "the thing" that arises in the description.
> This circularity, this connection between action and experience, this inseparability between a particular way of being and how the world appears to us, tells us that *every act of knowing brings forth a world*. . . . All this can be summed up in the aphorism *All doing is knowing, and all knowing is doing.* (Maturana and Varela 1987: 26)

Emotion, music, and dance become one system of ontogenic coordination of actions. Together, they bring about changes in being and changes in the music event. Although it is the individual who experiences the emotion, it is the group and its domain of coordinations that triggers the emotion. The changes in the neurophysiology of the listener are not attributable simply to the brain and body of a self-contained individual. They occur through the group processes of recurrent interactions between co-defined individuals in a rhythmic domain of music.

Thinking of the relationship of emotion and music and trancing as a biological process with a co-defined, historically enacted ontology, as a group creation in which self-contained individuals have undergone structural changes through their interaction with other self-contained individuals, helps to provide an integrated embodied analysis of the relationship of music and emotion and trancing. By this approach, the trancer is not isolated as the wild card in a description or analysis of trance events, but can be seen as closely interconnected to everyone else who is participating.

Rhythmic Entrainment

Rhythmic entrainment occurs when two or more seemingly independent processes mutually influence each other to converge in a common pattern. Musical rhythmic entrainment can be seen as structural coupling, of a changed interior, personal consciousness in a musical domain of coordination. Bodies and brains synchronize gestures, muscle actions, breathing, and brain waves while enveloped in music. Many persons, bound together by common aims, may experience revitalization and general good feeling. The situation is communal and individual, music descends on all alike, while each person's joy is his or her own.

Rhythmic entrainment is usually thought of in terms of large groups of people participating in a common activity like dancing, singing, or listening to music.[2] Coordinating bodily rhythms may have a much more fundamental, more primal evolutionary development than we normally assume. On warm summer nights of July and August in Michigan, the grasses and the low bushes and trees are filled with fireflies. If you watch long enough, you will begin to notice that the blinking of these tiny bugs becomes synchronized. The same phenomenon has been reported among male fireflies in Southeast Asia who gather in large groups and flash on and off in unison to attract females (Benzon 2001: 47). Even inanimate objects will become entrained. As early as 1665, Christiaan Huygens noticed that two pendulum clocks with a common wall behind them with close but unsynchronized periods would, within a short period of time, "phase-lock" their strokes (Rider and Eagle 1986: 227).

Within the human community, rhythmic entrainment begins within minutes after birth. A newborn baby will demonstrate interactional synchrony with a caregiver within the first half-hour of its life (Benzon 2001: 26). Using what he calls "micro-behavioral analysis," William Condon has shown that speakers and listeners become immediately entrained to each other's speech rhythms. The dance of the speaker becomes the dance of the listener.

> Whatever body parts the listener happens to be moving at that moment will be organized and will follow the organization of the speaker's speech. Further, the listener's body often speeds up and slows down in relation to the softness or loudness of the speaker's speech. (Condon 1986: 67)

Our speech and our body motions exhibit wave-like characteristics that are both personal and cultural. Differences between the speech rhythms and the body rhythms of different cultural subgroups within the United States are often the source of profound dis-ease between, say, mid-Western Protestants and New York Jews, as has been vividly illustrated by Deborah Tannen (1984).

Frederick Erickson has studied the differences between the cultural rhythms of two teachers in classrooms at the Odawa Indian Reserve (Algonquin) in Northern Ontario, Canada; one teacher was an Odawa, the other a white American (Erickson and Mohatt 1982). Both were skilled, experienced teachers. Erickson made videotapes of their respective classrooms during a lesson and then analyzed the tapes almost frame by frame to discern the rhythms of the students in relation to their teachers, a technique he calls "microethnography."[3] In the classroom with the Native American teacher, the movements of students and teacher were so well synchronized that Erickson was able to "conduct" the classroom as we were viewing the video. In the classroom with the American teacher, there was a clear dis-synchrony, a lack of smoothly coordinated actions between teacher and student. Their rhythms were out-of-sync. The teacher whose rhythms were entrained with those of her students had a more successful class and it seems reasonable to assume that their mutually coordinated rhythms were a contributive factor.

If speech rhythms can entrain, if rhythmically flashing lights can entrain, if bodily gestures can entrain, how much more powerful is musical ritual entrainment with a pulse that penetrates to our bones, with melodies that thrill, and a cosmology that gives life meaning and purpose? The anthropologist Maurice Bloch once claimed, "You cannot argue with a song" (Bloch 1975: 71). Paraphrasing and expanding on Bloch, I would say, "You cannot argue with a song sung in soaring phrases, with drum rhythms you are feeling in your bones, surrounded by friends and family who are all, like you, structurally coupled, rhythmically entrained."

Conclusion

The music making, trancing, preaching, glossolalia, dancing, the murmuring of mantras within a ritual are all parts of a biological/historical process that has had a long tradition of continual self-recreation. The music, the trancing, and every other aspect of the ritual process bring forth the activities of each other, bring forth a world, a reality in which certain actions are expected and appropriate, and in which the reality brought forth by all is enacted by all. The knowing is embodied in the doing. A trance/music event is not just in the minds of the participants, it is in their bodies; like a language accent, trancing and playing music are personally manifested but exist supra-individually. All persons involved, musicians, trancers, and other participants seem to be acting as self-contained, bounded individuals, and indeed they experience whatever they experience as deeply personal and emotional, but the event as a whole plays itself out in a supra-individual domain.

Language, music, and dance become a system of ontogenic coordination of actions. Together, they bring about changes in being, and changes in the ritual involved. Whereas it is the individual who experiences trancing, it is the group and its domain of coordination that triggers trancing. There must be changes in the neurophysiology of the trancer for trancing to occur, but those changes are not attributable simply to the brain/body of a self-contained individual. They occur through the group processes of recurrent interactions between co-defined individuals in a rhythmic domain of music that is intrinsically social, visibly embodied, and profoundly cognitive. In trancing as in playing music, knowing and doing are inseparable.

Special modes of conscious experience such as rhythmic entrainment, emotional responses to music listening and trancing emerge as phenotypic features of humankind, as biological developments in the evolution of the species, emerging from both genetic and environmental influences. Emotion and music and trancing viewed as evolving together in the interaction of each individual with performances dissolves intractable dichotomies concerning nature versus culture, and scientific universalism versus cultural particularism.

Furthermore, for those of us who want to use the word "culture" but are inhibited by all the recent attacks on the term relating to essentialism, historical stasis, and reified, abstracted psychology, culture can be restored as a more precise, more useful term. Culture (redefined) can be understood as a supra-individual biological phenomenon, a transgenerational history of ongoing social structural couplings that become embodied in the individual and transmitted into the future through actions.

6   Magic through Emotion: Toward a Theory of Trance Consciousness

> Mediumistic possession in all its grades seems to form a perfectly natural special type of alternate personality, and the susceptibility to it in some form is by no means an uncommon gift, in persons who have no other obvious nervous anomaly.
>
> —William James [1890] *Principles of Psychology*

Introduction

In exploring the sources of and workings of human consciousness, one has to ponder the problem of how one can begin to describe the mind of another when our thoughts, feelings and emotions are not only utterly private but often unknown even to ourselves. This worry is strikingly apparent in trance study—not only can we not know the mind of the trancer, oftentimes her consciousness is opaque even to herself. In spite of these formidable obstacles, it is still possible, I believe, to make sensible hypotheses of consciousness based on what we can observe, what we are told and what we already know of human minds; (1) we can observe external manifestations such as specific behaviors and attentional focus; (2) we can listen to verbal reports by persons manifesting those behaviors, that is, the corresponding internal manifestations; and (3) we can hypothesize from the internal manifestations that we can verify in ourselves in equivalent situations (Damasio 1999: 83).

One could object that we do not all trance, but I believe that most of us have experienced "near trance," or at least some of the characteristics of trance at certain times in our lives, especially in relation to musical listening or musical performing. Many of us have experienced sensations of nonself, out-of-body sensations, of closeness to forces that seem to be beyond ourselves, of momentary feelings of eternity stimulated by some visual or oral perception. The inner experiences of trancers have corollaries, in weaker or stronger forms, in more mundane experiences of folks who never have and never will trance. Trancers are special, but not so special that most of us cannot imagine what that experience might be like.

In Chapter 5, I discussed the analytic gains of an analysis that views the trancer or deep listener as profoundly interconnected to her milieu and to others participating in the same event (embodment #3). This chapter returns to the approach of embodment (1) (the body as a physical structure), and (2) (the body as a site of first-person, inner life). The body as a physical structure has, until recently, been the sole focus of neuroscientists. Only an intrepid few are willing to also include first-person experience in the domain of their research. Francisco Varela once remarked, "The hard sciences deal with the soft questions and the soft sciences deal with the hard ones."[1] The scientific study of consciousness, the hardest question of all, is still in its infancy. Few neuroscientists have been bold enough to take on the most difficult problem of their field and fewer still include the role of emotions and inner life. Although some might claim that special kinds of consciousness such as trancing and deep listening should not be addressed until "everyday" consciousness is better understood, I would claim the opposite. A theory of the processes of consciousness, of the neural activity of producing consciousness needs to apply to extraordinary as well as to ordinary states of consciousness. Seeing a phenomenon in its extreme form may be necessary in order to see it at all. Trancing may be an exceptional kind of consciousness, but it is prevalent worldwide, it is institutionalized within religious practices, and its practitioners often enough are ordinary people leading ordinary lives. We should reexamine our medicalized, pathological trance categories such as "multiple personality *disorder*" or "dissociative *disorder*." Balinese *bebuten,* Sufi *hal,* or Pentecostal "slain in the Spirit" are not illnesses. They are socially sanctioned religious practices that may bring comfort, solace, and an experience of the numinous to their practitioners.

The theory of consciousness developed by the neuroscientist Antonio Damasio in his book *The Feeling of What Happens: Body and Emotion in the Making of Consciousness,* provides, I believe, a model on which one can begin to hypothesize about trance consciousness in a way that integrates what we know about trance phenomenology with what we know about neurophysiology. Rendering thinkable in terms of neural activity and chemical action the biological properties of a trancing consciousness with the phenomenology of trancing seems to me a first step toward moving trance from a "marvel" (Hacking 1995: 143) to a position whereby it may become a serious focus for scholarly, scientific research. Bringing the phenomenology of the trancer, the first-person experience of communion with special spirits or deities or God into dialogue with biological models of consciousness makes imaginable the unimaginable, makes speakable the unspeakable.

Emotion is key to understanding Damasio's theory of consciousness as it is key, I believe, to understanding the relationship between trance consciousness and music. The brain nuclei primarily concerned with homeostasis are closely interconnected with those concerned with emotion. This suggests that homeostasis of the body and the production of emotion are conjoined. This is the basis for the assumption that emotions are basic to survival and adaptation.

Initially, at least, emotional arousal most strongly stimulates neurons and bundles of neurons in the older, lower areas of the brain. Emotional arousal stimulates neurons in the hypothalamus, basal forebrain, and brain stem to release chemical substances into several other regions of the brain including the cortical areas associated with the "higher" functions of the brain.

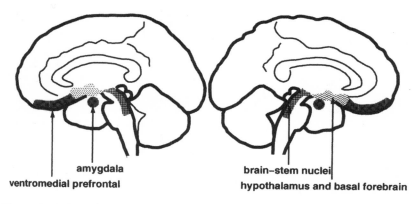

Figure 6-1. Principal emotion induction sites. From Damasio 1999: 61. Courtesy of Harcourt/H. and A. Damasio)

The intensity of the feeling of emotion is partially a result of the action of the chemicals released in response to the inducer of emotion (a perception or a thought).[2] In response to a particular perception or thought, a relatively small area of the brain (nuclei in the brain stem) releases monoamines and peptides; another small area (basal forebrain) alters the processes of many other brain circuits that affect behavior such as stimulating bonding or crying, and modifying the signaling of body states to the brain. From those small and ancient parts of the brain, chemicals wash throughout many other brain areas affecting not only what we feel and think but *how* we feel and think (Panksepp 1998b: 316; Damasio 1999: 67).

One result of this chemical bath can be the sensation of the mind slowing down as it continually processes images (Damasio 1999: 79–80). The slower the processing of mental images becomes, the more removed one feels from the "time" of living bodies progressing from sunrise to sunset in a nonstop succession of activities and mental images. Slowing the mind is one aim of meditation and, I suspect, a by-product of trance consciousness as well. Deep listening or performing music may induce the feeling of time stopping altogether.

> In the dimension of time, music modifies our consciousness of being to an even greater extent. It is an architecture in time. It gives time a density different from its everyday density. It lends it a materiality it does not ordinarily have and that is of another order. It indicates that something is happening in the here and now; that time is being occupied by an action being performed, or that a certain state rules over the beings present. (Rouget 1985: 121)

The way of being-in-the-world of both trancers and deep listeners differs from their more emotionally neutral, everyday inner experience of themselves and the world. Emotion changes our consciousness in small and large ways.

I suspect that many of the first-person "mystical" descriptions of trance experience, such as the sense of timelessness, of living in the eternal present, and the sense of closeness to the divine are related to the strong emotions enhanced by music of the trance experience. Long revered in humanistic scholarship and deeply treasured by all humans as the lynchpin of our enjoyment of life, until recently the biological underpinnings of emotion have remained largely guesswork.

Our rational minds, the part of our brain that plans for the future, that figures out problems, that writes elegant prose, that does our income tax returns has long been assumed to be exclusively neocortical, the most recently evolved part of the brain. But the "rational" decisions and choices made by patients with severe damage to some of the emotion producing, subcortical areas of the brain but no damage to the neocortex are severely compromised. Without input from the "emotional parts" of the brain, rational choice becomes impaired. Without input from our emotions, we, in fact, can't think clearly. Rather than reducing or diminishing the mystery of emotions, understanding their biological complexity only adds to their wonder.

Jaak Panksepp (1998a) has proposed another hypothesis of the basis of consciousness that has striking similarities to that of Damasio, and that also may allow for imagining trance consciousness. Panksepp, like Damasio, believes that the earliest, evolutionary roots of the self go back to the development of certain structures in the brain stem and in the midbrain that are related to the maintaining of basic metabolic survival mechanisms of which the emotional systems are a part. He maintains that the emotional structures of the brain are fundamental to the maintenance of the respiratory rate, heartbeat, skin temperature, and all the other autonomic body systems that create the homeostasis of the functioning body. In seeking to find the neurological source of what Panksepp calls the "primitive self" (similar to Damasio's core self), Panksepp looked for an area of the brain that both connected to other known centers of emotion and which can generate a primitive kind of action-readiness that he equates with a primitive intentionality and thus consciousness. He, like Damasio, believes that certain evolutionarily old structures in the brain stem and mid-brain areas qualify for the site of the early roots of consciousness (Panksepp 1998b: 309–15).

This chapter constitutes a speculation on a speculation. The theories of Panksepp and Damasio are bold, admittedly speculative and unproven. If these scientists are right, or even if they are not entirely right but somehow on the right track, what are the implications for the study of trancing and for the study of emotional reactions to music? What kind of theory of consciousness for musical trancing and musical listening would be consistent with a theory of normal, everyday consciousness?

Damasio's Theory of Two-Leveled Consciousness:
"Core Consciousness" and "Extended Consciousness"[3]

1. Core Consciousness

Our own bodily position, attitude, condition, is one of the things of which *some* awareness, however inattentive, invariably accompanies the knowledge of whatever else we know. We think; and as we think we feel our bodily selves as the seat of the thinking. (James 1950, vol. 1: 241–42)

Damasio's theory of "core consciousness" is based on two "facts" that give rise to a third; the first "fact" or the first given is what he calls the "proto-self," a nonconscious collection of information in the lower brain (mostly) concerning the ongoing stasis of the body, that is, the nonconscious monitoring of our heart beats, our respiration, our visceral systems, our entire internal milieu. The second given or "fact" is that perceptions or thoughts cause continual changes or perturbations to occur in the nonconscious proto-self/body state. These two givens, the proto-self and the perceptions or thoughts that precipitate the continuous small changes in the proto-self, give rise to the third given or "fact," the sensation that these changes are happening to someone, and that someone is "me."

Core consciousness, according to Damasio, emerges from the juxtaposition of an unconscious "proto-self" and a perception, a coupling that gives rise to a perceived sense of bodily change brought about by interaction with the world. Core consciousness arises from bodily awareness, from bodily knowing in relation to the surrounding milieu.

Damasio's core consciousness and extended consciousness are the equivalents of his "core self" and "autobiographical self." Core consciousness is not simple wakefulness, but is the sensation of knowing one's body-state in relation to a self. Extended consciousness builds upon core consciousness but includes the memory of our bodily interactions with our world and the sense of the continuity of our being throughout our life histories. We do not normally experience a distinction between these levels of self, but Damasio's clinical studies indicate that this distinction can be experimentally demonstrated.

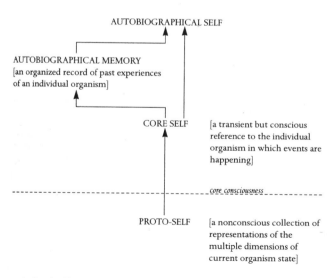

Figure 6-2. Kinds of self. From Damasio 1999: 199. Courtesy of Harcourt/H. and A. Damasio.

The two arrows pointing upwards to the autobiographical self indicates the two sources of that self, that is, continually updated autobiographical memory and continuous pulses of core consciousness, of body sense. The single arrow from the proto-self to the core self, crossing "core consciousness," indicates the transformation that occurs between the proto-self, or body-map, and the core-self, a conscious self.

Preceding core consciousness, there needs to occur a juxtaposition in the brain of two different first-order neural mappings. Damasio's "map" is not to be interpreted in an objectivist way. There is no one-to-one correspondence between the neural patterns that become "maps" and whatever it is in the world that is being attended to.

> The brain is a creative system. Rather than mirroring the environment around it, as an engineered information-processing device would, each brain constructs maps of that environment using its own parameters and internal design, and thus creates a world unique to the class of brains comparably designed. (Damasio 1999: 321–22)[4]

(Damasio's maps seem, to this humanist, congruent with Edelman's theory of neuronal group selection.) The first neural mapping is of the moment-by-moment internal physical state of the organism, called "body-map" or "proto-self." (See Figure 6-3.) The body-map or proto-self is ceaselessly updated and results from neural patterns at several levels in the brain, including the brain stem nuclei, the basal forebrain, the hypothalamus, and parts of the somatosensory cortices. We are not conscious of the proto-self.

> The proto-self is a coherent collection of neural patterns which map, moment by moment, the state of the physical structure of the organism in its many dimensions. (Damasio 1999: 154)

The proto-self has no powers of perception, no knowledge, no language.

The second neural mapping which precedes core consciousness is the mapping of "images" received from the senses or "images" internally generated. "Image" in Damasio's usage has a particular, specific meaning. He means a mental pattern that includes one's past history in relation to the perception and one's emotional evaluation of the perception. An "image" can be an entity projected from one of the senses, such as the sensation of seeing a friend, or hearing a melody, or an entity generated internally such as a vision or a memory. An image need not be visual, but can relate to any sense modality. It is important to stress that Damasio's definition of "image" is not objectivist. He, like Edelman, Maturana and Varela, and the other authors mentioned in the previous chapter, believes that our imaging of the world is part of a complex negotiation between our own bodies and the milieu of our bodies.[5]

An image is a first-person experiential knowing based on a neural pattern corresponding to an object/perception/thought conveying not only the look, sound, or feel of the object, but also one's emotional response to it, its relationship to other images, and one's own intentions regarding the image. An image

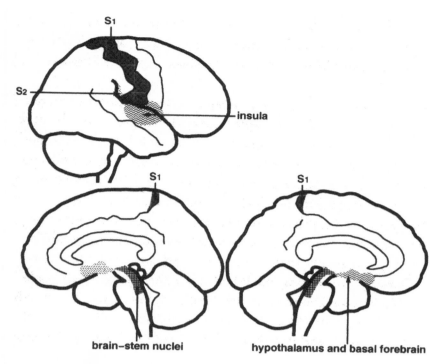

Figure 6-3. Location of some proto-self structures. From Damasio 1999: 155. Courtesy of Harcourt/H. and A. Damasio.

could be something seen, an idea, or a melody that becomes richly overlaid with emotion, knowledge about one's past experience with the image, and with values associated with the image.

> By *image* I mean a mental pattern in any of the sensory modalities, e.g., a sound image, a tactile image, the image of a state of well-being. Such images convey aspects of the physical characteristics of the object and they may also convey the reaction of like or dislike one may have for an object, the plans one may formulate for it, or the web of relationships of that object among other objects. (Damasio 1999: 9)

Core consciousness is the result of a *relationship* between a biological proto-self, that is, a non-conscious representation of the state of one's body at any given moment, and a perception or an image. The image, the perception, changes the nonconscious proto-self. It is the sensation of the changed proto-self that Damasio believes to be "core consciousness." This sensation of change leads to the sensation of a self who experiences the change. Core consciousness is thus the *relationship* between "something-to-which-knowing-is-attributed" and the "something-to-be-known." A body-state plus a perception which causes a perturbation in the body-state, the "something-to-be-known," brings forth a sense of self, a "something-to-which-knowing-is-attributed."

> All of a sudden, consciousness consisted of constructing knowledge about two facts: that the organism is involved in relating to some object, and that the object in the relation is causing a change in the organism. (Damasio 1999: 159)

Core consciousness, in addition to wakefulness, presumes low-level attention, a brief memory of the moment before, at least a background emotion and a sense of a self to whom some knowledge is being attributed (Damasio 1999: 95).

The core self, core consciousness, is the sense of *my* having these images and *my* knowing that they belong to *me*. This kind of here-and-now sense of a self, a knower of one's immediate situation is Damasio's core consciousness. Losing core consciousness while maintaining wakefulness and mobility seems, at first blush, to be unimaginable but can be illustrated in cases of epileptic automatism or absence seizures. Damasio describes one such situation: During the course of a normal conversation, the patient will freeze, stopping in mid-sentence, his face a blank mask. He may remain in this state for only a few seconds, or for nearly a minute. As he unfreezes, he may take a drink from a glass of water, get up and move toward the door, open it and walk down the hallway—always with the same visage, a blank stare. He may even go out of the building and walk down the street, an "epileptic fugue." After a short time, the episode will end and the patient appears bewildered, not knowing where he is or how he got there. He may have remained awake and attentive during the fugue, but will have no recollection of it.

> There would have been no plan, no forethought, no sense of an individual organism wishing, wanting, considering, believing. There would have been no sense of self, no identifiable person with a past and an anticipated future—specifically, no core self and no autobiographical self. (Damasio 1999: 96–99)

The utter flatness of emotion, the total lack of mood, and the loss of a sense of self is notable in absence seizures. With compromised core consciousness, patients do not exhibit any kind of emotion, not in facial expression, nor in language, nor in gestures. "Emotions and core consciousness tend to go together, in the literal sense, by being present together or absent together" (Damasio 1999: 100).

Let me put it another way.

The section above may seem reductive to the neuroscientists and formidable to the humanist. I will try to say the same thing differently. Following James's controversial thesis that we feel afraid because we tremble at seeing a bear (James 1950, vol. 2: 449–50), I draw on James's bear example to illustrate (and simplify) Damasio's core consciousness.

Imagining yourself in the woods of northern Michigan (not yet aware of a bear that is also not aware of you), the information basic to core consciousness would include the following: physical positioning (I'm in the woods), emotional state (well-being), thermal state (it's a bit chilly here), visceral state (I'm starting to feel hungry), aural impressions (a bird is singing), and all other immediate bodily impressions.

This type of consciousness is clearly not simple but already complex. Core consciousness changes from moment to moment, from birth till death. "Core" relates not to what we might imagine as enduring, as primal, as stable, but, rather, to the kind of consciousness of the "here and now," the immediacy of one's bodily relationship to the enveloping environment at the present moment.

Back to the woods. The bear moves and I hear the bear; I turn and see the bear, the "object" of perception. (My movement also causes the bear to perceive me.)

Core consciousness results from second-order mappings of the relationship between these two kinds of first-order mappings, that is, a mapping of the "object" (that which is perceived or thought about and which becomes an image), and the body-map or proto-self.

The second-order mapping of the relationship between them results in a new body-map and a new core consciousness. Now, I am a startled person in the woods of northern Michigan.

But Damasio also holds that an enhancement of the image results from the second-order mapping of the relationship between body-map and image. The image enhancement is achieved via chemicals released from the basal forebrain and brain stem percolating through the thalamus to the upper cortices (Damasio 1999: 193–94). An image carries emotional import, infused with and enhanced by our projections. I experience not just a bear but a special sort of bear. Maybe I experience a very large bear, and most certainly experience a very threatening bear. (The bear may be experiencing me as very large and threatening also.)

The sense of a *changed* body-map, a result of the relationship between the image and body-map, gives rise to the sense that these images belong to a *self*. Now, a terrified core self who has no doubt that the terror belongs to me.

2. Extended Consciousness: The Autobiographical Self

Damasio's extended consciousness is linked to our personal history, our lifelong memories and our social sense of who we are. For this reason, his alternate term for extended consciousness is the term "autobiographical self." Although core consciousness is constantly recreated moment by moment, we believe in a certain continuity or "nontransient collection of unique facts and ways of being" in the establishment of the autobiographical self.

> Our traditional notion of self, however, is linked to the idea of identity and corresponds to a nontransient collection of unique facts and ways of being which characterize a person. . . . The autobiographical self depends on systematized memories

of . . . an organism's life—who you were born to, where, when, your likes and dislikes, the way you usually react to a problem or a conflict, your name, and so on. (Damasio 1999: 17)

Extended consciousness, according to Damasio, relates to the notion of identity and involves long-term memory, a sense of personal history, the narrative of own's life. In humans, extended consciousness is also a languaged consciousness encompassing not only a personal but a cultural history as well. Core consciousness becomes extended consciousness when multiple other maps, or neural patterns, are stimulated by the image-map, the body-map, and the second-order relationship map.

Although extended consciousness is not possible without core consciousness, the reverse is not the case. "Transient global amnesia" describes one such situation of the impairment of extended consciousness but the retention of core consciousness.

The most astonishing examples of impaired extended consciousness occur acutely and dramatically in a condition known as transient global amnesia. The condition is benign in the sense that patients return to normal. Transient global amnesia can occur in the setting of migraine headaches, sometimes as a prodrome to the headache, sometimes as a substitute for the headache. In transient global amnesia, beginning acutely and lasting for a period of a few hours, usually less than a day, an entirely normal person is suddenly deprived of the records that have been recently added to the autobiographical memory. (Damasio 1999: 202–04)

One of Damasio's patients, a highly intelligent and successful editor, wrote down a diary-like account of her experiences during a mild episode of transient amnesia. Below is an abridged version of her story.

Thursday, Aug. 6, 11:05—*At my desk. Suddenly a strange episode. Feel like I'm about to faint or be ill. Vision clear, but whole being concentrates on strange episode. Lean back from my desk. Close eyes. Concentrate on not being ill. . . . Never lose awareness of surroundings, but am intensely centered on self and odd feeling. . . . Coming out of it feel warm, ask my office mate something about heat in office (by now, five minutes later, don't recall what I said), she indicates it's OK (I think). Now feel right. It's 11:18. But am not quite focused on what I am doing.*

Looking at my work. Don't recognize the page of manuscript I am editing! Flip back and forth, but can't make up my mind what exactly I was doing . . .

Looking at my calendar to enter note of the "event," I find names of people I dealt with in last ten days that disturb me: I am not sure who they are. Most entries, though, are clear to me.

11:23—*Reading back. I recall starting to write this but can't recognize the top lines! Feel quite clear-headed now, but still slightly confused about implications, if any? Of what I just experienced. . . . I don't dare look at my work to see if it makes better sense than ten minutes ago.*

11:25—*I read back what I wrote at beginning of the first page: I don't recognize the wording I used! I remember starting to write this, but I'm interested that the beginning of it seems strange . . .*

Every time I read back some of what I have written, I find statements that puzzle

me because I don't remember putting them down. Trivial wordings, but still they puzzle me because I don't recognize them. (Note: all along, I have been sure of what, who, where I am and what I am doing here.)
[Confusion about her work continues, and she goes to lunch]
1:00—Got to lunch all right. Felt unsure of identity of old friends in the hall. But conversed OK. Got to the lunch line and had moment of panic about how to sign in, then remembered. . . . Took a healthy lunch, tuna salad and milk. Sat alone. Lingered a bit, thinking of implications of this episode and whether to report it at once to someone? Go home to rest? Ignore it?
[She returns to work after lunch, regains feeling of normality and resumes work]
(Damasio 1999: 204–06)

Although emotion is absent from patients suffering from compromised core consciousness, patients suffering from a breakdown of extended consciousness may demonstrate the full range of emotional expression, from background moods, to primary emotions, to secondary emotions. Continual emotional displays accompany normal activity and thought where both core and extended consciousness are intact.

One of the aspects of Damasio's theory of consciousness that seems to make it relevant to the experience of trance possession is his belief in two distinct levels of consciousness. Trancers are fully conscious; they respond appropriately to their milieu, moment by moment. But they may not always attribute their trancing experience to their autobiographical selves.[6] The trancing experience may belong to the trance persona and not to the autobiographical self of the Balinese villager who trances.

Music and Core Consciousness: "Becoming the Music"

Trancers' core consciousness includes the fact that trancers are aware of the changing events around them, of themselves in relation to those events. In one ritual I witnessed, the elaborate headdress of the man playing Rangda became loose. Even though trancing, Rangda momentarily stopped her infernal prancing about, stood still until an attendant had repaired the loose headdress, and then, after a moment's stillness, began the drama again in earnest.

In the Barong/Rangda ritual, the trancer also hears the Balinese gamelan play without pause. The drama is totally enveloped in the brilliant, vibrant, shimmering sounds of the gamelan. The rhythms of the gamelan and the intricate drum patterns are at every moment adjusted to the movements of whoever is at the center of attention at any dramatic moment. Drummers carefully watch the dancing, prancing ritual characters and align melodies, tempos, and rhythms to every large and small gesture. Gamelan musicians, drummers, and actors become one in a rhythmically coordinated domain.

The dramatic climax of the ritual, the hostile encounter between the trancers and Rangda is accompanied by fast, loud, short temporal cycles played on the gamelan. (See Figure 6-4.) In Balinese gamelan music, short, loud temporal

"Encounter" Theme

Figure 6-4. "Encounter" music. Transcription by J. Becker.

cycles with no melodic elaboration indicate the presence of demons and fighting. No Balinese music is more demonic, louder, or more minimalist than that which signals the encounter between the witch Rangda and the entranced men who attempt to thwart her power. The driving, incessant ostinatos of these themes are iconic of the emotions of fear and rage and the action of fighting. They undergird and sustain the manic frenzy of both the witch and her attackers. The gamelan music impacts physically on the men who participate; groups of neurons in the brains and bodies of the trancers are firing synchronously with the gamelan rhythms. The clanging bronze keys of the metallophones, the booming gongs, and the pulsing rhythms of drums and cymbals, all synchronized, become one with the body and brain of the trancer.

"Encounter" Theme

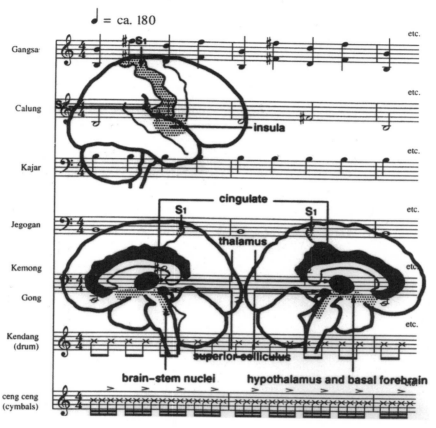

Figure 6-5. A "musicked" core consciousness? Graphic by J. Becker.

Gamelan music as image is juxtaposed with the body-map of the trancer. (See Figure 6-5.) The second-order mapping of the relationship between the two results in a changed body-map and changed sense of core self. What are the ways in which the trancers' body-maps, their proto-selves, unknowing and unawares, respond to the insistent gamelan ostinatos? And how does this "musicked" proto-self change core consciousness? What would a "musicked" core consciousness look like?

Musicians often use the expression "I become the music" to describe their sense of self when playing music. Within the frame of a "musicked" core consciousness, the phrase "I become the music" doesn't appear to be so metaphorical. Roland Barthes (1986) writes of "the body in a state of music," and T. S. Eliot (1943), "you are the music while the music lasts."

Music and Extended Consciousness in Trancing: The Loss of the Autobiographical Self

We asked: "And when they are stabbing their own breast, are they not even a little conscious of themselves?" To which Rena answered: "Not at all. I do not remember myself (*awak*) even a little bit; all I remember is the desire to stab my breast."
GM: "And if you have no *kris* [dagger], and, for instance, you try to get one from someone else, can't you remember who gave it to you?"
Rena: "At such a time I don't remember myself at all. For instance, if my head-cloth should fall off and someone picked it up and did not return it to me, I would not be able to remember who it was who picked it up."
GM: "What does it feel like when you have just been sprinkled with holy water?"
Rena: "When you've had holy water, then for the first time you feel like a person who has just awakened and got up from his bed." (Belo 1960: 105)

One of the salient features of possession trance is the apparent absence of, or inactivity of, or substitution for the autobiographical self. Trancers temporarily lose the sense of their private, autobiographical self in favor of the sense of the special self of trance possession. Trancers' extended consciousness must include long-term memories of previous encounters with Rangda that become activated upon seeing her again. They know what to feel and how to behave in relation to Rangda. This alternate trance self is necessarily impoverished in relation to their usual autobiographical self. The years of daily experiences, of interactions with persons and things, the laid-down memories of personal history have not occurred in relation to the extended self of trance possession. The entranced self is only experienced for a few minutes, or perhaps an hour or so, say, every few weeks. While the experience of the trance self lasts, the autobiographical self may be forgotten. The amnesia of trancers is in striking contrast to meditators who have crystal-clear memories of the processes and contents of their minds during meditation. Trance amnesia, I suspect, may be a result of the absence or inactivity of the autobiographical self during the trance period.[7]

The repertoire of pieces used in the Rangda/Barong ritual are largely specific to that ritual. All the memories, all the neural dispositions summoned by hearing the gamelan melodies will refer to other instances of the same ritual. The possessed self is a self whose personal history and culture is largely circumscribed by the narrative script of the ritual event, the music that accompanies the changing scenes of the drama and the cosmology it invokes. The extended consciousness of the trancers and thus their physical, emotional, and cognitive behavior is prescribed and stylized. They dance, they gesture, they react to others in the drama not as autobiographical selves but as the persona that the drama

requires. Not until they are later brought out of trance w
of the temple is their full, rich, Balinese, autobiographic

A crucial aspect of the autobiographical self is the on
ing, the internal monologue that accompanies nearly all o
Ernest Becker used the term "inner newsreel" for this phen
clude visual imaging. Ortega y Gasset used the Spanish tern
be inside oneself" and thought that this ongoing continual mo
sisted of ideas (Ortega y Gasset 1957: 18). A. L. Becker pursue:
how learning a second language, profoundly learning a second l
affects one's inner languaging and one's sense of self.

> . . . that personal, unuttered commentary on the present mixed with replays of the
> past and preplays of the future. It is the world each of us lives in, the individual
> *lebenswelt*, the personal noosphere, consciousness, the arena of meditation . . . there
> are many, many names for "it." Not so long ago "it" was called by Emerson *the soul,*
> and before that *psykhe*, that which most Christians believe is eternal and most Bud-
> dhists insist is the ultimate illusion. The question that formed over my years of
> studying Southeast Asian languages is: how does "it" change when one learns a dis-
> tant language? In other words, how do we become, internally and in our relations
> to the rest of the world, different persons in Burmese? (A. L. Becker 1995: 13)

William James equated consciousness with the inner language, that continuous internal thinking and imaging, emphasizing the fact that we feel as though
our internal monologue is without interruption, even though he felt that it included gaps, lapses, and ellipses.

> Consciousness, then, does not appear to itself chopped up in bits. Such words as
> "chain" or "train" do not describe it fitly as it presents itself in the first instance. It
> is nothing jointed; it flows. A "river" or a "stream" are the metaphors by which it is
> most naturally described. *In talking of it hereafter, let us call it the stream of thought,*
> *of consciousness, or of subjective life.* (James 1950, vol. 1: 239)

Conflating "consciousness" with inner languaging, as so many scholars have
done, is one of the common-sense notions that Damasio wishes to make more
complicated. He believes that inner languaging is a function of extended or biographical consciousness but not of core consciousness. Core consciousness does
not need language and needs only the briefest time span of memory.

> We can infer that the thoughts in our minds are created in our individual perspec-
> tive; that we own them; that we can act on them; that the apparent protagonist
> of the relationship with the object is our organism. As I see it, however, core con-
> sciousness begins before those inferences: *it is the very evidence, the unvarnished*
> *sense of our individual organism in the act of knowing.* (Damasio 1999: 125)

If inner languaging is coterminous with the autobiographical self, and if core
consciousness may remain intact without the autobiographical self, then the
temporary halting of the inner language in trancers seems to indicate (1) continued presence of core consciousness and (2) temporary suspension of extended consciousness, the unique autobiographical self. This biological, neuro-

model supports the epistemology of possession trance that another self temporarily displaced the autobiographical self. Friedson's description of his own trancing provides experiential evidence that confirms both the loss of the inner languaging and the priority of core consciousness, body consciousness, in unusual types of consciousness. His description also indicates another common first-person description of trancing; one senses a kind of knowing that feels different, qualitatively, from everyday knowing.

> As I sat there, I became aware that my internal dialogue, that voice of consciousness, had stopped. My conscious awareness seemed to be much more diffused throughout my entire body, as opposed to being centered in my head. It seems that my physical body had experienced *vimbuza* as much as my thinking self had, if not more. But this is a way of interpreting experience which assumes that the mind and body are somehow separate entities, and implicit in this assumption is the priority of the mind over the body. If anything—at least according to Merleau-Ponty's phenomenology—in actuality the body always has priority, for conscious awareness comes out of this realm of existence. (Friedson 1996: 19)

Benzon, echoing Friedson, speculates that the "flow" experience, the "peak" experience so often associated with music alone, may be related to the cessation of inner languaging. He feels that the total involvement with the narrative of the music, a narrative that includes all other experiences of that particular piece are a part of a special autobiography, a musicked autobiography that is in place for the duration of the performance, similar to my suggestion that a trancing autobiography is in place for the duration of the trance performance.

> Thus it is perhaps not so strange that an altered sense of one's own body parallels the cessation of inner speech. Think of the system for inner speech being coupled with the integrated body sense as a system we could call the Self System. An alteration in one component might affect the other as well. It is as though the mere existence of inner speech serves to anchor one's sense of intentionality in one's body. When that speech ceases, the anchor is gone and one floats free, outside one's body. (Benzon 2001: 154–55)

Benzon's Self System seems to combine elements of Damasio's core consciousness (integrated body sense) and autobiographical consciousness (languaged consciousness). Damasio's theory of the distinction between core consciousness and autobiographical consciousness better allows me to imagine the neurophysiology of trance as the substitution of a trance persona during trancing, a circumscribed, alternate autobiographical trancing self who enacts a prescribed role within a stable, sacred narrative.

How might this happen?

It may be that learning to control deep-brain ANS emotional responses, respiration, blood pressure, and skin temperature allows some persons to so change their consciousness that trancing becomes "allowed" and under voluntary control. Because emotional arousal is a precondition for deep listening and trancing, music may play as central a role as a precipitator of trancing as it does as a precipitator of transcendent feelings in deep listeners.

Music enhances the sense of a different imaginary world, provides a rhythmic template for the trancing body, increases emotional excitement, and may facilitate the experience of a different self. The transformed consciousness of the trancers allows for alternate mental images, the accompanying emotions, and behavior that may be remote from quotidian ways of interacting with the world. I suspect that the power of music to stimulate emotion, to create an imaginary world, to invoke the presence of the denizens of heaven or hell, while entraining the minds and bodies of the trancers helps propel the trancers into an alternate extended consciousness.

Trancing and Pain

The analgesic properties of music and trance are often dramatically enacted in rituals of religious trance. From the *tarantismo* of Apulia, to the self-stabbing of the Sulawesi *bissu* and the Balinese *bebuten* trances, trancing individuals transcend their normal bodily limitations and perform feats of physical endurance that are unthinkable in ordinary states of consciousness.

> Thus trance may be recognized, among other signs, by the fact that one can walk on burning coals without being burned, pierce one's own flesh without bleeding, bend swords one would normally be unable to curve, confront danger without flinching, handle poisonous snakes without being bitten . . . give acrobatic displays beyond one's normal ability, bend backwards to make a perfect arc, compose poems in one's sleep, sing for days and nights on end without a break, dance without difficulty despite being crippled. Thus trance always manifests itself in one way or another as a transcendence of one's normal self, as a liberation resulting from the intensification of a mental or physical disposition, in short, as an exaltation—sometimes a self-mutilating one—of the self. (Rouget 1985: 13–14)

Trance events are musical situations that may not be, in any direct way, about pain or suffering or healing, but which may result in extraordinary stamina and a modulation of the sensation of pain. Many kinds of music can, it seems, express sorrow (Meyer 1956; Dahlhaus 1982; Kivy 1989), and most any kind of music can help a patient realign his own bodily rhythms and contribute to healing and the ensuing diminution of pain (Sacks 1984). By contrast, music that accompanies religious trancing is not expressive of painful experiences, nor symbolic of pain, nor aimed at the reduction of pain. Rather, it is music whose primary function is to address, summon, or present an unseen world of gods, of deities, and of spirits.

The chemical bath stimulated by the emotions of the drama, the holiness of the event and the accompanying music may act as a powerful analgesic as well. The trancer who is emotionally excited by the sounds of the gamelan and who is imagining himself in the company of deities from the spirit world may well be releasing chemicals into his brain that include some of the natural opiates, or endogenous opioid peptides (Fields 1987: 114–17). Peptides such as beta-endorphins are potent natural painkillers. Long-distance runners, some anorexics, and meditators have been found to have elevated beta-endorphin levels (Hooper and Teresi 1986: 80). I suspect that those in trance do also. The ability to withstand turning a dagger on oneself, the ability to dance for hours, and the abatement of the pain of arthritis at a concert seem to be related phenomena. Balinese trancers not only do not feel pain when stabbing themselves but also rarely display any resultant physical trauma such as open, bleeding wounds. Do the chemicals released by emotional arousal have the ability not only to impede the sensation of pain, but to prevent the physical damage that would normally accompany the pain as well? Hearing the music enhances the emotion and the resultant stimulation of the production and release of certain hormones and monoamines, resulting in more intense feelings of rage. Along with rage, the trancers feel themselves to be in the presence of spirits from another realm, some of whom have temporarily taken over their bodies; for a while at least, the unseen world of powerful spirits is coterminous with their everyday Balinese world. They are enacting a cosmic narrative that is profoundly emotional, a drama that has changed the chemistry of their brains and their bodies.

Could it be that a lifetime of associating the pains and fatigues of everyday life to the autobiographical self sets up the mental images, the memories, whereby the pains and fatigues experienced while trancing are not associated with the trancing persona, but with the absent or replaced autobiographical self? Could it be that the trancing persona continues to ascribe his physical afflictions to his primary autobiographical self, and thus experiences a body-state that is impervious to pain and fatigue? Could it be that the mental images, the memories of the autobiographical self are temporarily inactive, or not attended to by the trancer, so that the trancing body does not interpret its body-map as "fatigue" or "pain"?[8] Could it be that the "I" who experiences the pain and fatigue is not, at the moment, paying attention?

> Knowing that you have pain requires something else that occurs after the neural patterns that correspond to the substrate of pain—the nociceptive signals—are displayed in the appropriate areas of the brain stem, thalamus, and cerebral cortex and generate an image of pain, a feeling of pain. But note that the "after" process to which I am referring is not beyond the brain, it is very much in the brain and, as far as I can fathom, is just as biophysical as the process that came before. Specifically, in the example above, it is a process that interrelates neural patterns of tissue damage with the neural patterns that stand for you, such that yet another neural pattern can arise—the neural pattern of you knowing, which is just another name for consciousness. If the latter interrelating process does not take place, you will never know that there was tissue damage in your organism—if there is no you and there is no knowing, there is no way for you to know, right? (Damasio 1999: 73)

I suggest that it is this syncope, this alternate self of religious trance, the extended trance consciousness accompanied by intense emotion, that provides the means by which Balinese daggers do not penetrate the skin and fatigue is for another day. As emotion plays a central role in Damasio's core consciousness, as emotions organize a whole host of chemical and neural activities that affect the entire body, might not emotions also be a key to the experience of another persona within one's own body? And might the emotional musical listening play a central role in this magical, mysterious process?

Postscript: Trancing, Deep Listening, and Human Evolution

To see the World in a Grain of Sand,
And a Heaven in a Wild Flower,
Hold Infinity in the palm of your hand,
And Eternity in an hour.

—William Blake [c. 1800] *Auguries of Innocence*

Trancing and deep listening are mind/body processes, kinds of consciousness that through history and across the globe some individuals have been able to master. Trancing and deep listening are, as far as we know, phenotypical characteristics of humans only. That is, they emerge only in certain types of human interactions with the environment, in some persons in very special circumstances. The potential for trancing may be genotypical of all humans, but if so, only a very small percentage ever actualize it—even in societies where trancing is much more common than in Western Europe and the United States. Trancing is everywhere something of an anomaly. Likewise, deep listeners seem to be a distinct minority.

Returning to the opening quotation of this study, William James suggested that there might be some use for extraordinary states of consciousness.

> Our normal waking consciousness, rational consciousness as we call it, is but one special type of consciousness, whilst all about it, parted from it by the filmiest of screens, there lie potential forms of consciousness entirely different. We may go through life without suspecting their existence; but apply the requisite stimulus, and at a touch they are there in all their completeness, definite types of mentality which probably somewhere have their field of application and adaptation. (James 1982 [1902]: 388)

The question "Does trancing have a field of application and adaptation somewhere?" must be speculative. There are scientists and humanists who feel that if a human trait has survived that must indicate that it has some evolutionary benefit; otherwise, it would have been eliminated long ago. This view of evolution that every characteristic of our biological being must be there for a purpose has sometimes been unflatteringly compared to the philosophical stance of the infamous literary character Pangloss, ridiculed by Voltaire in *Candide*.

> It has been proven . . . that things cannot be other than what they are, for since everything is made for an end, everything is necessarily for the best end. Observe that noses were made to wear spectacles, hence we have spectacles. Legs are pat-

ently devised to be breeched, and so we have breeches. . . . Therefore, those who have affirmed that all is well talk nonsense; they ought to have said that all is for the best. (Voltaire 1999 [1759]: 42)

Because trancing exists as a possible kind of consciousness for some people, does not of necessity imply any kind of evolutionary benefit. Nor does deep listening.

The evolutionary biologists Richard Lewontin and Stephen Jay Gould made the argument that organisms must be viewed as wholes, not as separable "traits," and that some feature may arise because it is correlated with another, clearly adaptive feature. Using the nonbiological example of the spandrels of San Marco, Milan (tapering triangular spaces formed by the intersection of two rounded arches at right angles), they argue that the spandrels are resultant by-products of an architectural design, that is, mounting a dome on rounded arches. The ornamentations on these spandrels are so compelling that one might view them as central to the architectural schema.

> Every fan vaulted ceiling must have a series of open spaces along the mid-line of the vault, where the sides of the fans intersect between the pillars. Since the spaces must exist, they are often used for ingenious ornamental effect. (Gould and Lewontin 1979: 582)

Similarly, the figure of David in Figure P-1, crouched between a pillar and an arch, is there because it is possible for it to be there. The pillar and the arch are structurally important to the design of the cathedral of San Marco in Milan. The artist's rendition of David is a fortuitous use of a space produced by design specifications that are unrelated to the painting.

Could it be that the ability to become a trancer or a deep listener is, like a spandrel, a resultant by-product of some other feature of our being that represents an evolutionary adaptive strategy?

Another alternative approach to the question of trancing, deep listening, and evolution might be as follows: Rather than believe that if a human trait has survived over the millennia it must have evolutionary benefit, we may believe that it is allowed to survive because it doesn't have a negative effect on survival. In other words, what is *not* proscribed is allowed; what does *not* negatively affect survival may continue. Natural selection may remove what is not compatible with survival but may allow whatever is *not* incompatible with survival (Varela, Thompson, and Rosch 1991: 195). Thus, trancing as a phenotypic human trait may have survived because it does not have any adverse effect on the evolutionary development of the species. Trancers, for the most part, lead normal human lives. Deep listeners seem to be indistinguishable from the population at large.

It seems to me that trancing and deep listening are skills that are not necessarily adaptive to survival but, rather, are life-enhancing, personally enriching skills that often bring deep rewards. Like learning any kind of physical skill, trancing may bring pleasure and satisfaction. We usually think of emotional control as meaning the ability to suppress or overcome emotional arousal. In the case of trancers and deep listeners, I believe it is the opposite. They are able to

Figure P-1. David, St. Mark's cathedral, Milan. From Perer 1998: 201. Courtesy of Banca Popolare de Milano.

intensify emotional arousal that can precipitate trance consciousness and result in a trancing body. Controlling emotional arousal by intensification during the service of a deeply believed religious drama can be thrilling. Deep listeners can induce thrills almost anytime.

Musical/rhythmic entrainment may present a stronger case for assisting in the evolution of the species. Synchronizing bodies and actions in musical performance, in musical listening is a unique characteristic of our species and may have evolutionary implications in terms of facilitating group activities directed toward finding food or fighting enemies. A bone flute has been discovered in a Neanderthal burial mound in Slovenia that has been determined to be between forty-three thousand and eighty-two thousand years old. No one knows what it was used for, but it clearly establishes great antiquity for some kind of musical behavior, a prerequisite for an evolutionary argument for promoting survival (Huron 2002: 50). Scholars such as Benzon and Freeman have made bold claims concerning the evolutionary importance of musical entrainment. Freeman suggests that musical entrainment has been a powerful evolutionary tool for forging a sense of identification between individuals and within groups of individuals that has clear evolutionary advantages (Freeman 2000: 411–24). He believes that something like musical entrainment has served as a survival necessity given the solipsism of the human brain. By solipsism he is referring to the demonstrated biological fact that our perception of the world outside of ourselves does not directly reflect sensory inputs but is a complex mental construct involving many areas of the brain in addition to those mainly involved with perception. We construe the world in accordance with our own fears and desires. Thus our mental images, our inner representations of the outside world may overlap with those of others in some ways, but are always in some sense *sui generis*. Freeman thus sees the necessity for some mechanism to overcome this solipsism and finds it in communal music and dancing. He uses the term "trance" to refer to the feeling of loss of self, of unity with others that occurs in situations of rhythmic entrainment.

> I conclude that music and dance originated through biological evolution of brain chemistry, which interacted with the cultural evolution of behavior. This led to the development of chemical and behavioral technology for inducing altered states of consciousness. The role of trance states was particularly important for breaking down preexisting habits and beliefs. That meltdown appears to be necessary for personality changes leading to the formation of social groups by cooperative action leading to trust. Bonding is not simply a release of a neurochemical in an altered state. It is the social action of dancing and singing together that induces new forms of behavior, owing to the malleability that can come through the altered state. It is reasonable to suppose that musical skills played a major role early in the evolution of human intellect, because they made possible formation of human societies as a prerequisite for the transmission of acquired knowledge across generations. (Freeman 2000: 422)

Freeman concludes that the ability to change consciousness that occurs in situations of communal dancing and singing, the "meltdown" of trancers and deep listeners, is a prerequisite for sustained human cultures. Are trancers and deep listeners thus deep learners as well? Is there any relationship between trancers, deep listeners and what Gregory Bateson has called "third-level learning," that is, that rare kind of learning that involves the replacements of the (largely) unconscious premises that underlie more gradual, more common learning patterns (Bateson 1972: 301–37)? That is, the kind of learning that shifts the foundational frame upon which we construct our understandings of ourselves and the relationship of ourselves to our world.

Taking up the theme of the evolutionary advantages of rhythmic entrainment, Benzon has elaborated and expanded on the idea of the singular importance of music-making and rhythmic coordination of bodies in the ongoing societal need to overcome private, nonsharable inner lives and to join in a community of our fellow creatures to build social coherence (Benzon 2001). Like Freeman, Benzon suggests that the evolution of music and the evolution of man as a social being are coterminous, that communal musical activity and rhythmic entrainment may have facilitated the survival of humankind by facilitating social bonding. Groups working together in hunting, in searching for food, in building shelters, in making clothing, and in raising children have a much better chance of survival than do individuals or single couples. Musical cohesion becomes a model for social cohesion. This is an attractive explanation for musical activity that otherwise might seem peripheral to more goal-oriented activities of humankind—an explanation that overcomes the current tendency to place musical activity outside the mainstream of productive behaviors.

Benzon has proposed a basic social principle reliant upon shared musical activity, upon rhythmic entrainment:

> The Social Principle: human beings create a uniquely human social space when their nervous systems are coupled through interactional synchrony. (Benzon 2001: 28)

Benzon uses the term "coupling" in the same way that Maturana and Varela use "structural coupling" to mean the mutual biological linkage of one person and another through interaction that affects the structure of both parties.

> If the whole village is listening and dancing, then the whole village is enacting a single pattern of musical activity, even though they are physically distinct individuals with distinct nervous systems. What makes this sonic communion possible is that all these physically distinct nervous systems are cut from the same mold, and all are attuned to the same pattern of sound. (Benzon 2001: 43)

Benzon's belief in the evolutionary, biological necessity of social bonding through participation in musical events leads him to a state of alarm concerning the reliance on deeply individual, non-participatory musical experience in so much of contemporary life. He feels, like Freeman, that musical participation is not just a pleasant pastime but a social necessity. We must all continue to share in each other's bodily rhythms in order to experience our common humanity, in order to promote enterprises for the common good.

A related argument has been made repeatedly by the ethnomusicologist Charles Keil in articles, books, at conferences, and on e-mail lists.

All humans were full participants once upon a time and I believe we still experience much music and perhaps some other portions of reality this way. I also believe we need more of this participatory consciousness if we are to get back into ecological synchrony with ourselves and with the natural world. (Keil and Feld 1994: 97)

But for all those trancers and deep listeners in the world, this conclusion would hardly suffice. They feel that the ability to be a deep listener or a trancer is a special blessing, a benediction. They have at their command a life-enhancing skill. Who would trade their ability to "listen deeply" or to trance with the resulting intensely felt emotion and feelings of transcendent numinosity for a more modulated reaction to music and to trance events? Who would willingly surrender their ability to temporarily abide in an eternity? Or to feel more purposefully alive and in direct communication with the Holy? Theirs is an enchanted world and is its own reward. "At any rate, they forbid a premature closing of our accounts with reality."

Notes

Introduction

1.   A few of the many well-documented forms of religious trancing with music not covered here include African examples such as the *zar* rituals of northeast Africa, the *bori* rituals of Tunisia, Algeria, and Morocco, the divinatory rituals of the Azande of southern Sudan, the *vodu* spirits and *orisha* of Guinea, and the *ng'oma* rites in central and southeastern Africa. I also will not discuss the Spiritual Baptists of Trinidad and St. Vincent, Haitian *vodun* practices, or *candomble* ceremonies in Brazil. I haven't included here the shamanic practices of Siberian peoples, of the Korean peninsula, and of the Temiar in Malaysia. I don't address the Sufi Muslim *dhikr* practices found throughout the Muslim world. My ethnographic examples are few compared to the vast number of possibilities. Furthermore, the issues addressed in this study do not necessarily relate to all instances of musical trancing in all places. However, I do claim that they relate to some and may be helpful in thinking about others.

2.   Notable exceptions are Charles Sanders Peirce and William James. Peirce rejected Cartesian dualism as well as the absolute separation between body and milieu, and an impermeable boundary between body and body. He also linked knowing and doing (Peirce 1931–35: 5. 400). James rejected mind/body dualism and, as the father of the discipline of psychology, held sophisticated and non-Cartesian, non-Enlightenment views about rationality (James 1950, 2 vols.).

3.   The nineteenth-century philosopher, Friedrich Schelling, has movingly made the same point.

> First and above all, an explanation must do justice to the thing that is to be explained, must not devaluate it, interpret it away, belittle it, or garble it, in order to make it easier to understand. The question is not "At what view of the phenomenon must we arrive in order to explain it in accordance with one or another philosophy?" but precisely the reverse: "What philosophy is requisite if we are to live up to the subject, be on a level with it?" The question is not how the phenomenon must be turned, twisted, narrowed, crippled so as to be explicable, at all costs, upon principles that we have once and for all resolved not to go beyond. The question is: To what point must we enlarge *our* thought so that it shall be in proportion to the phenomenon . . . ?" (Shelling, *Philosophie der Mythologie,* quoted in Zuckerkandl 1956: frontpage)

A Historical Interlude

1.   This was the method enacted and satirized in the Woody Allen movie *The Curse of the Jade Scorpion* (2001).

1. Rethinking "Trance"

1. On cite en preuve de pouvoir physique des sons la guerison des piquures des Tarentules. Cet exemple prouve tout le contraire. Il ne faut ni des sons absolus ni les mêmes airs pour guérir tous ceux qui sont piqués de cet insecte, il faut à chacun d'eux des airs d'une mélodie qui lui soit connüe et des phrases qu'il comprenne. Il faut à l'Italien des airs Italiens, au Turc il faudroit des airs Turcs. Chacun n'est affecté que des accens qui lui sont familiers; ses nerfs ne s'y prêtent qu'autant que son esprit les y dispose: il faut qu'il entende la langue qu'on lui parle pour que ce qu'on lui dit puisse le mettre en mouvement. Les Cantates de Bernier ont, dit-on, guéri de la fiévre un musicien François, elles l'auroient donnée à un musicien de toute autre nation (Rousseau 1970: 165).

2. Some skilled, experienced trancers often do remember their trance experiences.

3. Elsewhere, al-Ghazzali specifically recommends "forced ecstasy" as a pedagogic procedure for learning to trance. In this case he must be referring to "forced ecstasy" that aims at hypocrisy and is therefore blameworthy (al-Ghazzali 1901: 730).

4. Figure 1-2 demonstrates the irregularity of what is yet clearly a repeated drum pattern. These language-like patterns are called *wakyaya* "sentences."

   > Rhythm, force, tempo and expression are all woven into a beautiful design by the skilled drummer so that even minus the dancing it is an exhibitive display of drum music. One may say that this narrative style of drum play is not systematic and precise as it is a confusing medley of the mathematical fundaments of rhythm. But this incongruent arrangement of a number of rhythms and periods into a receptive demonstration is itself a system. (Kulatillake 1976: 40)

5. Below is an excerpt from a Romanized transcription (without diacritical marks) of the original text of this long recitation.

   > On namo kalingu nuvara sat mudukata edese sat sayur amal sayura kiri sayura vali sayura golu sayura kiri muhuda mat muhuda gomva muhuda nil muhuda mada vasattane karana maha kalu yakshaya yakshni rimdibisavu alle bisavu valle bisavu anda gana bisavu moragana bisavu dapila bisavu ethrabisavu atuluva ekamaduve keli pideni ganda varamgat rata yakuno maha kalu yakshaya yakshni me lamkadvipeta goda bamda ena tanedi solos dahas panshiyaka bosovaru pirivara gana satdenan satdena pirivaragana kurumbradan atadena pirivaragana istri avatarayak mavagan me lankamvipayata godabasimda ena gamanedi vesamuni rajjuruvo isvara deviyan langata andhagasa on kalu yaksha yakshani em em marettu varettu kiya suvamda mal bulat sarsa dun anubhaven adat mage rubara dola pideni kere dishtila mage anguru dunmala kere dishtila atakonen vara solos konen vara tumamamshalin vara anvuhaten vara muhudu haten vara sat sayuren vara mal sayuren vara kiri sayuren vara vali sayura hatte vara vil hakten vara pili haten vara kamdi haten vara korana haten vara gamga haten vara hagra pavraten ida hari isvara putraya nam mama tamayi adak me atura yage ata gata sandi gata naharagata nosamgi nomalaki gantahamchi bintahamdi hihiratahamchinu latahamchi kamduruta hamchi idahari da hasak hiravalakun igila igila vara vara yantra dishti mantra dishti mantra dishti bojana dishti maha kalu yakshaya yakshani vara vara dishti dishti eshvaah. (Egan 1969: 2.39–2.40)

6.   Allu Mari mi portati
      Se voleti che mi sanati
      Allu Mari, allu via:
      Cosi m'ama la Donna Mia
      Allu Mari, allu Mari;
      Mentre campo, t'aggio amari.

      Non fu Taranta, ne fu la Tarantella,
      Ma fu lo vino della garratella.
      Dove te mozico dill'amata dove fu,
      Ohime si fusse gamma, ohime mamma, ohime.

      Deu ti mussicau la Tarantella?
      Sotto la Pudia della vanella. (Kircher 1643: 760, 763)

7.   Probabile est motum velocissimum a musicis instrumentis aeri impressum, &
      ab aere cuti, mox spiritibus, & sanguini communicatum, incipientem eorun-
      dem coagulationem paulisper dissolvere, disgregare, excitare, & dissolutionis
      effectus crescere, sono ipso crescente; donec tandem per repetitas has succes-
      siones, ac veluti vibrationes pristinam fluiditatem humores acquisierint, quo
      facto aeger sensim reviviscit, membra movet, in pedes elevatur, suspirat, &
      vehemtissimas inchoat saltationes, donec evocatis sudoribus, veneni semina
      foris eliminata fuerint (Baglivi 1754: 321; from another printing of the 1723
      treatise).

8.   The *aulos,* featured prominently in rites in honor of Dionysus, was usually
      portrayed as a double *aulos,* that is, two pipes joined at the mouthpiece and
      splayed outward to form an inverted V. Most scholars believe it contained two
      double reeds and therefore is classified as an oboe rather than two single reeds
      and classified as a clarinet. (See Michaelides 1978: 42–44.)

2. Deep Listeners

1.   The theory is often called the James-Lange theory, because Carl Georg Lange
      (1834–1900), a Danish physiologist, almost simultaneously published a theory
      very similar to that of James.

2.   For an overview of recent theorizing on musical expression and emotion, see
      Gabrielsson and E. Lindstrom 2001: 223–48.

3.   The following table, compiled from recent neurological and psychological
      studies of music and emotion by Gabrielsson and Lindstrom Wik (2000),
      Krumhansl (1997), Nyklicek et al. (1997), and Panksepp (1995), indicates the
      range of musical emotions and supports the idea that although positive emo-
      tions are most common in relation to musical listening, a wide range of emo-
      tions occurs.

Scholar	Verbal Report of Musical Emotions as Experienced by Listeners
Gabrielsson, Alf and Lindstrom Wik, Siv (2000)	*Positive emotions* excitement, rapture, euphoria, happiness, sexual arousal, safety, warmth, peace, harmony

	Negative emotions
	fear, horror, panic, longing, frustration, grief
Krumhansl, Carol (1997)	*Positive emotions*
	surprised, happy, amused, contented, relieved
	Negative emotions
	afraid, angry, contemptuous, anxious, sad,
	disgusted
	Basic emotions
	sad, happy, fear
Nyklicek, Ivan, Thayer, Julian F.,	*Positive emotions*
and Van Doornen, Lorenz J. P. (1997)	happiness, serenity
	Negative emotions
	agitation, sadness
Panksepp, Jaak (1995)	*Positive emotions*
	happy/excited
	loving/accepting
	Negative emotions
	angry/frustrated
	anxious/fearful
	sad/melancholy

4.   The involvement of opioid systems in musical listening is also attested to by an early study conducted by Avram Goldstein (1968). Goldstein found that the experience of chills when listening to favorite musical examples diminished when subjects were injected with naloxone, an opioid antagonist, that is, a blocker of all things that activate the opioid receptors, endogenous or not.

5.   One of the surprising results of recent studies on emotion is that different emotions rely upon different brain patterns for their expression. Krumhansl found significant differences of configuration in the physiology of arousal associated with different emotions, a finding also supported by others (Panksepp 1995: 172; LeDoux 1996: 106; Nyklicek et al. 1997: 316; Damasio 1999: 61; Blood and Zatorre 2001: 11823).

> Sad was associated with changes in measures of cardiac and electrodermal systems, fear with changes in cardiovascular measures, and happy with respiration measures . . . the dynamic ratings of sad correlated strongest with the factors of blood pressure, skin conductance and temperature measures, and cardiac intercycle interval. The dynamic ratings of fear correlated strongest with the factors of pulse transmission time and amplitude. The dynamic ratings of happy correlated strongest with the respiration measures. (Krumhansl 1997: 439)

Thus all emotions involve brain-stem activation and all result in some form of visible and nonvisible physiological changes. Beyond that, sadness appears to affect blood pressure, skin conductance, and skin temperature, and cardiac intercycle interval while activating the brain stem, hypothalamus, and ventromedial prefrontal cortex. Happiness is strongly correlated with breathing, and fear with blood pressure. Arousal, whatever its form, changes our brains and our bodies.

6.   Musical listening or performing are not the only routes available for secular

ecstasy. Good sex is the most obvious example. The work of Maslow and Csikszentmihalyi demonstrates that many kinds of skillfully performed actions also have the potential to produce sensations parallel to religious ecstasy. Maslow reports the following sensations that may accompany very skillful action.

1. total attention on the object in question
2. complete absorption
3. disorientation in time and space
4. transcendence of ego
5. identification or even fusion of the perceiver and the perceived
6. occasionally described as sacred (Maslow 1968: 71)

Csikszentmihalyi has added the term "flow" to vernacular vocabulary, aptly describing the skillful movement of many musicians. His list of the attributes of flow suggests trancing as well.

1. effortless involvement in an activity
2. full concentration, absorption
3. altered perception of time
4. loss of self-consciousness (Csikszentmihalyi 1990)

7. Indian *rasa* theory was exported to Southeast Asia and was incorporated into aesthetic theory in Java, Indonesia (see J. Becker 1993).

8. I am indebted to David Huron for pointing out to me that "feeling state" subsumes the list of "Transitory Mental States."

9. I am indebted to Anthony Day for this translation. The roman transliteration of the original Javanese script is as follows:

Serat Tjentini, vol. 1, 44e Zang; dichtmaat: Potjoeng [verses 109–14]

kabeh baoed pada rasane nenaboeh
rereming irama
adoe wileting malatsih
oekoer djawil sadjedjantoeraning dalang

langkoeng roentoet rasaning gending pakantoek
dadya ngantak-antak
dangoe denira anggending
tan antara aneseg gendinge moenggah

pan adangoe saja goelet wiletpoen
reboet nges kesaman
naboehe samja birai
rahab berag rasa-rasa jen oewisa.

Sesegipoen ngendelong anoelja soewoek
Noelja sesendonan.

10. The poem is a *naat* in honor of the prophet Mohammad. I am grateful to Dr. Tahsin Siddiqi, Professor of Hindi/Urdu at the University of Michigan for providing the complete text in Urdu and the English translation.

Shams-ud duhaa, badr-ud dujaa

In you there is the exact light of Allah.
Khudaa kaa nuur tujh meN huu-ba-huu hai.

Allah is hidden, but you are face-to-face with Him.
Khudaa pinhaaN magar tuu ruu-ba-ruu hai.

Who can estimate the value of your greatness?
Terii 'azmat kaa andaazaa ho kis se?

Allah is first and you are second.
Khudaa hai aur khudaa ke baad tuu hai.

Your great honor is to be the sun of guidance, the moon of darkness.
Shams-ud duhaa badr-ud dujaa terii baRii tauqiir hai.

Oh king of the people, your form is the picture of Allah
Suurat terii shah-I umam, Allaah kii tasviir hai.

Such is your form, Oh Prophet.
Hai aisii suurat tirii kamliivale.

Not in this world but on the day of judgment you are my refuge, my support.
Duniyaa se k'yaa roz-i jazaa unkaa hai mujhko aasraa.

I, Mustafa (the prophet) am your slave. What a wonderful fate!
MaiN huuN ghulaam-I Mustafaa. Kaisii merii taqdiir hai.

3. Habitus of Listening

1.   Some *qawwals*, like Nusrat Fateh Ali Khan or the Sabri Brothers, became international performers, toured Europe and North America, made recordings and became rich. Although the "cross-over" *qawwal* seems like a modern phenomenon, and although international fame is certainly a result of contemporary technology, *qawwals* have operated in the public sphere and have been admired purely on aesthetic grounds for at least two hundred years (see D. Q. Khan 1989).

2.   For musical examples, listen to any of the many CDs of Nusrat Fateh Ali Khan.

3.   Accidents do happen. Belo describes one trancer who cut a deep gash in his chest (Belo 1960: 131).

4.   I heard Bateson propose this theory in a lecture given at the University of Michigan in the 1970s. I have been unable to find a reference to it in his published writings.

4. Trancing Selves

1.   For Descartes, the governing mechanism resided in the pineal gland (Dennett 1991: 104–105). In the book *Descartes' Error,* the neuroscientist Antonio Damasio demonstrates through his study of patients with various kinds of mental lesions that the reasoning/decision making parts of the brain and the emotion/feeling parts of the brain comprise the same collection of systems, that is, the ventromedial prefrontal cortices, the amygdala, and the somato-

sensory cortices. As Damasio states, reason and emotion "intersect" in these areas of the brain (see Damasio 1994: 70).

2. The "radical reflexivity" of Taylor is different from the "reflexivity" of contemporary anthropology and ethnomusicology. In the latter disciplines, reflexivity is the intent to make clear the role of the author in relation to what she writes about. To the degree that this technique, consciously or unconsciously, is used to enhance the authority of the writer, or to undermine the authority of a different writer, it may become yet another tool of mastery.

3. Not surprisingly, colonial evangelical congregations came to be dominated by women for whom "ecstatic expressivity" was more acceptable than for men (Isaac, personal communication)—an aspect of gendered selfhood that extends into our own time.

4. The church records mentioned in this quote came from the Chestnut Grove Baptist Church, 1773–79 and the Albemarle-Buck Mountain Baptist Church 1792–1811 (Isaac 1974: 354).

5. The term *Batara Guru* when used in Southeast Asia generally refers to Shiva and implies some Shaivite influence, but that does not seem to be the case here. Whereas Buginese contact with centers of medieval Shaivite beliefs such as Java and Sumatra were continual, the Buginese origin myth only peripherally touches on Shaivism.

6. Translated by the author from the French translation by Hamonic. The original Buginese is as follows:

Ana' tollao-lao ko mai
Ana' batara tungke' ko mai
Musulo' lanyu-lanyu
Mallarung maujangka
Balibonga sengngeng
Ri torowatu Ula'Naga
Ya.La.Ti.Nge. meggae
Pawewang simpuru' tasi
Aju taddelle' mulajaji
Wero' mawekke
Kua ile' tattere
Alumpang oddang
Musolo' mappesaga-saga
Batara tungke' ko mai
Nalanyu-lanyu anurungeng (Hamonic 1987: 56)

7. In his description of this part of the ceremony, Lathief (1983: 25) writes that the *bissu* attain *fana al fana*, "the passing away of passing away," the Sufi term for religious ecstasy in which one knows one's own nothingness and absolute dependence on Allah (al-Ghazzali 1990: xvi). Sufis were among the earliest Islamic missionaries in all Indonesia, so it is not surprising that Sufi terms and Sufi concepts have become a part of the way Bugis think about trance possession.

8. With the steady movement of all Indonesian Muslims toward a stronger orthodoxy, the pressures on the *bissu* increase. According to one source, many *bissu* have been killed and *bissu* rituals destroyed (Lathief 1983: 17). This may

have happened during the turbulent upheavals in Indonesia during the 1960s when thousands of people were killed throughout the archipelago because of suspicions of nonorthodoxy of one sort or another, especially Communism (or Lathief may be referring to more recent events). In any case, the narrative of the *bissu* rituals is one that becomes increasingly difficult to maintain in the present day.

5. Being-in-the-World

1. William Benzon, in his insightful book *Beethoven's Anvil*, uses the term "coupling" to designate what I am calling "structural coupling." He may have made the idea harder for his readers to understand by initially describing coupling as happening between brains rather than between whole bodies, "Music is a medium through which individual brains are coupled together in shared activity" (Benzon 2001: 23). Although later he speaks of coupled nervous systems and his examples include whole bodies, he still often inserts "brain" where "bodies" might have made his point more forceful. Nonetheless, his is an important and seminal book.

2. Some scholars who have studied rhythmic entrainment over the years are Walter and Walter 1949; Neher 1961/1962; Chapple 1970: 38; Hall 1977: 61; Pfeiffer 1982; Condon 1986; Rider and Eagle 1986; Petsche and Rappelsberger 1988; Vaughn 1990; and McNeill 1995: 6.

3. This material was presented in a lecture at the University of Michigan in the 1970s.

6. Magic through Emotion

1. Reported in Berman 1989: 116.

2. Neurochemicals can be either inhibitory or excitatory. In addition, at each synapse the impulse can be either modulated, duplicated exactly, reduced, increased, or delayed. As input from the senses percolates to different parts of the brain and the nervous system, it gets processed at every stage.

3. Other biological theories that include the concept of a layered consciousness include Edelman 1992 and Panksepp 1998a. The concept of levels of consciousness also has a long history within Buddhism. See, for example, Beyer 1978: 92–99; Hayward 1998; Snellgrove 1987; and Guenther 1976.

4. Below is Damasio's fuller definition of a "map."

> Maps
> When the light particles known as photons strike the retina in a particular pattern related to an object, the nerve cells activated in that pattern—say, a circle or a cross—constitute a transient neural "map." At subsequent levels of the nervous system, for instance, the visual cortices, subsequent related maps are also formed. To be sure, just as with the word representation, there is a legitimate notion of pattern, and of correspondence between what is mapped and the map. But the correspondence is not point-to-point, and thus the map need not be faithful. The brain is a creative system. Rather than mirroring the environment around it, as an engineered information-processing device would, each brain constructs maps of that environ-

ment using its own parameters and internal design, and thus creates a world unique to the class of brains comparably designed. (Damasio 1999: 321–22)

5. Below is my condensed versions of Damasio's definition of "image."

> When I use the term *image,* I always mean *mental* image. A synonym for image is *mental pattern.* I do not use the word image to refer to the pattern of neural activities that can be found, with current neuroscience methods, in activated sensory cortices—for instance, in the auditory cortices in correspondence with an auditory percept; or in the visual cortices in correspondence with a visual percept. When I refer to the neural aspect of the process I use terms such as *neural pattern* or *map.*
>
> Images can be conscious or nonconscious. Nonconscious images are never accessible directly. Conscious images can be accessed *only in a first-person perspective* (my images, your images). Neural patterns, on the other hand, can be accessed *only in a third-person perspective.* If I had the chance of looking at my own neural patterns with the help of the most advanced technologies, I would still be looking at them from a third-person perspective.
>
> By the term images I mean mental patterns with a structure built with the tokens of each of the sensory modalities—visual, auditory, olfactory, gustatory, and somatosensory. The somatosensory modality . . . includes varied forms of sense: touch, muscular, temperature, pain, visceral, and vestibular. The word image does not refer to "visual" image alone, and there is nothing static about images either. The word also refers to sound images such as those caused by music or the wind, and to the somatosensory images that Einstein used in his mental problem solving . . . Images in all modalities "depict" processes and entities of all kinds, concrete as well as abstract. Images also "depict" the physical properties of entities and, sometimes sketchily, sometimes not, the spatial and temporal relationships among entities, as well as their actions. In short, the process we come to know as mind when mental images become ours as a result of consciousness is a continuous flow of images many of which turn out to be logically interrelated. The flow moves forward in time, speedily or slowly, orderly or jumpily, and on occasion it moves along not just one sequence but several. Sometimes the sequences are concurrent, sometimes convergent and divergent, sometimes they are superposed. *Thought* is an acceptable word to denote such a flow of images.
>
> Images are constructed either when we engage objects, from persons and places to toothaches, from the outside of the brain toward its inside; or when we reconstruct objects from memory, from the inside out, as it were. The business of making images never stops while we are awake and it even continues during part of our sleep, when we dream. One might argue that images are the currency of our minds . . . Even the feelings that make up the backdrop of each mental instant are images, in the sense articulated above, somatosensory images, that is, which mostly signal aspects of the body state. The obsessively repeated feelings that constitute the self in the act of knowing are no exception. (Damasio 1999: 317–19)

6. My application of Damasio's theory seems more directly applicable to possession trance than to shamanic trance, in which the autobiographical self of the shaman is a crucial aspect of the ceremonies. Sufi ecstasy likewise doesn't fit easily into my hypothesis. I suspect that there may be different kinds of consciousness coterminous with differing kinds of trancing.

7. What is more difficult to explain, I believe, is the fact that experienced, skilled trancers oftentimes do remember their trances. Is this "lucid trancing" related to the phenomenon of "lucid dreaming" in which a self seems to occupy two

different mental spaces simultaneously? Is the "lucid trancer" simultaneously the trance persona *and* his/her autobiographical self?

8. I cannot remember where I read it, but I distinctly recall the story of the hospitalized old woman with severe bodily affliction who also suffered from mental lesions who remarked that she knew there was pain somewhere in the room but she didn't know to whom it belonged.

Bibliography

Abu-Lughod, Lila
   1986   *Veiled Sentiments: Honor and Poetry in a Bedouin Society.* Berkeley: University of California Press.
Alkon, Daniel L.
   1992   *Memory's Voice: Deciphering the Mind-Brain Code.* New York: Harper Collins Publishers.
Ames, Adelbert, Jr.
   1960   *The Morning Notes of Adelbert Ames, Jr.,* ed. Hadley Cantril. New Brunswick, N.J.: Rutgers University Press.
Appadurai, Arjun
   1996   *Modernity at Large: Cultural Dimensions of Globalization.* Minneapolis: University of Minnesota Press.
Aristotle
   1950   "The Politics." In *Source Readings in Music History: From Classical Antiquity through the Romantic Era,* ed. Oliver Strunk: 13–24. New York: W. W. Norton and Co.
Arnheim, Rudolph
   1958   "Emotion and Feeling in Psychology and Art." *Confinia Psychiatrica* 1: 69–88.
Baglivi, Giorgio
   1723 [1695]   *The Practice of Physick.* 2nd English ed. London.
   1754   *Opera omnia medico-practica, et anatomica.* Venetiis: typis Remondinianis.
Balasaraswati, T.
   1985   "The Art of Bharata Natyam: A Personal Statement." *Dance as Cultural Heritage,* ed. B. T. Jones, 2: 1–7. Dance Research Annual XV. New York: Congress on Research in Dance.
Baldwin, James
   1953   *Go Tell It on the Mountain.* New York: Knopf.
Bandem, I Made
   1994   "Taksu Dalam Seni Pertunjukan Bali." *Catatan Kebudayaan: Jurnal Sastra dan Budaya Sanggar Minum Kope Bali* 1: 22.
Barnard, Malcolm
   1995   "Advertising: The Rhetorical Imperative." In *Visual Culture,* ed. Chris Jenks: 26–41. London and New York: Routledge.
Barthes, Roland
   1986   "Rasch." In *The Responsibility of Forms: Critical Essays on Music, Art, and Representation,* trans. Richard Howard: 299–312. New York: Hill and Wang.
Bateson, Gregory
   1972   *Steps to an Ecology of Mind: A Revolutionary Approach to Man's Understanding of Himself.* New York: Ballantine Books.

Baxandall, Michael
    1974   *Painting and Experience in Fifteenth Century Italy: A Primer in the Social History of Pictorial Style.* London and New York: Oxford University Press.
Becker, A. L.
    1995   *Beyond Translation: Essays Toward a Modern Philology.* Ann Arbor: University of Michigan Press.
    1999   "A Short, Familiar Essay on Person." *Language Sciences* 21: 229–36.
Becker, Ernest
    1971   *The Birth and Death of Meaning: An Interdisciplinary Perspective on the Problem of Man.* New York: Free Press.
Becker, Judith
    1979   "Time and Tune in Java." In *The Imagination of Reality: Essays in Southeast Asian Coherence Systems,* ed. A. L. Becker and Aram A. Yengoyan: 197–210. Norwood, New Jersey: Ablex Publishing.
    1983   " 'Aesthetics' in Late 20th Century Scholarship." *The World of Music* 25 (3): 65–80.
    1988   "Earth, Fire, *Sakti,* and the Javanese Gamelan." *Ethnomusicology* 32 (3): 385–91.
    1993   *Gamelan Stories: Tantrism, Islam, and Aesthetics in Central Java.* Tempe: Arizona State University Press.
    2000   "Listening Selves and Spirit Possession." *The World of Music* 42 (2): 25–50.
    2001   "Anthropological Perspectives on Music and Emotion." In *Music and Emotion: Theory and Research,* ed. Patrik Juslin and John Sloboda: 135–60. Oxford: Oxford University Press.
Becker, Judith, and Alton Becker
    1981   "A Musical Icon: Power and Meaning in Javanese Gamelan Music." In *The Sign in Music and Literature,* ed. Wendy Steiner: 203–215. Austin: University of Texas Press.
Belo, Jane
    1960   *Trance in Bali.* New York: Columbia University Press.
Benamou, Marc
    1998   *Rasa in Javanese Musical Aesthetics* (Ph.D. dissertation, University of Michigan). Ann Arbor, Mich.: UMI Dissertation Services.
Benveniste, Emile
    1971   "Subjectivity in Language." In *Problems in General Linguistics,* trans. M. E. Meek: 223–30. Coral Gables, Fla.: University of Miami Press.
Benzon, William L.
    2001   *Beethoven's Anvil: Music in Mind and Culture.* New York: Basic Books.
Berk, Laura E.
    1994   "Why Children Talk to Themselves." *Scientific American* (Nov.): 78–83.
Berman, Morris
    1989   *Coming to our Senses: Body and Spirit in the Hidden History of the West.* New York: Simon and Schuster.
Beyer, Stephan
    1978   *The Cult of Tara: Magic and Ritual in Tibet.* Berkeley: University of California Press.
Blacking, John
    1973   *How Musical Is Man?* Seattle: University of Washington Press.
Blake, William
    1968   *Auguries of Innocence.* New York: Grossman Publishers.

Bloch, Maurice

1975   "Symbol, Song, Dance and Features of Articulation." *European Journal of Sociology* xv (1): 55–81.

Blood, Anne J., and Robert J. Zatorre

2001   "Intensely Pleasurable Responses to Music Correlate with Activity in Brain Regions Implicated in Reward and Emotion." *Proceedings of the National Academy of Sciences* 98: 11818–23.

Blumhofer, Edith

1993   *Restoring the Faith; The Assemblies of God, Pentecostalism and American Culture.* Bloomington: Indiana University Press.

Boor, M.

1982   "The Multiple Personality Epidemic: Additional Cases and Inferences Regarding Diagnosis, Dynamics and Cure." *Journal of Nervous and Mental Disease* 170: 302–04.

Borchgrevink, Hans M.

1982   "Prosody and Musical Rhythm are Controlled by the Speech Hemisphere." In *Music, Mind, and Brain: The Neuropsychology of Music,* ed. Manfred Clynes: 151–57. New York and London: Plenum Press.

Bourdieu, Pierre

1977   *Outline of a Theory of Practice,* trans. Richard Nice. Cambridge: Cambridge University Press.

Brennan, Teresa, and Martin Jay, eds.

1996   *Vision in Context: Historical and Contemporary Perspectives on Sight.* New York and London: Routledge.

Brown, Donald E.

1991   *Human Universals.* Philadelphia: Temple University Press.

Bruner, Jerome

1990   *Acts of Meaning.* Cambridge, Mass.: Harvard University Press.

Buranelli, Vincent

1975   *The Wizard from Vienna.* London: Peter Owen.

Caciola, Nancy.

1994   *Discerning Spirits: Sanctity and Possession in the later middle ages* (Ph.D. dissertation, University of Michigan). Ann Arbor: UMI Dissertation Services.

Callaway, John, trans.

1829   *Yakkun Nattannawa: A Cingalese Poem.* London: Printed for the Oriental Translation Fund.

Chadwick, Henry, trans.

1991   *Saint Augustine Confessions.* New York: Oxford University Press.

Chalmers, David J.

1995   "Facing Up to the Problem of Consciousness." *Journal of Consciousness Studies* 2 (3): 200–19.

Chapple, Eliot D.

1970   *Culture and Biological Man: Explorations in Behavioral Anthropology.* New York: Rinehart and Winston.

Chomsky, Noam

1972   *Language and Mind.* New York: Harcourt Brace Jovanovich.

Churchland, P. S.

1986   *Neurophilosophy: Toward a Unified Science of the Mind-brain.* Cambridge, Mass.: MIT Press.

Clynes, Manfred
    1986   "When Time Is Music." In *Rhythm in Psychological, Linguistic and Musical Processes*, ed. James Evans and Manfred Clynes: 169–224. Springfield, Ill.: Charles C. Thomas.
Condon, William S.
    1986   "Communication: Rhythm and Structure." In *Rhythm in Psychological, Linguistic and Musical Processes*, ed. James Evans and Manfred Clynes: 55–77. Springfield, Ill.: Charles C. Thomas.
Coomaraswamy, Ananda K.
    1957   *The Dance of Shiva*. New York: Noonday Press.
Cornelius, Randolph R.
    1996   *The Science of Emotion: Research and Tradition in the Psychology of Emotions*. Upper Saddle River, N.J.: Prentice Hall.
Cox, Harvey
    1995   *Fire from Heaven: The Rise of Pentecostal Spirituality and the Reshaping of Religion in the Twenty-first Century*. Reading, Mass.: Addison-Wesley Publishing Company.
Crow, Douglas Karim
    1984   "Sama': The Art of Listening in Islam." In *Maqam: Music of the Islamic World and Its Influences*, ed. Robert Browning: 30–33. New York: Alternative Museum, Athens Printing Company.
Csikszentmihalyi, Mihaly
    1990   *Flow: The Psychology of Optimal Experience*. New York: Harper and Row.
Csordas, Thomas J.
    1994   *The Sacred Self: A Cultural Phenomenology of Charismatic Healing*. Berkeley: University of California Press.
Dahlhaus, Carl.
    1982   *Esthetics of Music*, trans. William W. Austin. Cambridge: Cambridge University Press.
Damasio, Antonio
    1994   *Descartes' Error: Emotion, Reason, and the Human Brain*. New York: Grosset/Putnam.
    1999   *The Feeling of What Happens: Body and Emotion in the Making of Consciousness*. New York, San Diego, and London: Harcourt Brace and Company.
Danziger, Kurt
    1990   *Constructing the Subject: Historical Origin of Psychological Research*. Cambridge: Cambridge University Press.
Darnton, Robert
    1968   *Mesmerism and the End of the Enlightenment in France*. Cambridge, Mass.: Harvard University Press.
    1984   *La Fin Des Lumières: Le Mesmerisme et la Révolution*, trans. Marie-Alyx Revellat. Paris: Librairie Academique Perrin.
Darwin, Charles
    1872   *The Expression of the Emotions in Man and Animals*. London: J. Murray.
Date, Henry
    1894   *Pentecostal Hymns No. 1: A Winnowed Collection for Evangelistic Services, Young People's Societies and Sunday-Schools*. Chicago: Hope Publishing.

Davidson, Richard J.
1992   "Prolegomenon to the Structure of Emotion: Gleanings from Neuropsychology." *Cognition and Emotion* 6: 245–68.

Davies, John Booth
1978   *The Psychology of Music.* London: Hutchinson.

Decker, Hannah
1986   "The Lure of Nonmaterialism in Materialist Europe: Investigations of Dissociative Phenomena, 1880–1915." In *Split Minds/Split Brains,* ed. J. M. Quen: 31–62. New York: New York University Press.

Dennett, Daniel C.
1991   *Consciousness Explained.* Boston: Little, Brown.

Descartes, R.
1637   *Discourse on Method.* In *The Philosophical Works of Descartes,* 2 vols., trans. and ed. Elizabeth Haldane and George Ross. 1967. Cambridge: Cambridge University Press.

Deutsch, Diana
1982   "Organizational Processes in Music." In *Music, Mind, and Brain,* ed. Manfred Clynes: 119–36. New York and London: Plenum Press.

DeZoete, Beryl, and Walter Spies
1938   *Dance and Drama in Bali.* London: Faber and Faber.

Douglas, Mary
1992   "The Person in an Enterprise Culture." In *Understanding the Enterprise Culture: Themes in the Work of Mary Douglas,* ed. Shaun Hargreaves Heap and Angus Ross: 41–62. Edinburgh: Edinburgh University Press.

Dowling, W. Jay, and Dane L. Harwood
1986   *Music Cognition.* Orlando, San Diego, and New York: Academic Press.

Downey, James
1968   *The Music of American Revivalism.* Ph.D. dissertation [microfilm], Tulane University.

Dreyfus, Hubert L.
1991   *Being-in-the-World: A Commentary on Heidegger's Being and Time, Division I.* Cambridge, Mass.: MIT Press.

Dreyfus, Hubert L., and Stuart E.
1988   "Making a Mind Versus Modeling the Brain: Artificial Intelligence at a Branchpoint." *Daedalus,* Journal of the American Academy of Arts and Sciences (Winter): 15–43.

Edelman, Gerald M.
1989   *The Remembered Present: A Biological Theory of Consciousness.* New York: Basic Books.
1992   *Bright Air, Brilliant Fire: On the Matter of the Mind.* New York: Basic Books.

Egan, Michael J.
1969   *A Structural Analysis of a Sinhalese Healing Ritual.* Ph.D. dissertation, University of Cambridge.

Eiseman, Fred B., Jr.
1989   *Bali: Sekala and Niskala: Essays on Religion, Ritual, and Art,* vol. 1. Berkeley and Singapore: Periplus Editions.

Ekman, Paul
1980   "Biological and Cultural Contributions of Body and Facial Movement in the

Expression of Emotions." In *Explaining Emotions,* ed. Amelie Rorty: 73–101. Berkeley: University of California Press.

Ekman, Paul, R. W. Levenson, and W. V. Friesen

    1983   "Autonomic Nervous System Activity Distinguishes among Emotions." *Science* 221: 1208–10.

Eliot, T. S.

    1943   *Four Quartets.* New York: Harcourt, Brace.

Erickson, Frederick, and Gerald Mohatt

    1982   "Cultural Organization in Participation Structures in Two Classrooms of Indian Students." In *Doing the Ethnography of Schooling: Educational Anthropology in Action,* ed. George Spindler: 132–74. New York: Holt, Rinehart, and Winston.

Errington, Shelly

    1983   "Embodied *Sumange'* in Luwu." *Journal of Asian Studies* 42 (3): 545–70.

    1989   *Meaning and Power in a Southeast Asian Realm.* Princeton, N.J.: Princeton University Press.

Fales, Cornelia

    1998   "Issue of Timbre: Inanqa Chuchotee." *The Garland Encyclopedia of World Music* 1: 164–207.

    2002   "The Paradox of Timbre." *Ethnomusicology* 46 (1): 56–95.

Feld, Steven

    1982   *Sound and Sentiment: Birds, Weeping, Poetics, and Song in Kaluli Expression.* Philadelphia: University of Pennsylvania Press.

Ferdinandus, Epiphanius

    1621   *Centum Historiae seu Observationes et Casus Medici.* Venetiis.

Feynman, Richard

    1965   *The Character of Physical Law.* Cambridge, Mass.: MIT Press.

Fields, Howard L.

    1987   *Pain.* New York: McGraw-Hill.

Fish, Stanley

    1980   *Is There a Text in This Class? The Authority of Interpreting Communities.* Cambridge, Mass.: Harvard University Press.

Flanagan, Owen

    1991   *The Science of the Mind.* Cambridge, Mass.: MIT Press.

Foley, William A.

    1997   *Anthropological Linguistics: An Introduction.* Oxford: Blackwell Publishers.

Freeman, Walter

    1997   "Happiness Doesn't Come in Bottles." *Journal of Consciousness Studies* 4 (1): 67–70.

    2000   "A Neurobiological Role of Music in Social Bonding." In *The Origins of Music,* ed. Nils L. Wallin, Bjorn Merker, and Steven Brown: 411–24. Cambridge, Mass.: MIT Press.

Friedson, Steven M.

    1996   *Dancing Prophets: Musical Experience in Tumbuka Healing.* Chicago: University of Chicago Press.

Frith, Simon

    1987   "Towards an Aesthetic of Popular Music." In *Music and Society: The Politics of Composition, Performance and Reception,* ed. Richard Leppert and Susan McClary: 133–49. Cambridge: Cambridge University Press.

Fuller, Robert C.
 1982   *Mesmerism and the American Cure of Souls.* Philadelphia: University of Pennsylvania Press.
Gabrielsson, Alf, and Erik Lindstrom
 2001   "The Influence of Musical Structure on Emotional Expression." In *Music and Emotion: Theory and Research,* ed. Patrik Juslin and John Sloboda: 223–48. Oxford: Oxford University Press.
Gabrielsson, Alf, and Siv Lindstrom
 1993   "On Strong Experiences of Music." *Musik Psychologie* 10: 118–40. Wilhelmshaven: Florian Noetzel Verlag.
Gabrielsson, Alf, and Siv Lindstrom Wik
 2000   "Strong Experiences of and with Music." In *Musicology and Sister Disciplines: Past, Present, Future.* Proceedings of the Sixteenth International Congress of the International Musicological Society (London 1997), ed. David Greer: 100–08. Oxford: Oxford University Press.
Gabriesson, Alf, and Erik Lindstrom
 2001   "The Influence of Musical Structure on Emotional Expression." In *Music and Emotion: Theory and Research,* ed. Patrik Juslin and John Sloboda: 223–48. Oxford: Oxford University Press.
Gamman, Lorraine, and Margaret Marshment, eds.
 1988   *The Female Gaze: Women as Viewers of Popular Culture.* London: Women's Press.
Geertz, Clifford
 1973a   "The Impact of the Concept of Culture on the Concept of Man." In *The Interpretation of Cultures:* 33–54. New York: Basic Books.
 1973b   "Person, Time, and Conduct in Bali." In *The Interpretation of Cultures:* 360–411. New York: Basic Books.
 1983a   "Blurred genres: The Refiguration of Social Thought." In *Local Knowledge: Further Essays in Interpretive Anthropology:* 19–35. New York: Basic Books.
 1983b   "'Native's Point of View': Anthropological Understanding." In *Local Knowledge: Further Essays in Interpretive Anthropology:* 55–70. New York: Basic Books.
Geertz, Hildred
 1974   "The Vocabulary of Emotion: A Study of Javanese Socialization Processes." In *Culture and Personality: Contemporary Readings:* 249–64. Chicago: Aldine Publishing.
Gergen, Kenneth J.
 1991   *The Saturated Self: Dilemmas of Identity in Contemporary Life.* New York: Basic Books.
Gewehr, Wesley M.
 1930   *The Great Awakening in Virginia, 1740–1790.* Durham, N.C.: Duke University Press.
al-Ghazzali, Abu Hamid Muhammad
 1901–02   "Emotional Religion in Islam as Affected by Music and Singing," from *The Revivification of the Religious Sciences,* [*Ihya 'Ulum ad-Din*], art.VIII, XXVI, trans. Duncan B. Macdonald. *The Journal of the Royal Asiatic Society,* 195–252, 705–748 (1901), 1–28 (1902).
 1991   *The Alchemy of Happiness,* trans. Claud Field, revised and annotated by Elton Daniel. London: M. E. Sharpe.

1990   *Invocations and Supplications: Book IX of The Revival of the Religious Sciences,*
        trans. K. Nakamura. Cambridge: The Islamic Texts Society.

Gnoli, Raniero
    1956   *The Aesthetic Experience According to Abhinava Gupta.* Rome: Instituto Itali-
            ano per il medio ed Estremo Orient.
    1968   *The Aesthetic Experience According to Abhinava Gupta.* Varanasi, India:
            Chowkhamba Publications.

Goldhill, Simon
    1996   "Refracting Classical Vision: Changing Cultures of Viewing." In *Vision in
            Context: Historical and Contemporary Perspectives on Sight,* ed. T. Brennan
            and M. Jay: 17–28. New York and London: Routledge.

Goldstein, Avram
    1968   "Thrills in Response to Music and Other Stimuli." *Physiological Psychology* 8
            (1): 126–29.

Goodenough, Ward, H.
    1970   *Description and Comparison in Cultural Anthropology.* Chicago: Aldine.

Gould, Stephen Jay, and Richard C. Lewontin
    1979   "The Spandrels of San Marco and the Panglossian Paradigm: A Critique of
            the Adaptationist Programme." *Proceedings of the Royal Society of London*
            205: 581–98.

Greeley, Andrew, and William McCready
    1979   "Are We a Nation of Mystics?" In *Consciousness: Brain, States of Awareness
            and Mysticism,* ed. D. Goleman and R. J. Davidson: 178–83. New York: Har-
            per and Row.

Green, Elmer E., and Alyce M. Green
    1989   "General and Specific Applications of Thermal Biofeedback." In *Biofeedback:
            Principles and Practice for Clinicians,* 3rd ed., ed. John V. Basmajian: 209–21.
            Baltimore: Williams and Wilkins.

Griffith, Niall, and Peter M. Todd, eds.
    1999   *Musical Networks: Parallel Distributed Perception and Performance.* Cam-
            bridge, Mass.: MIT Press.

Grotowski, Jerzy
    1968   *Towards a Poor Theatre.* New York: Simon and Schuster.

Guenther, Herbert V.
    1976   *The Tantric View of Life.* Boulder, Colo. and London: Shambhala Publica-
            tions.

Hacking, Ian
    1995   *Rewriting the Soul: Multiple Personality and the Sciences of Memory.* Prince-
            ton, N.J.: Princeton University Press.

Hall, Edward
    1977   *Beyond Culture.* Garden City, N.Y.: Anchor Books.

Halverson, John
    1971   "Dynamics of Exorcism: The Sinhalese Sanniyakum." *History of Religions* 10
            (4): 334–59.

Hamonic, Gilbert
    1975   "Travestissement et bisexualité chez les 'bissu' du Pays Bugis." *Archipel* 10:
            121–34.
    1987   *Le Langage Des Dieux: Cultes et Pouvoirs Pre-islamique en Pays Bugis Celebes-*

Sud, Indonesie. Paris: Editions Du Centre National De La Recherche Scientifique.

Hayward, Jeremy
    1998   "A Rdzogs-Chen Buddhist Interpretation of the Sense of Self." *Journal of Consciousness Studies* 5 (5–6): 611–26.

Hebdige, Dick
    1995   "Fabulous Confusion! Pop before Pop?" In *Visual Culture,* ed. Chris Jenks: 96–122. London and New York: Routledge.

Heidegger, Martin
    1962   *Being and Time.* New York: Harpers.

Heimert, Alan, and Perry Miller, eds.
    1967   *The Great Awakening: Documents Illustrating the Crisis and Its Consequences.* Indianapolis and New York: Bobbs-Merrill.

Herdman, John
    1991   *The Double in Nineteenth-Century Fiction: The Shadow Life.* New York: St. Martin's Press.

Hobson, J. Allan
    1994   *The Chemistry of Conscious States: How the Brain Changes Its Mind.* Boston: Little, Brown.

Hooper, Judith, and Dick Teresi
    1986   *3-Pound Universe.* New York: Dell.

Huron, David
    2002   "An Instinct for Music: Is Music an Evolutionary Adaptation?" Lecture 2, The 1999 Ernest Bloch Lectures. *Annals of the New York Academy of Sciences* 930: 43–61.

Hutchins, Edwin
    1995   *Cognition in the Wild.* Cambridge, Mass.: MIT Press.

Ihde, Don
    1977   *Experimental Phenomenology: An Introduction.* New York: Capricorn Books, G. P. Putnam's Sons.

Imberty, Michel
    2000   "The Question of Innate Competencies in Musical Communication." In *The Origins of Music,* ed. Nils L. Wallin, Bjorn Merker, and Steven Brown: 449–62. Cambridge, Mass.: MIT Press.

Inglis, Brian
    1989   *Trance: A Natural History of Altered States of Mind.* Toronto: Grafton Books.

Irvine, Judith T.
    1990   "Registering Affect: Heteroglossia in the Linguistic Expression of Emotion." In *Language and the Politics of Emotion,* ed. Catherine Lutz and Lila Abu-Lughod, 126–61. Cambridge: Cambridge University Press.

Isaac, Rhys
    1974   "Evangelical Revolt: The Nature of the Baptists' Challenge to the Traditional Order in Virginia, 1765 to 1775." *William and Mary Quarterly* 31 (3): 345–68.

Jackson, George Pullen
    1964   *Spiritual Folk-Songs of Early America.* New York: Dover.
    1975   *White and Negro Spirituals: Their Life Span and Kinship.* New York: DaCapo Press.

James, William
    1890   "The Hidden Self." *Scribner's Magazine* 7: 361–73.

1950 [1890]   *The Principles of Psychology,* 2 vols. New York: Dover Publications.
1982 [1902]   *The Varieties of Religious Experience.* New York: Penguin Books.
Jamison, Kay Redfield
    1993   *Touched with Fire: Manic-Depressive Illness and the Artistic Temperament.* New York: Free Press.
Janet, Pierre
    1920   *The Major Symptoms of Hysteria: Fifteen Lectures Given in the Medical School of Harvard University.* 2nd ed. New York: Macmillan.
Jefferson, Thomas
    1994 [1776]   *Declaration of Independence and the Constitution of the United States of America: The Texts.* Washington, D.C.: National Defense Press.
Jenks, Chris, ed.
    1995   *Visual Culture.* London: Routledge.
Johnson, James H.
    1995   *Listening in Paris.* Berkeley: University of California Press.
Johnson, Mark
    1987   *The Body in the Mind: The Bodily Basis of Imagination, Reason, and Meaning.* Chicago: University of Chicago Press.
Kamus Bali-Indonesia.
    1991   Dinas Pendidikan Dasar Propinsi Dati I Bali.
Kapferer, Bruce
    1991   *A Celebration of Demons: Exorcism and the Aesthetics of Healing in Sri Lanka.* Washington, D.C.: Smithsonian Institution Press.
Katz, Richard
    1982   "Accepting 'Boiling Energy': The Experience of !Kia Healing among the !Kung." *Ethos* 19: 348.
Katz, Steven T.
    1978   "Language, Epistemology, and Mysticism." In *Mysticism and Philosophical Analysis,* ed. Steven T. Katz: 22–74. New York: Oxford University Press.
Kaudern, Walter
    1927   *Ethnographical studies in Celebes,* vol. 4. The Hague: Martinus Nijhoff.
Keijzer, Fred
    2002   "Representation in Dynamical and Embodied Cognition." *Cognitive Systems Research Journal,* Special Issue, 3 (3): 275–88.
Keil, Charles
    1987   "Participatory Discrepancies and the Power of Music." *Cultural Anthropology* 2 (3): 275–83.
Keil, Charles, and Steven Feld
    1994   *Music Grooves: Essays and Dialogues.* Chicago: University of Chicago Press.
Kenny, Michael G.
    1986   *The Passion of Ansel Bourne: Multiple Personality in American Culture.* Washington, D.C.: Smithsonian Institution Press.
Kern, Stephen
    1996   *Eyes of Love: The Gaze in English and French Painting and Novels: 1840–1900.* London: Reaktion Books.
Khan, Dargah Quli
    1989   *Muraqqa'-e-Delhi* [The Mughal Capital in Muhammad Shah's Time], trans. Chander Shekhar and Shama Mitra Chenoy. Delhi: Deputy Publication.

Khan, Hazrat Inayat
  1994   *The Mysticism of Music, Sound and Word: The Sufi Message,* vol. 2. Delhi:
           Motilal Banarsidass.
Kircher, Athanasius
  1643   *Editio secunda post Romanam multo correctior.* Coloniae Agrippinae.
Kivy, Peter
  1989   *Sound Sentiment: an Essay on the Musical Emotions.* Philadelphia: Temple
           University Press.
Krumhansl, Carol L.
  1997   "An Exploratory Study of Musical Emotions and Psychophysiology." *Cana-
           dian Journal of Experimental Psychology* 51 (4): 336–52.
Kulatillake, Cyril de Silva
  1976   *Metre, Melody and Rhythm in Sinhala Music.* Colombo: Sri Lanka Broadcast-
           ing Corporation.
Lacan, Jacques
  1968   *The Language of the Self: The Function of Language in Psychoanalysis,* trans.
           Anthony Wilden. Baltimore, Md., and London: Johns Hopkins University Press.
Laderman, Carol
  1996   "The Poetics of Healing in Malay Shamanistic Performances." In *The Per-
           formance of Healing,* ed. Carol Laderman and Marina Roseman: 115–41. New
           York: Routledge.
Lakoff, George
  1987   *Women, Fire and Dangerous Things: What Categories Reveal about the Mind.*
           Chicago: University of Chicago Press.
Lathief, Halilintar
  1983   *Tari-Tarian Daerah Bugis.* Yogyakarta: Institut Press Yogyakarta.
Lazarus, Richard S.
  1991   *Emotion and Adaptation.* Oxford: Oxford University Press.
Leach, Edmund
  1981   "A Poetics of Power." *New Republic* 184: 14.
LeDoux, Joseph
  1996   *The Emotional Brain: The Mysterious Underpinnings of Emotional Life.* New
           York: Simon and Schuster.
Lerdahl, Fred, and Ray Jackendoff
  1983   *A Generative Theory of Tonal Music.* Cambridge, Mass.: MIT Press.
Lévi-Strauss, Claude
  1962   *The Savage Mind.* London: Wiedenfeld and Nicholson.
Levy, Robert I.
  1984   "Emotion, Knowing, and Culture." In *Culture Theory: Essays on Mind, Self,
           and Emotion,* ed. Richard Shweder and Robert LeVine: 214–37. Cambridge:
           Cambridge University Press.
Lewis, Michael, and Linda Michalson
  1983   *Children's Emotions and Moods: Developmental Theory and Measurement.*
           New York/London: Plenum Press.
Lewis, Michael, and Carolyn Saarni, eds.
  1985   *The Socialization of Emotions.* New York/London: Plenum Press.
Little, Lewis Peyton
  1938   *Imprisoned Preachers and Religious Liberty in Virginia.* Lynchburg, Va.: J. P.
           Bell.

Livingston, Robert B.
  1978   *Sensory Processing, Perception, and Behavior.* New York: Raven Press.
Lovejoy, Arthur O.
  1948   *Essays in the History of Ideas.* Baltimore, Md.: Johns Hopkins Press.
  1964 [1936]   *The Great Chain of Being: a Study of the History of an Idea.* Cambridge,
          Mass.: Harvard University Press.
Lovejoy, David S.
  1969   *Religious Enthusiasm and the Great Awakening.* Englewood Cliffs, N.J.: Pren-
          tice Hall.
Lutz, Catherine A.
  1986   "Emotion, Thought, and Estrangement: Emotion as a Cultural Category."
          Cultural Anthropology 1: 287–309.
  1988   *Unnatural Emotions: Everyday Sentiments on a Micronesian Atoll and Their
          Challenge to Western Theory.* Chicago: University of Chicago Press.
Lutz, Catherine A., and Lila Abu-Lughod, eds.
  1990   "Introduction: Emotion, Discourse, and the Politics of Everyday Life." In
          Language and the Politics of Emotion: 1–23. Cambridge: Cambridge Univer-
          sity Press.
Maslow, A. H.
  1968   *Towards a Psychology of Being.* 2nd ed. New York: Van Nostrand Reinhold.
Masson, Jeffrey M., and M. V. Patwardhan
  1969   *Santarasa.* Poona: Bhandarkar Oriental Research Institute.
  1977   "The Dhvanyaloka and the Dhvanyalokalocana: A Translation of the Fourth
          Uddyota," Pts. 1–2. *Journal of the American Oriental Society* 97 (3): 285–304,
          (4): 423–40.
Maturana, Humberto, and Francisco Varela
  1987   *The Tree of Knowledge: The Biological Roots of Human Understanding.* Boston
          and London: New Science Library.
McClary, Susan
  1991   *Feminine Endings: Music, Gender, and Sexuality.* Minneapolis: University of
          Minnesota Press.
McDaniel, June
  1995   "Emotion in Bengali Religious Thought: Substance and Metaphor." In *Emo-
          tions in Asian thought: A Dialogue in Comparative Philosophy,* ed. J. Marks
          and R. T. Ames: 39–63. Albany: State University of New York Press.
McNeill, William H.
  1995   *Keeping Together in Time: Dance and Drill in Human History.* Cambridge,
          Mass.: Harvard University Press.
Mead, George Herbert
  1962 [1934]   *Mind, Self and Society: From the Standpoint of a Social Behaviorist.*
          Chicago: University of Chicago Press.
Melzack, Ronald,
  1992   "Phantom Limbs." *Scientific American* 266 (4): 120–26.
Merleau-Ponty, Maurice
  1962   *Phenomenology of Perception,* trans. Colin Smith. London: Routledge and
          Kegan Paul.
  1963   *The Structure of Behavior,* trans. Alden Fischer. Boston: Beacon Press.
  1964   *The Primacy of Perception.* Evanston, Ill.: Northwestern University Press.

Merriam, Alan P.
   1964   *The Anthropology of Music.* Evanston, Ill.: Northwestern University Press.
Meyer, Leonard
   1956   *Emotion and Meaning in Music.* Chicago: University of Chicago Press.
Michaelides, Solon
   1978   *The Music of Ancient Greece: An Encyclopaedia.* London: Faber and Faber Limited.
Minsky, Marvin
   1982   "Music, Mind and Meaning." In *Music, Mind and Brain: The Neuropsychology of Music,* ed. Manfred Clynes: 1–19. New York and London: Plenum Press.
Mitchell, W. J. Thomas
   1986   *Iconology: Image, Text, Ideology.* Chicago: University of Chicago Press.
Mora, George
   1963   "An Historical and Sociopsychiatric Appraisal of Tarantism and Its Importance in the Tradition of Psychotherapy of Mental Disorders." *Bulletin of the History of Medicine* 37: 417–39.
Morley, David
   1995   "Television: Not So Much a Visual Medium, More a Visible Object." In *Visual Culture,* ed. Chris Jenks: 170–89. New York and London: Routledge.
Mozart, Wolfgang A.
   1790   *Cosí fan Tutte:* An Opera in Two Acts. New York: Broude Brothers (1940).
Myers, Fred R.
   1979   "Emotions and the Self: A Theory of Personhood and Political Order among Pintupi Aborigines." *Ethos: Journal of the Society for Psychological Anthropology* 7: 343–70.
Narmour, Eugene
   1990   *The Analysis and Cognition of Basic Melodic Structures.* Chicago: University of Chicago Press.
Needham, Rodney
   1967   "Percussion and Transition." *Man* 2: 606–14.
   1981   *Circumstantial Deliveries.* Berkeley: University of California Press.
Neher, Andrew
   1961   "Auditory Driving Observed with Scalp Electrodes in Normal Subjects." *Electroencephalography and Clinical Neurophysiology* 13: 449–51.
   1962   "A Physiological Explanation of Unusual Behavior in Ceremonies Involving Drums." *Human Biology* 34: 151–60.
Nettl, Bruno
   1983   *The Study of Ethnomusicology: Twenty-nine Issues and Concepts.* Urbana: University of Illinois Press.
Nuñez, Raphael E.
   1997   "Eating Soup with Chopsticks: Dogmas, Difficulties and Alternatives in the Study of Conscious Experience." *Journal of Consciousness Studies* 4 (2): 143–66.
Nyklicek, Ivan, Julian F. Thayer, and Lorenz J. P. Van Doornen
   1997   "Cardiorespiratory Differentiation of Musically-Induced Emotions." *Journal of Psychophysiology* 11: 304–21.
O'Neill, John
   1995   "Foucault's Optics: The (in)Vision of Mortality and Modernity." In *Visual Culture,* ed. Chris Jenks: 190–201. London and New York: Routledge.

Ornstein, Robert, and Richard F. Thompson
 1984   *The Amazing Brain.* Boston: Houghton Mifflin Company.
Ortega y Gasset, José
 1957   *Man and People,* trans. Willard R. Trask. New York: W. W. Norton.
Ortony, Andrew, Gerald L. Clore, and Allan Collins, eds.
 1988   *The Cognitive Structure of Emotions.* Cambridge: Cambridge University
          Press.
Oughourlian, Jean Michel
 1991   *The Puppet of Desire: the Psychology of Hysteria, Possession and Hypnosis.*
          Stanford, Calif.: Stanford University Press.
Panksepp, Jaak
 1992   "A Critical Role for Affective Neuroscience in Resolving What Is Basic About
          Basic Emotions." *Psychological Review* 99: 554–60.
 1995   "The Emotional Sources of 'Chills' Induced by Music." *Music Perception* 13
          (2): 171–207.
 1998a   "The Periconscious Substrates of Consciousness: Affective States and the
          Evolutionary Origins of the Self." *Journal of Consciousness Studies* 5–6: 566–82.
 1998b   *Affective Neuroscience: The Foundations of Human and Animal Emotions.*
          New York: Oxford University Press.
 2001a   "On the Subcortical Sources of Basic Human Emotions and the Primacy of
          Emotional Affective (Action-Perception) Process in Human Consciousness."
          Evolution and Cognition 7 (2): 134–40.
 2001b   "The Neuro-evolutionary Cusp between Emotions and Cognitions: Emer-
          gence of a Unified Mind Science." *Evolution and Cognition* 7 (2): 141–63.
Peirce, Charles
 1931–38 *The Collected Papers of Charles Sanders Peirce,* 6 vols., ed. Charles Hart-
          shorne and Paul Weiss. Cambridge, Mass.: Harvard University Press.
Pelras, Christian
 1976   "Notes to the Recording *Les Musiques de Celebes Indonesia: Musique Toradja
          et Bugis.*" Paris: Société Française de Productions Phonographiques.
 1996   *The Bugis.* Oxford: Blackwell.
Perer, Maria Luisa Gatti, ed.
 1998   *La Chiesa di San Marco in Milano.* Banca Popolare de Milano.
Peretz, Isabelle, and Jose Morais
 1988   "Determinants of Laterality for Music: Toward an Information Processing
          Account." In *Handbook of Dichotic Listening: The Theory, Methods and Re-
          search,* ed. Kenneth Hugdahl: 323–58. Chichester: John Wiley and Sons.
Persische Miniaturen
 1960   Photography by Werner Forman, Text by Vera Kubickova. Praha: Artia.
Petsche, H., K. Lindner, and P. Rappelsberger
 1988   "The EEG: An Adequate Method to Concretize Brain Processes Elicited by
          Music." *Music Perception* 6 (2): 133–59.
Pfeiffer, John E.
 1982   *The Creative Explosion: An Inquiry into the Origins of Art and Religion.* New
          York: Harper and Row.
Piaget, Jean
 1959   *The Language and Thought of the Child.* London: Routledge and Kegan Paul.
 1969   *Judgment and Reasoning in the Child.* London: Routledge and Kegan Paul.

Pinker, Steven
   1994   *The Language Instinct.* New York: William Morrow.
Piszczalski, Martin, and Bernard A. Galler
   1982   "A Computer Model of Music Recognition." In *Music, Mind, and Brain: The Neuropsychology of Music,* ed. Manfred Clynes: 399–416. New York and London: Plenum Press.
Plutchik, Robert
   1980   *Emotion: A Psychoevolutionary Synthesis.* New York: Harper and Row.
Prince, Morton
   1930   *The Dissociation of a Personality: A Biographical Study in Abnormal Psychology.* London: Longmans, Green, and Co.
Qureshi, Regula Burckhardt
   1986   *Sufi Music of India and Pakistan: Sound, Context and Meaning in Qawwali.* Cambridge: Cambridge University Press.
Racy, Ali Jihad
   1991   "Creativity and Ambience: An Ecstatic Feedback Model from Arab Music." *The World of Music* 33 (3): 7–28.
   2003   *Making Music in the Arab World: The Culture and Artistry of Tarab.* Cambridge: Cambridge University Press.
Raffman, Diana
   1993   *Language, Music, and Mind.* Cambridge, Mass.: MIT Press.
Rider, Mark S., and Charles T. Eagle, Jr.
   1986   "Rhythmic Entrainment as a Mechanism for Learning in Music Therapy." In *Rhythm in Psychological, Linguistic and Musical Processes,* ed. James Evans and Manfred Clynes: 225–48. Springfield, Ill.: Charles C. Thomas.
Rosaldo, Michelle Z.
   1980   *Knowledge and Passion: Ilongot Notions of Self and Social Life.* Cambridge: Cambridge University Press.
   1984   "Toward an Anthropology of Self and Feeling." In *Culture Theory: Essays on Mind, Self, and Emotion,* ed. Richard Shweder and Robert Levine: 137–57. Cambridge: Cambridge University Press.
Roseman, Marina
   1991   *Healing Sounds from the Malaysian Rainforest.* Berkeley: University of California Press.
   1996   " 'Pure Products Go Crazy': Rainforest Healing in a Nation-State." In *The Performance of Healing,* ed. Carol Laderman and Marina Roseman: 233–69. New York: Routledge.
Rouget, Gilbert
   1980   *La Musique et la Transe: Esquisse d'une Theorie Generale des Relations de la Musique et de la Possession.* Paris: Edition Gallimard.
   1985   *Music and Trance: A Theory of the Relations between Music and Possession,* trans. Brunhilde Biebuyck. Chicago: University of Chicago Press.
Rousseau, Jean-Jacques
   1970 [1781]   *Essai sur l'origine des langues : où il est parlé de la mélodie et de l'imitation musicale,* ed. Charles Porset. Bordeaux: G. Ducros.
   1986   *The First and Second Discourses and Essay on the Origin of Languages.* New York: Harper and Row.
Rowell, Lewis
   1992   *Music and Thought in Early India.* Chicago: University of Chicago Press.

Russell, James A.
    1991a   "Culture and the Categorization of Emotions." *Psychological Bulletin* 110: 326–450.
    1991b   "In Defense of a Prototype Approach to Emotion Concepts." *Journal of Personality and Social Psychology* 60: 37–47.

Ryle, Gilbert
    1949   *The Concept of Mind.* London: Hutchinson.

Sacks, Oliver
    1984   *A Leg to Stand On.* New York: Summit Books.

Scarry, Elaine
    1985   *The Body in Pain: The Making and Unmaking of the World.* New York: Oxford University Press.

Schank, Roger C., and Robert P. Abelson
    1977   *Scripts, Plans, Goals and Understanding: An Inquiry into Human Knowledge Structures.* Hillsdale, N.J.: Lawrence Erlbaum Associates.

Scherer, Klaus R., and Marcel R. Zentner
    2001   "Emotional Effects of Music: Production Rules." In *Music and Emotion: Theory and Research,* ed. Patrik Juslin and John Sloboda: 361–92. Oxford: Oxford University Press.

Schieffelin, Edward
    1996   "On Failure and Performance: Throwing the Medium Out of the Séance." In *The Performance of Healing,* ed. Carol Laderman and Marina Roseman: 59–89. New York: Routledge.

Searle, John R.
    2002   "End of the Revolution." Review of *New Horizons in the Study of Language and Mind* by Noam Chomsky. *The New York Review of Books* 49 (3): 33–36.

Seeger, Anthony
    1987   *Why Suya Sing: A Musical Anthropology of an Amazonian People.* Cambridge: Cambridge University Press.

Serafine, Mary Louise
    1988   *Music as Cognition: The Development of Thought in Sound.* New York: Columbia University Press.

Shankar, Ravi
    1968   *My Music, My Life.* New Delhi: Vikas Publications.

Shepherd, John, and Jennifer Giles-David
    1991   "Music, Text and Subjectivity." In *Music as Social Text:* 174–85. Cambridge: Polity Press.

Shirokogoroff, S. M.
    1935   *Psychomental Complex of the Tungus.* London: Kegan Paul, Trench, Trubner, and Co.

Showalter, Elaine
    1993   "Hysteria, Feminism, and Gender." In Sander L. Gilman, Helen King, Roy Porter, G. S. Rousseau, and Elaine Showalter, *Hysteria beyond Freud:* 286–344. Berkeley: University of California Press.

Shweder, Richard A.
    1985   "Menstrual Pollution, Soul Loss, and the Comparative Study of Emotions." In *Culture and Depression: Studies in the Anthropology and Cross-cultural Psychiatry of Affect and Disorder,* ed. Arthur Kleinman and Byron Good: 182–215. Berkeley: University of California Press.

Shweder, Richard A., and Bourne, Edmund J.
  1984   "Does the Concept of the Person Vary Cross-Culturally?" In *Culture Theory: Essays on Mind, Self, and Emotion,* ed. Richard Shweder and Robert Levine: 158–99. Cambridge: Cambridge University Press.
Siddiqui, Mahmud Husain
  1979   *The Memoirs of Sufis Written in India.* Baroda, India: Maharaja Sayajirao University.
Sigerist, Henry E.
  1944   *Civilization and Disease.* Ithaca, N.Y.: Cornell University Press.
Slater, Don
  1995   "Photography and Modern Vision: The Spectacle of 'Natural Magic.'" In *Visual Culture,* ed. Chris Jenks: 218–37. London and New York: Routledge.
Sloboda, John
  1985   *The Musical Mind: The Cognitive Psychology of Music.* Oxford: Clarendon Press.
  1991   "Music Structure and Emotional Response: Some Empirical Findings." *Psychology of Music* 19: 110–20.
Small, Christopher
  1987   *Music of the Common Tongue: Survival and Celebration in Afro-American Music.* London: John Calder; New York: Riverrun Press.
Smith, J. C., and Carla Ferstman
  1996   "Knowledge and the Languaging Body." In *The Castration of Oedipus: Feminism, Psychoanalysis, and the Will to Power,* ed. J. C. Smith: 52–79. New York: New York University Press.
Snellgrove, David L.
  1987   *Indo-Tibetan Buddhism: Indian Buddhists and Their Tibetan Successors,* 2 vols. Boston: Shambhala Publications.
Sparshott, Francis
  1983   "Prospects for Aesthetics." *The World of Music* 25 (3): 3–12.
Soeradipoera, R. Ng., Poerwasoewignja, R., and R. Wirawangsa, eds.
  1912–15   *Serat Tjentini: Babon Asli Saking Kita Leiden ing Negari Nederland.* 8 vols. Batavia: Ruygrof.
Solie, Ruth A.
  1993   *Musicology and Difference: Gender and Sexuality in Music Scholarship.* Berkeley: University of California Press.
Solomon, Robert C.
  1984   "The Jamesian Theory of Emotion in Anthropology." In *Culture Theory: Essays on Mind, Self, and Emotion,* ed. Richard Shweder and Robert LeVine: 238–54. Cambridge: Cambridge University Press.
Sparshott, Francis
  1983   "Prospects for Aesthetics." *The World of Music* 25 (3): 3–12.
Spiro, Melford E.
  1984   "Some Reflections on Cultural Determinism and Relativism with Special Reference to Emotion and Reason." In *Culture Theory: Essays on Mind, Self, and Emotion,* ed. Richard Shweder and Robert LeVine: 323–46. Cambridge: Cambridge University Press.
Spivak, Gayatri Chakravorty
  1988   *In Other Worlds: Essays in Cultural Politics.* New York: Routledge.

Squire, Larry R.
  1987   *Memory and Brain.* New York: Oxford University Press.
Stanislavsky, Konstantin
  1936   *An Actor Prepares,* trans. Elizabeth R. Hapgood. New York: Theatre Arts
          Books.
  1958   *Stanslavski's Legacy: A Collection of Comments on a Variety of Aspects of an
          Actor's Art and Life,* ed. and trans. Elizabeth R. Hapgood. New York: Theatre
          Arts Books.
Steiner, George
  1984   "The Retreat from the Word." In *George Steiner: A Reader:* 283–304. New
          York: Oxford University Press.
Stoller, Paul
  1996   "Sounds and Things: Pulsations of Power in Songhay." In *The Performance
          of Healing,* ed. Carol Laderman and Marina Roseman: 165–84. New York:
          Routledge.
Stone, Ruth
  1982   *Let the Inside be Sweet: The Interpretation of Music Event among the Kpelle of
          Liberia.* Bloomington: Indiana University Press.
Strunk, Oliver
  1950   *Source Readings in Music History from Classical Antiquity through the Roman-
          tic Era.* New York: W. W. Norton and Co.
Sutton, R. Anderson
  1995   "Performing Arts and Cultural Politics in South Sulawesi." *Bijdragen Tot de
          Taal, Land-en Volkenkunde* 151: 672–99.
Tambiah, Stanley Jeyaraja
  1985   *Culture, Thought and Social Action: An Anthropological Perspective.* Cam-
          bridge, Mass.: Harvard University Press.
Tannen, Deborah
  1984   *Conversational Style: Analyzing Talk among Friends.* Norwood, N.J.: Ablex.
Taylor, Charles
  1985   "How Is Mechanism Conceivable?" In *Human Agency and Language: Philo-
          sophical Papers I:* 164–86. Cambridge: Cambridge University Press.
  1988   "The Moral Topography of the Self." In *Hermeneutics and Psychological
          Theory: Interpretive Perspectives on Personality, Psychotherapy, and Psycho-
          pathology,* ed. Stanley B. Messer, Louis A. Sass, and Robert L. Woolfolk: 298–
          320. New Brunswick, N.J.: Rutgers University Press.
  1989   *Sources of the Self: The Making of the Modern Identity.* Cambridge, Mass.:
          Harvard University Press.
Terhardt, Ernst
  1982   "Impact of Computers on Music: An Outline." In *Music, Mind and Brain:
          The Neuropsychology of Music,* ed. Manfred Clynes: 353–69. New York: Ple-
          num Press.
Thomas, David
  1774   *The Virginia Baptists, or, A View and Defence of the Christian religion, as it is
          Professed by the Baptists of Virginia.* Baltimore, Md.: Printed by Enoch Story,
          living in Gay Street [microfilm].
Todd, Peter M., and D. Gareth Loy, eds.
  1991   *Music and Connectionism.* Cambridge, Mass.: MIT Press.

Tolbert, Elizabeth
    1992   "Theories of Meaning and Music Cognition: An Ethnomusicological Approach." *The World of Music* 34 (3): 7–21.
Tramo, Mark Jude
    2001   "Music of the Hemisphere." *Science* 291: 54–56.
Treitler, Leo
    1993   "Reflections on the Communication of Affect and Idea through Music." In *Psychoanalytic Explorations in Music*, 2nd series, ed. S. Feder, R. Karmel, and G. Pollock: 43–62. Madison, Conn.: International Universities Press.
Tupa, Nursiah
    1997   "Sistem Pronomina Persona Bahasa Bugis." In *Bunga Rampai: Hasil Penelitian Bahasa dan Sastra:* 139–212. Ujung Pandang: Balai Penelitian Bahasa.
Turino, Thomas
    1993   *Moving Away from Silence: Music of the Peruvian Altiplano and the Experience of Urban Migration*. Chicago: University of Chicago Press.
Turner, Victor
    1983   "Body, Brain, and Culture." *Zygon* 18: 221–45.
van Noorden, Leon
    1982   "Two Channel Pitch Perception." In *Music, Mind and Brain: The Neuropsychology of Music*, ed. Manfred Clynes: 251–69. New York and London: Plenum Press.
Varela, Francisco J., Evan Thompson, and Eleanor Rosch
    1991   *The Embodied Mind: Cognitive Science and Human Experience*. Cambridge, Mass.: MIT Press.
Vaughn, Kathryn
    1990   "Exploring Emotion in Sub-structural Aspects of Karelian Lament: Application of Time Series Analysis to Digitalized Melody." *Yearbook for Traditional Music* 22: 106–22.
Viswanathan, Tanjore, and Jody Cormack
    1998   "Melodic Improvisation in Karnatak Music: The Manifestation of Raga." In *In the Course of Performance: Studies in the World of Musical Improvisation*, ed. Bruno Nettl and Melinda Russell: 219–33. Chicago: University of Chicago Press.
Voltaire
    1999 [1759]   *Candide,* trans. and ed. Daniel Gordon. Boston and New York: St. Martin's.
Vos, Joos, and Rudolf Rasch
    1982   "The Perceptual Onset of Music Tones." In *Music, Mind, and Brain: The Neuropsychology of Music*, ed. Manfred Clynes: 299–319. New York and London: Plenum Press.
Vygotsky, Lev
    1986   *Thought and Language*. Cambridge, Mass.: MIT Press.
Wacker, Grant
    2001   *Heaven Below: Early Pentecostals and American Culture*. Cambridge, Mass.: Harvard University Press.
Wallin, Nils L.
    1991   *Biomusicology: Neurophysiological, Neuropsychological, and Evolutionary Perspectives on the Origins and Purposes of Music*. Stuyvesant, New York: Pendragon Press.

Walter, V. J., and W. Grey Walter
1949   "The Central Effects of Rhythmic Sensory Stimulation." *Electroencephalography and Clinical Neurophysiology* 1 (1): 57–86.
Weinberger, Norman M., and Thomas M. McKenna
1988   "Sensitivity of Single Neurons in Auditory Cortex to Contour: Toward a Neurophysiology of Music Perception." *Music Perception* 5 (4): 355–89.
Weisberger, Bernard A.
1958   *They Gathered at the River: The Story of the Great Revivalists and Their Impact upon Religion in America.* Boston and Toronto: Little, Brown.
Wittgenstein, Ludwig
1958   *Philosophical Investigations.* 3rd ed., trans. G. E. M. Anscombe. New York: Macmillan.
Wood, William W.
1965   *Culture and Personality Aspects of the Pentecostal Holiness Religion.* The Hague/Paris: Mouton.
Wong, Deborah
2001   *Sounding the Center: History and Aesthetics in Thai Buddhist Performance.* Chicago: University of Chicago Press.
Young, James O.
1999   "The Cognitive Value of Music." *The Journal of Aesthetics and Art Criticism* 57 (1): 1–54.
Ziemke, Tom
2002   "Introduction to Special Issue on Situated and Embodied Cognition." *Cognitive Systems Research Journal,* Special Issue 3 (3): 271–74.
Žižek, Slavoj
1991   *Looking Awry: An Introduction to Jacques Lacan through Popular Culture.* Cambridge, Mass.: MIT Press.
1996   "'I hear you with my eyes'; or, The Invisible Master." In *Gaze and Voice as Love Objects,* ed. Renata Saleci and Slavoj Žižek: 90–126. Durham, N.C.: Duke University Press.
Zuckerkandl, Victor
1956   *Sound and Symbol: Music and the External World,* trans. Willard R. Trask. New York: Pantheon Books.

Index

monoamines, 133, 148; neuropeptides, 9; neurotransmitters, 9, 118; oxytocin, 53, 56; peptides, 133, 148

brain parts: amygdala, 50–51, 56, *133,* 162; auditory cortex, 37, 112, 115, 165; basal forebrain, 56, 132–133, *133,* 136, *137,* 139; brain stem, 47, *48,* 50–51, 117, 132, 134, 139, 148, 160; brain stem nuclei, 56, *133,* 136, *137;* cortex, 47, 50–51, 56, 111, 132, 139, 148, 164; frontal lobe, *48,* 90, 112, 114–115; hypothalamus, 50, 56, 132, *133,* 136, *137,* 160; limbic system, 50, 115, 117; neocortex, 49, 56, 134; neuron, 3, 9, 112–118, 132, 142; somatosensory cortices, 50, 136, 162–163, 165; temporal lobe, *48,* 114–115; thalamus, 56, 139, 148; ventromedial prefrontal cortex, 56, *133,* 160, 162

Brazil, 73, 157

Brennan, Teresa, 70

Brouillet, Pierre-André, painting of Charcot's classroom, *21*

Bruner, Jerome, 5

Buddha, 30, 42

Buddhist, 30, 57, 60, 88, 145, 164

Bugis, 100–102, 104–106, 163

Buranelli, Vincent, 16–18

Caciola, Nancy, 13–14, 62

Canada, 128

Cartesian. *See* Descartes, René

catatonic state, 1

Catholic Church. *See* Roman Catholic Church

Chadwick, Henry, 80

Chalmers, David J., 118

Chapple, Eliot D., 164

Charcot, Jean Martin, 13, 20–21, *21,* 22–23

chills, 11, 52–56, 63, 160

Chomsky, Noam, 5

Christian, 1, 42–43, 61–62, 79, 94–95, 99, 106, 118, 145

Church of England, 93–94

Churchland, P. S., 122

Clore, Gerald L., 49

Clynes, Manfred, 122

cognitive science, 6, 8–9, 117, 121–122

Collins, Allan, 49

computer studies, 5–6

Condon, William, 128, 164

Congo, 52

consciousness: core, 11, 134–141, 145–146, 149; core and music, 141, 143, *143;* double, 20, 24, 38–39; extended, 11, 134–135, 139–141, 144–145, 147; states of, v, 3, 22, 38, 57–58, 60, 76, 108, 118, 127, 132, 146–147, 150, 153, 164–165; theory of, 2, 4, 9, 11, 29, 43, 111, 117–118, 122, 131–132, 134, 141; trance, 3, 7, 11–12, 24, 38–40, 45, 56, 66, 68, 82, 84, 89, 124, 126, 131–134, 144, 147–148, 150–151, 153. *See also* emotion, consciousness and; self, autobiographical; self, core

Coomaraswamy, Ananda K., 76

Cormack, Jody, 73

Cornelius, Randolph, 46–47

Cox, Harvey, 99

Crow, Douglas Karim, 60, 82

Csikszentmihalyi, Mihaly, 161

Csordas, Thomas J., 30

Dahlhaus, Carl, 147

Damasio, Antonio, 4, 9, 11, 29, 47–51, 67, 88, 91, 117, 120, 131, 133, 145–146, 148–149, 160; definition of image, 165; definition of map, 164–165; *Descartes' Error,* 162–163; *The Feeling of What Happens,* 132; theory of consciousness, 111, 132, 134–141

dance, 1, 4, 7, 10, 29, 31–32, 34–36, 54, 57, 62, 70, 74, 76, 78, 80, 83, 86, 94–95, 97, 99, 103–104, *104,* 106, 114, 118, 124, 126–129, 141, 144, 147–148, 153–154, 158; *Bharata Natyam,* 76

Darnton, Robert, 17

Darwin, Charles, 9, 49

Date, Henry, 98

Davidson, Richard J., 73

Davies, John Booth, 26

Decker, Hannah, 15, 22

deity, 14, 27, 40, 42–44, 83–84, 102–105, 132, 147

demon, 13, 27, 30–32, 34, 40, 42, 83–84, 142. *See also* possession trance, demonic

Dennett, Daniel C., 29, 122, 162

Descartes, René, 90–92, 162; theory of being (Cartesian dualism), 4–6, 90–92, 97, 100, 106, 157

Deutsch, Diana, 5

devil, 14–15

DeZoete, Beryl, 85

Dhadi, Chalbal, 81

Dibia, I Wayan, 55, 88

Dionysus, 159

dissociative disorder, 1, 18, 22, 24–25, 40, 132

Douglas, Mary, 91–92

Dowling, W. J., 5

Downey, James, 94

dream, 3, 58, 113, 165

Dreyfus, Hubert L., 4, 118

Dreyfus, Stuart E., 4
Druid, 90–91, 107

Eagle, Charles T., Jr., 128, 164
Eastern, 40
ecstasy, 2, 4, 8, 10, 14, 28, 30, 38–40, 42–43,
    54–55, 61–62, 77–79, 81–83, 86, 94, 99, 117–
    118, 123, 126, 158, 161, 163, 165
Edelman, Gerald M., 9, 11, 109, 112–117, 122,
    136, 164
Egan, Michael J., 31–32, 158
Eiseman, Fred B., Jr., 40
Ekman, Paul, 47, 73
Eliot, T. S., 144
embodiment, 14, 127, 129–130; multiple
    senses of, 8–9, 37–38, 45, 85–86, 107, 117,
    131–132; of music, 6
Emerson, Ralph Waldo, 145
emotion: aesthetic, 11, 52, 56–60, 80–81
    (see also rasa, theory); background, 51,
    138, 141; and cognition, 8, 123; conscious-
    ness and, 10–11, 131–134, 138, 141, 146–
    149; definition of, 45, 46, 47–54, 57–59, 72,
    75–76; primary, 49–50, 50, 51–52, 56, 58–
    59, 67, 76, 141; secondary, 49–50, 50, 51, 58–
    59, 141; and trance, 10–12, 29, 43, 45, 52,
    59, 62–63, 66, 68, 84–85, 87, 94, 96–97, 105,
    113, 117, 121, 124, 127, 129, 142, 146–148,
    151, 153, 155. See also music and emotion;
    rasa
Enlightenment, 11, 14–15, 72, 91, 100, 157
Erickson, Frederick, 128
eroticism. See music and emotion; trance,
    eroticism/sexuality and
Errington, Shelly, 88, 101–103
ethnomusicology, 3, 7, 10, 71, 89, 106, 155, 163
euphoria, 53, 55, 159
Europe, 1–2, 7–8, 11, 13, 15, 21–22, 69, 72, 74,
    93, 118, 150, 162
evangelical, 87, 93–95, 95, 96–97, 100, 105, 163
evolution, 9, 49, 51, 128–129, 134, 149, 151,
    153–154
exorcism, 15, 84

Fales, Cornelia, 5
feeling, 2, 29, 45, 47, 49, 54, 69, 71, 73, 79, 82–
    83, 115, 118, 127, 131, 133, 140, 155, 161
Feld, Steven, 27, 73
Ferdinandus, Epiphanium, 36
Ferstman, Carla, 7
Feynman, Richard, 12
Fields, Howard L., 148
film, 21, 24, 70, 123; The Curse of the Jade

Scorpion, 157; Sybil, 24; The Three Faces
    of Eve, 24
Fish, Stanley, 69
Flanagan, Owen, 4, 9
Foley, William A., 9, 117, 126–127
France, 14, 17, 23, 26; Paris, 13, 15–17, 20,
    22–23
Franklin, Benjamin, 17
Freeman, Walter, 111, 153–154
Freud, Sigmund, 18, 22–23, 87, 122
Friedson, Steven M., 3, 29, 39, 106, 124,
    126, 145
Friesen, W. V., 47
Frith, Simon, 74
fugue state, 1, 138
Fuller, Robert C., 20

Gabrielsson, Alf, 11, 52, 54–55, 59, 159
Galler, Bernard A., 5
gamelan, 3, 38, 40, 60, 84, 89, 141–143, 142–
    143, 144, 147, P7
Gamman, Lorraine, 70
Gassner, Father, 15
gaze, 30, 70, 110
Geertz, Clifford, 51, 72, 88–89
Geertz, Hildred, 73
gender studies, 72
Gergen, Kenneth J., 69
Germany, 14, 17, 26; Bavaria, 15
Gewehr, Wesley M., 93–94
al-Ghazzali, Abu Hamid Muhammad, 10,
    28, 30, 42, 62, 68, 77, 79, 82, 158, 163;
    The Alchemy of Happiness, 78
Giles-David, Jennifer, 74
glossolalia. See speaking in tongues
Gnoli, Raniero, 57–60, 75, 126
gnosis, 76, 78, 81, 100. See also trance,
    knowledge/gnosis and
God, 12, 14, 39–40, 42–43, 60, 62, 68, 77, 93,
    95, 97, 99–100, 132
gods, 13, 147
Goldhill, Simon, 70
Goldstein, Avram, 60, 160
Goodenough, Ward H., 72
Gould, Stephen Jay, 151
Great Britain, 72
Greeley, Andrew, "Are We a Nation of
    Mystics?," 45
Green, Alyce M., 68
Green, Elmer E., 68
Griffith, Niall, 6
griot, 74–75, 84–85
Grotowski, Jerzy, 47

Lazarus, Richard S., 52
Leach, Edmund, 71–72
"Leaning on the Everlasting Arms," 97, *98*
LeDoux, Joseph, 3, 49, 160
Lennon, John, "Imagine," 2
Lerdahl, Fred, 5, 122
Levenson, R. W., 47
Lévi-Strauss, Claude, 72
Levy, Robert I., 72
Lewis, Michael, 49
Lewontin, Richard, 151
Liberia, 73
Lindner, K., 5
Lindstrom, Erik, 159
Lindstrom, Siv, 54–55
Lindstrom Wik, Siv, 11, 52, 54, 59, 159
linguistics, 5, 8, 41, 87–88, 101, 117, 124, 126
Little, Lewis Peyton, 93
Livingston, Robert B., 110–111
Locke, John, 90, 92
Lovejoy, Arthur O., "The Great Chain of Being," 72
Lovejoy, David S., 94
Loy, D. Gareth, 6
Lutz, Catherine A., 72, 88

magic, 11, 131
Mahavamsa (Buddhist chronicle), 30
Malawi, 88, 106
Malaysia, 101, 157
mapping, 5, 112–114, *114,* 115–116, *116,* 120, 136, 139–140, 143, 164–165
Marshment, Margaret, 70
Mascou, J. J., 72
Maslow, A. H., 161
Masson, Jeffrey M., 75
Maturana, Humberto, 7, 9, 11, 29, 117, 119–122, 127, 136, 154
Max Joseph of Bavaria, Prince, 15
McClary, Susan, 72
McCready, William, "Are We a Nation of Mystics?," 45
McDaniel, June, 75–76
McKenna, Thomas M., 5
McNeill, William H., 164
Mead, George Herbert, 87
meditation, 1, 3, 54, 66, 78, 101, 133, 144–145, 148
medium, 34, 39–40, 126
melody, 5, 17, 25–26, 37, 39, 60, 75–76, 80, 84, 114, 129, 136–137, 141–142
Melzack, Ronald, 88
Merleau-Ponty, Maurice, 8, 68, 118–119, 146; *Phenomenology of Perception,* 108

Merriam, Alan P., 52
Mesmer, Franz Anton, 13, 15–16, *16,* 17–20
mesmerism, 18, 20–21, 23
Meyer, Leonard, 5, 147
Michaelides, Solon, 159
Michalson, Linda, 49
Middle Ages, 13–14, 57–58, 62, 89
Miller, Perry, 95
Minsky, Marvin, 5
Mitchell, W. J. Thomas, 70
Mohammed, 161
Mohatt, Gerald, 128
Monteverdi, Claudio, *Orfeo,* 75–76
Mora, George, 35, 62
Morais, Jose, 5
Morley, David, 70
Morocco, 78, 157
Mozart, Wolfgang Amadeus, *Cosí fan Tutte,* 17, *19*
multiple personality disorder, 1, 13–15, 22–24, 36, 39, 132
music and emotion, 1–2, 4–6, 10–12, 26, 28–29, 45, 49, 51–53, 56–57, 59–60, 63, 68–69, 71–76, 79–80, 82, 84, 97, 115, 118, 121, 123–124, 127, 129, 134, 137, 147–149, 159; eroticism/sexuality and, 60–61, 63
music and trance, 3–4, 8, 10–12, 17, 25–27, 35–39, 42, 45, 54–56, 63, 78, 82–84, 86–89, 92, 99–100, 105, 108, 112, 115–116, 119, 122, 124–125, *125,* 126–127, 129, 131–132, 134, 144, 147, 153, 157
music cognition, 3–7, 43, 122, 129
music theory, 4, 5
music therapy, 17
musical accompaniment, 1, 16, 27, 38, 67, 78, 83, 87, 104, *104,* 105, 144, 147
musical instruments, 17, *18,* 31, 37, 54, 97; aulos, 37, 159; clapper, 74, 104; clarinet, 159; cymbal, 104, 142; *dholak,* 77; drum, 30–31, *31,* 32, 35, 37, 40, 74, 77–78, 97, 104–105, 122, 124, 129, 141–142, 158; flute, 35, 153; glass harmonica, 16; *godji,* 126; gong, 104–105, 142; guitar, 97; harmonium, 77; metallophone, 142; oboe, 37, 104, 159; organ, 97; piano, 16–17, 40, 67–68, 97; plate, 104; rattle, 103, *103,* 105; *sitar,* 69, 75, 85; synthesizer, 40, 97; *tabla,* 75; *tambura,* 75; violin, 16–17, 35, 126; woodwind, 17. *See also* gamelan
musician, 10, 17, 26–27, 35–36, 38, 60–61, 74–75, 77–80, 97, 118, 122–124, 126, 129, 141, 161
musicking, 4, 7–8, 122–124, 127, 143, *143,* 146
musicology, 7, 9

representation, 5–6, 76, 111, 118, 121, 164
rhythm, 32, 37, 39, 54, 60, 62, 66, 76, 79–
	80, 98, 114, 119, 127–129, 141–142, 147,
	154, 158
rhythmic entrainment, 10–11, 39, 60, 119,
	121, 127–129, 153–154, 164
Rider, Mark S., 128, 164
Roman Catholic Church, 4, 14–15, 89
Romanticism, 90
Rosaldo, Michelle A., 71–72, 88
Rosch, Eleanor, 4, 109–110, 117, 151
Roseman, Marina, 27, 39
Rosicrucian, 18
Rouget, Gilbert, 1, 3, 27, 84, 133, 147; *La
	Musique et la transe*, 25–26, 37, 43
Rousseau, Jean-Jacques, 10, 26, 158
Rowell, Lewis, 58
Russell, James A., 73, 82
Ryle, Gilbert, 9

Saarni, Carolyn, 49
Sabri Brothers, 63, 162
Sacks, Oliver, 147
Sacred Harp, 95
sama', 8, 11, 30, 61, 77–78, 80–82, 123
Scarry, Elaine, 2
Schank, Roger C., 82
Schelling, Friedrich, 157
Scherer, Klaus R., 5
Schieffelin, Edward, 34
schizophrenia, 39
Schubert, Franz, 70
science, 1, 7, 10, 12–13, 17–18, 22–24, 28, 34,
	36, 43, 56, 69, 72, 90–91, 93, 108, 117–118,
	122, 129, 132, 134, 150
scientific method, 3–4, 8, 16, 90, 122
script, 82, 85, 123
séance, 23, 34
Searle, John R., 6
Seeger, Anthony, 27, 73
self, 11, 38–39, 59, 76–77, 87–94, 97, 101, 105–
	106, 108, 121, 134–135, *135,* 136–140, 143–
	147, 153; autobiographical, 11, 91, 135, *135,*
	136, 138–139, 141, 144–146, 148, 165–166;
	core, 134–135, *135,* 136, 138–139, 143;
	proto-, 120, 135, *135,* 136–137, *137,* 139,
	143. *See also* trance, and selfhood
semiotic, 10, 26, 63, 124
Senegal, 74
Separate Baptist, 93–96, 100
Serafine, Mary Louise, 5
Serat Centhini (Javanese poem), 60
shaman, 126, 157, 165
Shankar, Ravi, 75

Shepherd, John, 74
Shirokogoroff, S. M., 126
Shweder, Richard A., 72–73, 88
Siberia, 157
Siddiqui, Mahmud Husain, 80
Sigerist, Henry E., 35–36, 63
Slater, Don, 70
Sloboda, John, 5, 52
Slovenia, 153
Small, Christopher, 7
Smith, J. C., 7
Snellgrove, David L., 164
social science, 72
Soeradipoera, R. Ng., 61
Solie, Ruth A., 72
solipsism, 120, 153
Solomon, Robert C., 73
somnambulism, 1, 14–15, 21–22
song, 6, 10, 31–32, 34–36, 39, 75, 77–83, 89,
	93–97, 103, 105, 114, 126, 128–129, 147, 153
soul, 4, 9, 14–15, 39, 42, 62, 77, 80, 93, 95, 145
South Africa, 73
Sparshott, Francis, 57
speaking in tongues, 4, 34, 55, 99–100,
	102, 129
Spies, Walter, 85
spirit, 7, 10, 13–15, 23, 28, 34, 39–40, 42–43,
	75, 83–84, 86–88, 94, 97, 99–106, 125–126,
	132, 147–148, 157; "Baptism in the Holy
	Spirit," 34, 55, 99; Holy Spirit, 14, 34, 40,
	55, 79, 88, 99–100, 105–106
Spiro, Melford E., 72
Spivak, Gayatri Chakravorty, 72
Squire, Larry R., 3
Sri Lanka, 10, 30–31, 42, 44
Steiner, George, 44
Stevenson, Robert Louis, *The Strange Case of
	Dr. Jekyll and Mr. Hyde,* 23
Stoic, 90
Stoller, Paul, 126
Stone, Ruth, 73
structural coupling, 11, 60, 113, 119, 121–123,
	126–127, 129–130, 154, 164
Strunk, Oliver, 37
Sudan, 157
Sufi, 6–8, 10–11, 30, 42–43, 56, 61–63, 78–82,
	85, 99, 123–124, 132, 157, 163, 165, *P3*
sumange', 101–103, 105
Suryani, Luh Ketut, 40
Sutton, R. Anderson, 101, 104
Swedenborg, Emanuel, 18

Tambiah, Stanley, Jeyaraja, 31
Tannen, Deborah, 128

JUDITH BECKER, an authority on the music of Southeast Asia, is also director of the Center for Southeast Asian Studies, a unit of the International Institute at the University of Michigan. She is a co-founder of the Center for World Performance Studies at the University of Michigan and was its first director. She has written numerous articles for such publications as *The Galpin Society Journal*, *Ethnomusicology*, *Journal of Music Theory*, *Journal of Musicological Research*, *The World of Music*, *Asian Music*, *The New Grove Dictionary of Music and Musicians*, *The New Grove Handbook of Ethnomusicology*, *The New Grove Handbook of World Music*, *Leonardo Music Journal* and *The Musical Quarterly*.

Becker is the author of *Traditional Music in Modern Java* and *Gamelan Stories: Tantrism, Islam and Aesthetics in Central Java*. She is the editor of *Art, Ritual and Society in Indonesia* and the three-volume set of translations entitled *Karawitan: Source Readings in Javanese Gamelan and Vocal Music*. These three volumes are the first-ever substantial set of translations of musical works written by Southeast Asian scholars and musicians.

She has received awards from the Society for Ethnomusicology, the National Endowment for the Humanities, the Smithsonian Institute, the Social Science Research Council, the Rockefeller Foundation, and the Fulbright Foundation. She was the first recipient of Michigan's John D'Arms Award for graduate student mentorship and was recently awarded the Glenn McGeoch Collegiate Professorship of Music by the School of Music.

Her current research focuses on the relationships between music, emotion and trance in institutionalized religious contexts. She is exploring the common ground between humanistic, cultural, anthropological approaches and scientific, cognitive, psychological approaches.